America's Problem Youth

Education and Guidance of the Disadvantaged

America's Problem
Education and

OSCAR G. MINK

Director of the Senior College Division
of the Regional Educational Laboratory
for the Carolinas and Virginia in Durham, N.C.

INTERNATIONAL TEXTBOOK COMPANY

Youth
Guidance of the Disadvantaged

BERNARD A. KAPLAN

Department of Education
Division of Research, Planning, and Evaluation
State of New Jersey

an **Intext** *publisher*   *Scranton, Pennsylvania 18515*

To those haves and have-nots who are
working together for a human world

Parable of the Teacher-Counselor

It came to pass that a certain student fell among evil companions. They stripped him of his allowance, induced him to forsake his studies, left him outcast by his elders, wounded in pride, and fallen by the wayside.

And by chance there came that way a Keeper of Records who saw that the student had fallen. And, as is the custom of record keepers, he recorded it. And he said unto the student, Every student who falls by the wayside should be helped. There should be no partiality. Would that I could help all students, then I could help thee! And so saying, he consulted his book and found that it was so written, and he passed by on the other side.

And there likewise came that way a Test Maker and he looked upon the student and it appeared that he was sorely beaten. He examined his allowance and found that it was ninety-eight percent empty. He consulted his companions and discovered that seven out of ten of them were evil. He talked to the elders and learned that they had all rejected him. He devised an ingenious method of measuring the extent to which the student's pride had been wounded. He at last became convinced that here, indeed, was a student who had fallen by the wayside!

And the Test Maker assembled paper and pencils and wrote a mighty dissertation recommending that help be provided. And he filed his dissertation and passed by on the other side.

And there also came that way an Interviewer. And he looked upon the fallen student and said, How feelest thou? And the student answered saying, My pride is wounded, my companions were false, the elders have forsaken me, there is no hope! And the Interviewer said, Thou feelest, then, that there is no hope. And the student cried, Woe is me, my mistakes are grievous, I have been false to my heritage, leave me that I may mourn alone! And the Interviewer said, Thou wouldst have me go. And the student answered, Thou sayest. And the Interviewer made note of it and passed by on the other side.

But there also came that way a certain teacher. And beholding the fallen student, he had compassion on him. He sought out linen and oil and with these helped the student bind up his wounded pride. He directed his footsteps to an agent who obtained employment for the student so that he might replenish the misspent allowance. He helped the student to again discover his studies. And he assisted him in declaring unto his elders that he should no longer be rejected, and they did believe it to be so.

Now which of these four, sayest thou, was counselor unto him who had fallen?

GEORGE A. PIERSON
Queens College, Flushing, N.Y.

Preface

This publication is the result of a series of workshops designed for school personnel desiring to improve educational programs for disadvantaged youth and potential dropouts. The workshops were conducted at Cornell University, Ithaca, N.Y., during the summers of 1964 through 1967. Both editors of this publication were actively involved in these four workshops, Dr. Kaplan as workshop director and Dr. Mink as assistant director and later contributing lecturer.

The chapters comprising this publication represent, in part, papers presented at the aforementioned workshops. Some of the papers have been entirely rewritten and updated. Several chapters have been especially prepared for this publication.

A great deal has happened in the field of educating the disadvantaged since 1964 and some of this is reflected in the writing that follows. In the early days, for example, much time and energy were directed to questions of definition (Who are the culturally deprived? Is it appropriate to describe students in this way?) and strategy (How should selection of pupils for these programs be handled? How can the charge of special treatment and "favoritism" be avoided? How can pupils be placed in specially designed programs without stigmatizing them or their parents?).

Subsequent concerns embraced appropriate and effective programs, evaluation of these efforts, and the role of integration and race relations in the schools.

This publication, then, represents the thinking of a number of educators addressing various aspects of the problem over the last five years. Questions of severity, dimension, strategy, and approach are addressed. A special effort has been made to include suggestions for specific programs and approaches.

This publication, like the original workshops from which it evolved, is directed to public school educators at all levels and variety of assignment. We hope that it provides insight, guidance, and inspiration to the end that disadvantaged pupils are more effectively and consistently adequately educated by the public schools.

BERNARD A. KAPLAN
OSCAR G. MINK

Morgantown, West Virginia
May, 1970

Contents

part IV   Counseling

part V   Action Projects

prologue

Neighbors of the President*

Paul A. Fine

"We are near the end of a long journey. Vivid scenes continue to explode in the mind. There is Oscar, so outraged at the trash in his yard, so terrified of Steven's gang and of the crooked buildings that look as if they are going to fall on him. There is Bill, disgusted at the "Winos," chasing the dog out of his backyard, drawing back from the parking meter he is about to smash, saying to himself, "I tricked the Devil." Bill, with his vision of two sides of the street, wanting only to get on to the good side.

"There is Victor hanging by his wrists from a pipe near the ceiling, taking the beating, and Albert taking his from a cop in the corner of a jail cell. There is Eric going to school in his stepsister's shoes and having his blanket and mattress stolen from his bed by his stepmother. And Don rolling out of the way as his father falls drunkenly into bed, and laughing, then crying, then getting sick as he gets kicked by a policeman.

"There are school teachers who treat children far worse than they treat dogs, and children becoming animals because they are treated like animals. There is Steven, who wants to drive a bus so that he will be safe when the inevitable collision comes, running out of the alley where his gang is hiding, taunting the enemy to lead them into the trap he has prepared for them. There is Norris, hungry and ragged himself, whose heart goes out to the pregnant girl sleeping on rags in the closet. There is Wentworth at age fourteen, who spent five years in prison, who cannot bear to be 'cooped' up saying to us, 'I don't think America, you know, think as much as they should about teen-agers. It's not their fault— they don't have the stuff to live right.' (The Second Precinct, where all this takes place is six blocks from the White House. The moon is 238,000 miles away.)

"And perhaps the most incredible fact about this whole situation is that it is quite literally true that the distance to the moon is likely to be bridged first."

*Paul A. Fine, *Neighbors of the President—A Study of the Patterns of Youth Life in the Second Precinct, Washington, D.C.* (New York: Paul A. Fine Associates).

America's Problem Youth

Education and Guidance of the Disadvantaged

part I

Milieu

1

School Dropouts and Job Outlook

Herbert Bienstock

Schools prepare youngsters to enter the labor market, and the degree of education a youth completes will definitely affect his occupations. This in turn influences his social and economic adjustment to society.

The increased focus on manpower trends and problems in recent years reflects an awareness of the close relationship between education and training and socioeconomic status. This was particularly true in the 1960's, when increases in automation and technological change and an unprecedented growth in the labor force in the United States mark the problem more significant than ever before.

It is not that training and education have suddenly gained importance. It is the relationship that has developed between education and occupational level that is of great concern.

POPULATION AND LABOR FORCE TRENDS

The population of the United States is expected to increase to 222 million in 1975, and while this increase of some 42 million people in 15 years is of great significance in many areas, it becomes even more significant when one thinks of the distribution of population in terms of age.

By 1975, for example, about 47 percent of our population will be under 25. If one adds to this group persons who are 65 or over, just about three out of every five people in the United States are excluded from the hard-core years of working life (ages 25-64). The upward extension of the school age and the lowering of retirement age are vital factors in this phenomenon.

In 1965 the young people reaching age 18 annually jumped to 3.8 million, a million more than in the previous year! A more dramatic way of looking at this figure of 3.8 million is to consider that in 1967 there are some 2 million more youngsters age 16-17 than in 1965. Another important development that will have great significance in terms of the adjustment of young people to the work force of the nation is what is happening to a particular older group, the age category of 35-44.

3

Over the entire period of 1960-70 the labor force was expected to jump about 20 percent—an increase of 12.5 million. That is the part of the population that works for income, the part of the population considered to be in the labor force because they are either employed or seeking employment.

Table 1-1
Projected Labor-Force Changes by Age, 1965-70 (millions)

Age	Actual, 1965	Projected, 1970	Change, 1965–70
Both Sexes			
Under 35	31.8	37.3	+5.5
35–44	17.2	16.5	−.7
45 and over	29.3	32.3	+3.0
Men			
Under 35	21.2	24.7	+3.5
35–44	11.5	10.9	−.6
45 and over	19.0	20.2	+1.2

While the overall increase is expected to be about 20 percent, the sharpest increase is expected to be in the age group under 25. This group during the decade of 1960 will number 26 million, which compares with 19 million in the decade of the 1950's, or about a 40 percent increase in the number of youngsters who in this decade are entering the work force. Youth will be increasing in the work force at about twice the average rate.

At the same time, there is a 20 percent overall increase in the work force within the age group 35-44. This will actually decline by some 300,000 over the period 1960 and 1970, and by about another 300,000 in 1970 to 1975, or well over half a million in the entire period 1960-75. Again, that is the age category in which the hard-core age of working life of 35-44 takes place.

In this group is found the experienced supervisor, the working foreman, the college teacher, the people who have a certain amount of know-how and experience in industry. This shrinkage in the number of persons in mid-working life should open up many new opportunities for young people to move ahead into many categories of occupations.

Such opportunities should improve but they will improve only if the younger people have the education and training required by the nation's job structure. In other words, the working situation is facing improved opportunities for those who are educationally prepared to meet them.

WOMEN WORKERS

Women in the labor force are a vital factor. It has become commonplace for women to work before marriage and retire from work during the time of marriage and family rearing. Then they increasingly come back to work during their forties. In fact, the modal age of participation in the work force for women is now age 45-54. Twenty years ago the average age for the working woman was 28, and typically she was single and had no children. Now the average age is 41, and typically she is married and has children. Approximately eight out of every ten women work for income some time in their lives; by 1970, one out of every three workers will be a woman. Obviously one cannot ignore girls anymore. They too need some kind of job orientation in the area of vocational guidance.

PEOPLE AVAILABLE TO THE WORK FORCE

In October 1963 the Bureau of Labor Statistics made a study of people available to the work force. In round numbers, of the total population at that time 31.5 million were between the ages of 14 and 24. Of this number, 16.5 million were in school, 1.5 million were in the armed forces, and 8.3 million were employed.

These figures indicated that there were approximately 5.3 million young people age 14-24 who were neither employed nor in the armed forces. For the sake of obtaining a clearer statistic, subtract from this latter figure the nearly four million young women age 14-24 who were neither employed nor in the armed forces.

This is how one arrives at the figure that has provoked concern in terms of social dynamite 1,359,000 young people age 14-24 who are neither in school nor at work.

Of these nearly 1.4 million young people, more than 1 million say they are looking for work but can't find it. This leaves 337,000 who are not in the labor force and not in school. They tell the census taker they are not in school, they are not at work, and they are not even looking for work. These youngsters, who are almost completely disoriented from society, can be found on street corners of almost every large city of the country. And it is important to remember that 337,000 is not a small or insignificant number.

Before leaving that number, however, one must put it into the total perspective. While being concerned with some 1.4 million who are out of school and out of work, including those who are looking for work and those who are not looking for work, one should keep in mind that the 1.4 million related to the 31.6 million of the total population age 14-24 means that roughly 29 out of every 30 youngsters in that age group are in a relatively satisfactory adjustment. This point needs emphasis because too often it's merely an afterthought. Many of the 8 million that hold jobs may not be in satisfactory job situations, but for the most part they are in a comparatively sound and healthy situation. However, that doesn't make the problem of dealing with those who need our concern and care any the less severe.

THE WORLD OF WORK—TECHNOLOGY AND AUTOMATION

What's been happening in the world of work? What types of jobs are developing and what's happening in terms of job opportunities for young people who are entering the work force?

At the outset, it should be noted that 1950 was the first year since the American Revolution that employment in the *service* industries was higher than employment in the *production* industries.

These two occupational categories are used in the broadest sense. *Production* industries refers to all the industries that make or produce goods—manufacturing, mining, construction, agriculture. *Service* industries refers to such occupations as wholesale and retail business, personal services like that of barbers, tailors, small businesses, finance and real estate, and many, many others.

The classic economist reports that the first dollars earned are spent on food, clothing, and shelter. Only as more affluence is attained are more dollars spent in other areas—what the economists heartlessly call the nonessential spending areas. Today, people in this country are spending more and more of their dollars in these areas, and consequently more and more new job opportunities are becoming available. This has great significance for the job market and high school dropouts.

Thus society is now feeling the impact of technology and automation. What has been happening in the last two decades is the introduction of machinery that replaces men largely at the lower end of the skill level. At this level one finds the kinds of job a machine can do less expensively than a human being. The unskilled worker has been more or less eliminated as such machinery has been introduced. This worker is the fellow who didn't graduate from high school, whose education was prematurely terminated. What's happened to him in the labor force is that he has been squeezed out and more and more others have been prevented from replacing him.

A very simple but dramatic example of the impact of automation is the automatic elevator. It has been suggested that in the city of New York alone some 40,000 jobs were eliminated because automatic elevators were substituted for hand-operated ones. In other words, thousands of jobs have been eliminated. One may wonder about the value of a life spent riding up and down in an elevator; nevertheless, it's a better than a life spent walking up and down the streets looking for a job.

The problem is how to retrain and provide education for the jobs that are available. There are at the present time in this country literally millions of jobs going unfilled. There are jobs for secretaries all over the city of New York, but can one put unemployed Scranton coal miners to work as secretaries? The answer to that is obviously no, but there are closer areas of displacement and job openings where retraining can do it.

Some of this has been accomplished for older workers through the Manpower Development and Training Act. But there is much to be done about the impact of automation and its effects upon the young dropout. What has been happening in the last decade or two is quite unique. It is not simply the old story of technological development. Workers are being replaced at the lower end of the skill range in unprecedented numbers, and at a time when more and more young people are entering the work force than ever before!

Manufacturing firms are just about the largest employers of labor in the country. In the total labor force of about 70 million, the wage and salary work force is roughly in the range of 50 million, and of that number close to 16 million are in manufacturing. In other words, manufacturing accounts for just about 30 percent of the nation's nonfarm work force. Within this important industrial sector and in a period when the labor force has been steadily increasing, there was an actual decline in manufacturing. It is in the nation's factories, particularly, where you have the largest numbers of unskilled and semiskilled workers. They are the operators, the people who work on the assembly lines. These are the jobs that automation has really been eliminating.

Not all job change is the result of automation. To a very large extent one of the important factors is the change in consumer preference—how dollars are spent. For example, since 1957 employment in the service industries has been turning upward while employment in transportation has turned slightly downward. When these two industrial groupings are considered it becomes more evident that automation is only one of the factors influencing job displacement and job change.

Within the transportation, communication, and public utilities sector of our economy one can readily see the impact of pure automation in the case of the telephone operator. Those who call "Information" to get a phone number in a neighboring community ("directory assistance") are given a string of digits that are almost impossible to remember. The general public is now doing some of the work the telephone operators once did. Machinery is doing the rest of the work of the operator, and thus one has an example of job deletion because of pure automation.

Note, though, that transportation alone provides an excellent example of job displacement and change that is *not* due to automation. Few vacationists ride the railroad anymore. Vacations are taken in automobiles. Automobiles are driven by owners. For that matter, cars are driven to work more and public transportation is used less. A recent study of consumer spending patterns found that by 1960, 14 cents out of every consumer dollar went for automobile purchase and repair. This compares with about 5.6 cents for medical care. In other words, we spend roughly twice as much for the care and repair of our automobiles as we do for the care and repair of our bodies. The significant and relevant point here is the fact that instead of people being employed on the railroads or other public transportation, they are employed in the service category—pumping gas and repairing automobile engines, tires, and the like. Therefore, service employment is increasing, while transportation, communication, and public utilities employment is decreasing.

Changes in consumer preference are not the only factors that lead to job change. Ways of handling jobs, methods, and the flow of materials also have an impact. Thirty or forty years ago trolley cars were run by two men—one the motorman and the other the conductor. Now we move the same number of people (or more) in a bus with only a driver. This represents an increase of 100 percent productivity and one job less in the transportation industry. Again a job has disappeared; it isn't all automation. It's just a matter of continuous change in the structure of jobs.

The impact on jobs then is this: Change seems almost inevitably to result in jobs being eliminated at the lower end of the skill level and increased at the upper end.

THE NATION'S FARMS AND PRODUCTIVITY

One of the most important factors involved relates to something that has not yet been mentioned. In thinking of automation and productivity, there is a tendency to think only in terms of the nation's factories and industries. The truth of the matter is that the sharpest productivity gains in the last two decades, if not in the last half century, have been made on the nation's farms. On the farms, under the influence of improved agricultural equipment, improved fertilizers, and improved seeds, more and more is being produced by fewer and fewer people. At the turn of this century just about one out of every five American workers worked on farms. Now the ratio is down to about one out of every 15, representing a huge gain in productivity. In fact, so much is being produced now that supply exceeds need and creates a problem of disposal.

It's the farm labor force that perhaps has been most seriously affected in job displacement. This has a very real impact for the school dropout. What has occurred has been the shift of population from the farm to the urban centers. There was a time on the farm when the high school dropout was an economic asset. During those times many farm families waited for the young healthy son to drop out of school and to help the family full time with the farm work—which he had been trained in from childhood.

With the shift in population from rural to urban centers and increased productivity, the high school dropout is no longer the asset he once was on the farm. In fact, he has become something of an economic drag on the market because the kinds of jobs that are developing are not those that high school dropouts can fulfill.

INDUSTRIAL PATTERNS

Another way of looking at the problem is to look at industrial patterns. Because industries have had differing patterns, there has occurred a real change in the overall job picture. For example, in construction, about 80 percent are blue-collar jobs, while only about 20 percent are white-collar jobs. On the other hand, in finance, insurance, and real estate there are close to 90 percent white-collar jobs. Finance is one of the long-term continuing growth industries and it has a tremendous white-collar work force—90 percent—while manufacturing, which is just about 70 percent blue collar, is on the decline.

Here, then, are the real problems that have developed for the high school dropout. The white-collar and skilled groups continue to grow sharply and have shown accelerated growth since 1940. The white-collar, skilled, professional, and managerial category also continue to grow.

The real story of the last decade and a half is that the white-collar, skilled, professional, and managerial workers are continuing to show large-scale increases. The service categories are also rising, reflecting an improved standard of living. However, since 1956 the unskilled laborer in construction and the unskilled factory worker for the first time in any decade show no increase whatsoever. This is in the face of a 20 percent increase in the work force and a 40 percent increase in young people coming into the work force, among them large numbers of high school dropouts. On the basis of present trends, approximately 7.5 million people are expected to drop out of the present labor force during this decade. At the same time we foresee a complete drying up of the number of job opportunities for unskilled workers.

EDUCATION AND UNEMPLOYMENT

The total years of education for professional and technical workers in 1962 averaged 16.2 years of education or two-tenths of a year beyond the bachelor degree. Clerical and sales workers in 1962 were averaging 12.5 years—a half year beyond a high school diploma. This means that the educational competition for a high school dropout is becoming increasingly greater as he struggles to get a foothold in the world of work.

With educational attainment continuously rising, the dropout is even in a worse position than he might otherwise be, for the simple reason that employers' standards are rising. Under the pressure of a more highly educated work force the employer can demand higher standards, whether or not these are needed for satisfactory job performance. There are more people available with this educational requirement. Consequently the high school dropout is at at even greater disadvantage.

Currently the unemployment rate for the high school dropout runs about four times as high as the rate for persons with some college education and twice as high as the rate for high school graduates. Certainly in the years ahead, as the demand for skills increases and the demand for unskilled workers declines, the untrained, unskilled dropout will find the going especially difficult in the labor force of the space age.

REFERENCES

Hamel, H. R. "Employment of High School Graduates and Dropouts in 1965." Special Labor Force Report No. 66, Reprint No. 2489, U.S. Department of Labor, *Monthly Labor Review*, 1966.

United States Department of Labor. "Economic Background to the Occupational Outlook in the Mid-Sixties (charts and graphs)." New York: U.S. Department of Labor, 1966.

2

Education, Psychological and Social Aspects of Disadvantaged Youth

Jim Amos

INTRODUCTION

Since many of the difficulties individuals experience are intricately meshed with their perceptions of themselves and the perceived expectations of those with whom they interact, social class may be a plausible approach to the question of self-esteem and self-concept as they relate to the disadvantaged or deprived. The term *social class*, being a comparative term, refers to a set of positions in a social heirarchy which assumes some reference to one or more higher classes. Using social class as an approach, the people with whom we are vitally concerned are lower-class—that is, individuals with a slight percentage of intact families, a large number of children, poor housing, low income and little education. Interaction with any numerous combinations of these conditions would seem to significantly influence an individual's perception(s) of himself or themselves.

Vital for the educator interested in teaching the disadvantaged is the need to realize how his student perceives the world. In order to do this, the educator must attempt to understand the student's self-concept—the problems and conditions that are active in its formation, how it may affect learning, and how it might be altered. In regard to the latter point, the would be ambitious educator may have to use the sparse amount of information and material available and a large amount of ingenuity. Documenting the characteristics does not necessarily identify the cause nor outline the courses of remedy. In addition, the concerned educator and researchers are faced with the enigma of those circumstances under which certain characteristics and conditions result in success and under which others result in failure. The need also remains for the development of more sensitive and accurate procedures for the assessment of potential for development as well as for behavioral change; in addition, they must determine those conditions necessary for appropriate development where existing pedagogical principles and technology are inappropriate or irrelevant for the learning experiences of the disadvantaged. (Gordon, 1965)

This discussion shall begin by attempting to identify some general problems of self-concept of the disadvantaged and then relate these to the more specific problems encountered when a disadvantaged child enters the educational system—the first two of the three aforesaid points regarding the student's self-concept.

FORMATION OF SELF-CONCEPT

In the process of coping with one's environment, each individual finds certain forms of behavior more effective than others. These selected behaviors are further modified and perpetuated via the reinforcements and punishments which the social milieu applies to individuals. Since an individual's behavior is consistent with his perceptions of himself, and since experiences that are inconsistent with one's self-concept tend to be rejected (Hawk, 1967), the end results are behavior patterns which seem to be congruent with an individual's self-concept and his perceived roles in various social groups. Consequently, the self-concept of an individual becomes organized through the reward system of significant others (individuals who are important to him), his community, and the social situations or institutions in which he participates. The self-concept, like fashion, may well determine the way an individual looks, feels, and communicates.

CULTURAL AGENTS AND SELF-CONCEPT

Since the majority of human reinforcements are mediated by other people some individuals can be effective only when they behave in concert with the existing social practices of the cultural agents (Smith, 1966); the family, the school, and the occupation can be identified as some of the cultural agents that interact to shape an individual's conception of himself.

Apparently the family, as one of the principal contexts in which the self-concept develops, asserts itself early in the developmental process and is not only concerned with biological reproduction but with maintenance, socialization, and status placement. (Keller, 1965) Often lower-class families are involved in a continuous crisis condition. Efforts to find money, to eat, and to keep shelter provide constant psychological irritants. Their homes usually crowded, noisy, discordant, disorganized, and austere, are characterized by preoccupation with day-to-day subsistence.

In spite of the deplorable environment, the home may afford the deprived child, as Rees reminds us, with "... his only source of security and safety, which are among his greatest needs." (Rees, 1968)

In some cases it is economically essential that large family groups live together. The family may consist of one or more parents and other adults, such as grandparents or aunts and uncles, and the child is usually one of a number of children—brothers, sisters, or cousins. In many cases both parents work and in time of need the other adults serve as substitute parents for the children. (Rees, 1968)

The advantages of such an extended family is expressed by Riessman (Rees, 1965); the lessening of self-concern and the danger of overprotection, and learning early in life the meaning of simple cooperative living and sharing. As Keller (1965, p. 25) stated,

> Lower-class life is neither to be preferred entirely nor rejected entirely. Every way of life gives some satisfactions and the question if whether or not these satisfactions are gained at the price of objective suffering or whether they might not be retained along with improvements in objective living conditions.

The extended family seems to be fostered by more than economic essentiality. Keller (1965) noted the deprived increase their security and enhance their power through establishing kinship relationships that are reciprocal, durable, and nonthreatening. Their ties with neighbors and co-workers are of a more superficial and less binding nature. They tend to exhibit a reluctance to associate readily with people other than close kin. This writer has noted that while the members of some of these families seem to adhere to close relationships which should foster emotional security in reality form emotional dependency which tends to increase insecurity. Weller (1965) mentions similar observations in dealing with the Appalachia poor. This may be due in part to the almost total dependency of the children on the family for social relationships. As a result any form of rejection, disapproval, or ridicule from the family is greatly feared by the children. (Keller, 1965) Weller (1965) suggests that a plausible and contributing factor is that these children achieve premature independence and are made to depend upon their own choices early in life. A good deal of them realizing their inadequacies seek the security of the parents and adults of the extended family who are assumed to possess good decision-making abilities, thus creating a sense of insecurity and emotional dependency in the child. Since their security is not based within themselves, the family may not be a mutually supporting cultural agent in which each member gives of himself for the good of the others. Instead, it tends to be an agency in which each member requires support from the others. Therefore it is not uncommon for a teenager to verbalize intensive dislike for his family but be unable to be separated from them for an extended period of time.

While these people may be reluctant to make new acquaintances or to interact with strangers, they are sensitive and concerned about being accepted and well liked by others. Since they tend to lack confidence in their ability to interact appropriately with strangers they become anxious and uncomfortable in such encounters. Consequently, they continue to seek the comfort and security of the established kinship relationships. (Keller, 1965)

There exists in the lower-class milieus various contradictory and conflicting patterns of conduct. It is possible to experience family security and parental dissertion within a short period of time. The children learn the "street" culture long before they are of school age. Stable and unstable groups are meshed together sharing hallways and kitchens. The religious and the law abiding are engulfed by gambling, drinking, narcotics, fornication, and prostitution. The children growing up in this setting are generally exposed to an incoherent and fragmented view of a world governed simultaneously by opposing principles. Frequently they are torn between the wishes of their family and their peer groups. Often a child attempts to hid his role with his peers from his family, and vice versa. By being one thing at home and another while on the street, compartmentalization of values and of actions may result, thus allowing an individual to be morally inconsistent without guilt and to justify his actions according to an arbitrary context. Hence if consistent moral values are necessary for the development of an integrated image of one's self and the world, it is probable that this consistency and the resultant integration are weak if not lacking in the lower-class families. (Keller, 1965)

The early and repetitive exposure to a transient existence helps to develop the moral sophistication of a world traveler before the child can develop a firm moral character of his own. Though they may be ignorant of the middle-class standards of behavior, they repeatedly experience the consequences of this ignorance as they encounter teachers and other such representatives of middle-class institutions. (Keller, 1965)

In their relationships with the opposite sex the men expect their women to satisfy them sexually, back them up in arguments or fights, share their earnings with them when they work, have supper ready on time, refrain from clinging to them and making excessive demands for money or material goods, stick with them through good and hard times, be faithful, and above all do not give the husband's money to other men. Though the women have fantasies about romantic love, an idealized image of a husband as a steady worker who brings his paycheck home and provides the family with a comfortable and pleasant life, they seem satisfied if their men work when possible, refrain from excessive drinking or gambling or becoming involved with other women to the extent of squandering the house money. In addition, they expect their men to satisfy them sexually, show some interest in their children, and to refrain from beating them excessively. (Keller, 1965)

THE SCHOOL AS A CULTURAL AGENT

As one could have surmised from the foregoing descriptive account of deprived families, they typically lack many of the cultural artifacts associated with the development of school readiness such as books, artwork, variety of toys, and self-instructional equipment. (Gordon, 1965) Generally, the low educational achievement of the parents and the fatigue and drudgery that frustrate adult learning adversely affects the intellectual stimulation of the children, despite the fact that many parents verbalize the positive value of education for their offspring. (Schwebel, 1963) Yet the verbalization is not functional regarding occupational growth but valued as being "good," like God and motherhood.

Almost all are, have been, or will be high school dropouts with academic achievement levels significantly lower than the last year of school attended. The median age, 16-21, has completed approximately ten years of education. The range of reading ability is very wide, with the median reading level predicted at approximately the seventh-grade level and arithmetic grade levels still yet lower. Vocational training is minimal. Readiness to learn may be reduced by extended lack of success in prior school contacts and deprivation of intellectual and social stimulation from early childhood. The classroom may be perceived as a symbol of embarrassment and humiliation, and the teachers as symbols of authority who are unsympathetic or indifferent. Leaving school may be viewed as the termination of years of academic frustration.

The native intelligence of many of these young people is within or in excess of the average range. However, in some cases, intelligence test scores may be lower than true ability because of their unfamiliarity with testing procedures, meager verbal skills, and the effect of sociocultural factors which make up the items of the test. These factors tend to handicap the disadvantaged who are schooled in a society that places great value on intelligence and school achievement. The only academic recognition in our educational system is given to those obtaining high grades and/or producing work of outstanding or unusual intelligence.

An educational setting arouses negative feelings in both the parent and child. As previously mentioned, many of the adults in the lower class are high school dropouts, the label itself being an anathema. When these adults have contacts with their children's teachers, the disadvantaged person will approach the meeting with a feeling of less than equality. Likewise the disadvantaged child bearing low grades and emotional battle scars derived from the frustration and humiliation of chronic inadequate classroom performances often sees himself as something less than his learned classroom peers. The effect on his internalized success expectancy will often be one of failure, so "Why try"? These children need teachers who are emphatically involved with the difficult factors a disadvantaged child experiences in his formal learning situations. Without them, the disadvantaged child's self-concept will increasingly become lower until he joins his parental ranks—and "drops out" concluding he has little control over academic payoff.

The teacher of these children should also be aware of some of their problem-solving handicaps. As a group they demonstrate a poor capacity for persistent or intense intellectual concentration. In attempting to solve abstract problems as in math, many tend to approach the problem as though hoping to be "inspired with an answer," and ultimately they merely guess at it. Generally, they are unable to disclose the process by which they arrived at the answer, even if correct. In instances like this the answer usually is arrived at not by sharp concentration on facts and logical steps but by hunches.

This unique group is noted for its distractibility and impressionability. Generally speaking, they are highly suggestible, and easily influenced by another's opinion, by the pressure of real or imagined external expectations, by fads, and by current prejudices and excitements.

They are not, as a rule, intellectually curious. In intellectual matters they demonstrate an impressionistic style of cognition comprised of hunches and quick, relatively passive impressions which tend to stop at the obvious—whatever is easily and immediately seen.

They are generally deficient in factual knowledge in contrast to motor skills. For example, they may be very unrealistic in their estimate of "how far it is from New York to Chicago," or they may respond "George Washington" to the question "Who discovered America?", but they may be relatively successful at assembling a complex puzzle or reproducing a given pattern of blocks.[1] Their style of cognition does not accumulate facts but impressions which easily displace or fuse with one another, thus losing distinctness and factual sharpness. Such cognitive practices may account for some of the reasons why deprived children become less able to succeed at intellectual and linguistic tasks as they move thorugh school. Usually an individual is able to retain informative facts and relationships if they appeal to his needs and interests. Regarding learning, Durking and Wiesley report (Gordon, 1965) that lower-class children learn more quickly when given a material incentive than when given a nonmaterial one. They found just the opposite to be true of middle-class children.

OCCUPATION AS A CULTURAL AGENT

Contrary to the popular beliefs, most of the adults whose families reside in poverty, are employed. In spite of an unusually large proportion of elderly persons and women household heads among the poor, two-thirds of all poor household heads worked in 1966. One-third of this group was employed full time, working at least 39 hours per week for 50 to 52 weeks. (Newman, 1969)

These people are unable to fulfill their role as an adequate provider not because of their inability to find work but rather because of inadequate earnings determined by the low wages paid for the jobs they are able to obtain. The heavy concentration of the deprived in unskilled and service jobs probably accounts, at least in part, for their low income levels. As a comparison in 1966, the national median income of all men who worked as waiters, cooks, or bartenders, both full and part time, was $2,912, and the national median income of all nonfarm laborers was $2,580 while the national median income of all male, professional, technical, and kindred workers was $8,330—approximately three times greater. (Willacy, 1969)

The deprived's perception of the world of work tends to be colored by family and personal experience. They bear the full blunt of the truism that in

[1] A small portion of the test items on the Wechsler Intelligence Scale for Children.

our society, status and prestige are obtained primarily through the occupation of the men in the family. Generally the lower class are employed in the occupations that carry the lowest status and prestige. Parents and neighbors are service workers, domestics, manual laborers, migrant workers, or low-level industrial workers. Because of the type of jobs available to them and the level of their marketable skills, many view work as tiring, humiliating, and difficult to obtain. Though unemployment is more prevalent among Negro males than among whites, their average duration of unemployment was approximately the same. More than half of the unemployed poverty males had last held semiskilled and unskilled jobs. This helps to account for the higher jobless rate of Negro men—over four-fifths had last worked in these jobs, while only three-fifths of the white males had. (Willacy, 1969)

CHANGING SELF-CONCEPTS

The preceding pages may seem to indicate that an individual's self-concept is learned through a gradual process of interacting with the world around him and that as Freudian psychology and learning theory implies (Miller, 1968, p. 5), "human behavior, including social and economic failure, is not a matter of personal responsibility but rather a product of the impersonal force of the environment." Whether one takes such a deterministic viewpoint or whether one prefers to think of man as having a free will and being capable of choice, the alteration of self-concepts is a difficult task.

Regarding the change of self-concepts, Hawk (1967) starts with two propositions: first, the self is difficult to change; second, when change does occur, it is very gradual. Once an individual's self-image is formal, his behavior tends to be somewhat compulsive and predictable. In addition, the person has preconceived notions of subsequent relationships, and the more nearly these expectations are met the more assured one can be that the concept of self will not change. For example, the deprived child has certain misgivings about teachers, and teachers may communicate, through their behavior to the child, certain stereotype beliefs and adverse labels about the socially disadvantaged. Such interactions only reinforce the child's negative self-image rather than alter it in a positive direction.

The changing of the concept of self is further hampered by it acting as a censor of one's perceptions. Instead of perceiving what actually occurs in his physical and social environment, one tends to perceive those aspects that relate to, enhance, and maintain the self. This tendency has moved therapists, like Albert Ellis to focus largely on what the patient tells himself about what happened or is happening to him. That is, in the ABC's of rational psychotherapy, A is what the individual perceives, B is what he tells himself about what he perceives, and C is the reaction of the individual, not to A but to B.

Hawk (1967) is in agreement with the advice given at the beginning of this chapter to the educator interested in teaching the disadvantaged. In part of this article he quotes Combs as saying "It is people who see themselves as unliked, unwanted, unworthy, unimportant or unable who fill our jails, our mental hospitals, and our institutions." (p. 201) Hawk reports that in order to help an individual gain a more positive view of himself, the would be helper first has to see the person as the person sees himself. He advises that, difficult as it is to see the world from the disadvantaged child's viewpoint, one possible substitute for a common background of experience is to listen with objectivity and warmth so that in getting to know the child you can feel *with* him, not *about* him.

With this accomplished, the child is in a position to be accepted. Acceptance, according to Hawk, is the key word in improving an individual's concept of self. An individual learns that he is adequate by being treated *as if* he were adequate. And in a learning situation, a child—or any person for that matter—learns feelings of adequacy and competence by performing successfully on tasks that are appropriate to his level of competence.

Though Hawk accepts the proposition that an individual's behavior is linked with his perceived self, he recommends that if negative comments are necessary they should be made about behavior and not about the person. He believes that negative statements about behavior may not have the self-deprecating effects that negative statements about the person might have. He warns that ignoring a child may be even more damaging than negative statements. If you have accepted him, he will accept being corrected; but to be ignored or overlooked may be perceived as being rejected.

REFERENCES

Gordon, Edmund W. "Characteristics of Socially Disadvantaged Children," *Review of Educ. Res.,* Vol. 35, No. 5 (December 1965), pp. 377-385.

Hawk, Traves L. "Self-Concepts of the Socially Disadvantaged," *Elementary School J.*, Vol. 67, No. 4 (January 1967), pp. 296-206.

Keller, Suzanne. "The American Lower-Class Family." Report prepared for New York State Division for Youth, 1965, pp. 1-87.

Miller, Robert W., Frederick A. Zeller, and Harry R. Blaine. "Implications of Social Class Differences in Beliefs Concerning Causes of Unemployment." Office of Research and Development, Appalachian Center, West Virginia University, April 1968.

Newman, Dorothy K. "Changing Attitudes About the Poor," *Monthly Labor Review* (February 1969), pp. 32-36.

Rees, Helen E. *Deprivation and Compensatory Education.* Boston: Houghton Mifflin, 1968.

Schwebel, Milton. "Learning and the Socially Deprived," *Personnel and Guidance J.* (March 1963), pp. 646-652.

Smith, Wendall I., and J. William Moore. *Conditioning and Instrumental Learning.* New York: McGraw-Hill, 1966.

Weller, Jack E. *Yesterday's People.* Lexington: U. of Kentucky Press, 1965.

Willacy, Hazel M. "Man in Poverty Neighborhoods: A Status Report," *Monthly Labor Review* (February 1969), pp. 23-31.

3

Difficulties in "Helping" the "Disadvantaged"

C. E. Smith

A good deal of confusion reigns, emotionality runs rampant, and cliché assumptions abound in both lay and professional discussions about "help," particularly for the "disadvantaged." The purpose of this brief paper is to sample some of the difficulties in conceptualizing effective help for the disadvantaged. To accomplish this purpose, the current status of some manpower retraining programs are surveyed and both deficiencies and effective elements noted.

Evaluation of manpower training programs depends on an awareness of social phenomena which surround such undertakings. While such an assertion has a ring of obviousness—even naiveté—about it, typical evaluative statements usually are confounded by conflicting and shortsighted assumptions about goals, process, outcome, methods, and social need for retraining programs.

Critics of the social reconstruction enterprise and helping professions in general tend to have a mistaken view that such activities are new social functions which "mollycoddle" people, encourage irresponsibility and dependency, enforce conformity, or other similarly value-laden and emotionally charged generalizations. An example of such a mistaken and widespread view was reported in a recent study of differences in beliefs among social classes regarding reasons for unemployment. In the social classes deemed successful, beliefs tended to be represented by statements such as the following.

"If an individual fails to become socially and economically self-sufficient, it is his own responsibility for not having decided to exert proper effort." (Miller, Zeller, Blaine, 1968, p. 68) The implication is that being helped is somehow not quite respectable, and that "rugged individualism" is the truly righteous path. An attitudinal set of this sort provides the basis for the mystique of the "self-made" man whose frequent benedictions and sanctimonious self-aggrandizement consequently are socially and self-reinforced.

Where a "rugged-individualist" point of view falters, however, is in its failure to realize that man's existence and progress in a complex society is best described as a process of interdependency—of reciprocal sharing and accepting, giving and receiving. Further, genuine helping functions have always existed in Western civilization. Until rather recent times, however, most such functions were typically performed exclusively by parents, venerable elders, "self-made" men, church leaders, and other influential adults of the community. At the risk of oversimplification, one may state that over the past several decades there has developed in the United States a professionalized structure of variable sophistication which gradually has assumed responsibility for the performance of this same set of functions as were always performed. The emergence of a professionalized structure is due predominantly to rampant social changes such as rapid industrialization, massive population shifts, and numerous other well-known factors, all of which have resulted in the overwhelming complexity of contemporary society. The resultant "technological juggernaut" with dominant characteristics of insatiable demands for higher-level skills, pressures toward increased specialization, and instant obsolesence of many salable skills requires not only the intensified development of a professional body of helpers but also an expanded concept of who the consumers of the help actually are. If some theorists (such as Super) are accurate, the social need for professional helpers conceivably could be extended to include all members of a complex and specialized society throughout their lifetime. For example, it is naive today to attach much viability to the nineteenth-century model of "helping" a child make a specific occupational choice, thereby preparing for a career he expects to follow most of his life. Statistics abound to cast doubt upon such a model: 70 percent of the jobs today's elementary school children will eventually hold do not now exist; on the average, a worker needs retraining by the age of 30; workers need retraining, on the average, every seven years. (Wrenn, 1962) Clearly then, the emphasis in education and training must be on the processes of continual choosing and learning, and on the acquisition of basic skills, attitudes, and knowledge to continue learning and making wise choices.

John Diebold, a recognized authority on automation, summarizes the point.

> No longer can we afford complete confidence in the permanency of a way of life or in the continuence of existing trends. Counselors should no longer emphasize a choice of one career as a lifetime pursuit . . . the future is in the planning for change. In helping a person plan for his occupational life, a counselor should keep uppermost in mind the importance of avoiding overemphasis on specific skills at the expense of developing basic capabilities. Special skills can become obsolete quickly. General capabilities, on the other hand, have the necessary foundation for acquiring new special skills.

The failure of public schools to operationalize a system to achieve general capabilities for great numbers of students is in part responsible for the need for "retraining" programs. Paradoxically, retraining efforts largely repeat the failure on both a conceptual and an operational basis.

SOME DIFFICULTIES OF CURRENT PROGRAMS

A dismaying but necessary way to begin examining problems of current manpower retraining programs is to look critically at some present shortcomings of some existing programs. Two broad kinds of ineffectual retraining programs may be identified. The first of these is exemplified by the following letter written by a group of Appalachian men enrolled in such a program. The letter reflects sheer criminal prostitution of human dignity and public monies.

> We were in the building and maintenance class under MDTA that took up on April 10 and ended September 29. They told us each day we would have two hours of electricity, plumbing, carpentry and painting but for the most of it, all we did was paint school buildings and repair and cover the roofs of the schools. When some of the men bucked on painting so much, they was told the government would buy around a thousand dollars of lumber a month for us to work with. We unloaded plenty of new lumber and racked it up on the racks. For awhile we used some and then we was told we could buy it for 25 cents a foot and they said it wasn't for sale but it still got missing. In electricity, all we had were nine days; on our certificate of training, it says we got 320 hours. They just didn't care much if we learned a thing or not we was just putting in time. . . . (Ciardi, 1968, p. 16)

While relatively uninteresting from a theoretical standpoint, this sort of gross corruption clearly exemplifies the first type of ineffectual retraining program and apparently occurs with some regularity in current reality. The trainees invested nothing in a nonexistent program and gained even less from it. Unfortunately, hypocritical disregard for effective help for disadvantaged people will probably continue to exist as a cancerous growth on the quest for social health from some time to come. The solution, moreover, to this type of ineffectiveness is simple to state: Don't entrust programs to people who don't care.

The second type of ineffectual manpower development program is more common, although it is somewhat more difficult to analyze precisely. Ineffectual programs can result even when projects are entrusted to people who do care deeply whether others "learn a thing or not." In a recent vice-presidential address to the American Association for the Advancement of Science entitled, somewhat tongue-in-cheek, "Dare We Take the Social Sciences Seriously"? economist Kenneth Boulding (1967) spoke of the negative effects of the widespread presence of a good deal of relatively accurate general knowledge about social systems.

> If we want to navigate a satellite or produce a nuclear weapon, we do not call in the old wives. In social systems the old wives, or at least their husbands, are called in all the time. Creating a peaceful world, abolishing slums, solving the race problem, or overcoming crime and so on, are not regarded as subjects for scientific technology but are re-

garded as fields where a pure heart and a little common sense will do all that is really necessary.

The point is, of course, that a "pure heart, deep caring, and common sense" are all critically necessary, but they are not sufficient ingredients for successful manpower retraining programs. The truth of the matter is there is a body of scientific theory and applied methods which can be demonstrated to work in most cases, assuming one knows where one wants to go. Lloyd Homme (1967, p. 1) states the case this way:

> There is a widespread misconception in our society that not much is known about the control of behavior. One of the ways this shows itself is in the often repeated assertion that, in order for a breakthrough in education to occur, "We need to know more about the learning process." This simply does not square with the facts. Psychologists have long pointed out . . . that by taking seriously the fundamental laws of behavior already well established, we can promote great changes for the better in our society. This can occur without the discovery of hitherto unknown laws, without any elaborate new theories, without knowing any more about the chemistry of the brain, without knowing any more about the fundamentals of behavior than we know today.

Scientists may agree among themselves that theory and applied methods in the social and behavioral sciences may be at a level only a foot off the floor if the ceiling represents most of the answers. Practice, however—even in formal institutions of learning—is typically the height of a speck of dust on the same floor. Inadequate conceptualization of program design is even more extensive.

A pointed example of the inadequately conceptualized retraining program is found in adult basic education classes for the school "dropout." The dropout, sent as an adult back to the same schoolroom he dropped out of, meets with the same old instructor again, fails to learn the same old material, and perhaps even sits in the same old desk. While popular songs assert love is better the second time around, the analogy does not hold for the dropout simply because he now is an adult and "settled down."

Yet another example of shortsightedness is the case where trainees are given limited entry-level technical training for jobs that will, in all likelihood, be obsolete in the near future. (Smith, 1968) Or, consider the naive, assembly-line model of education or training where the trainee "raw material" is taken into the training factory and tooled up as a finished product; the task is then over.

Another aspect of conceptual inadequacy is failure to design for the avoidance of negative psychological effects of nonmeaningful work. A recent article, for example, describes dramatic differences observed between two groups of young trainees, one of which was offered to role playing to prepare for a job interview and the other group which had a bonefide interview scheduled the next day. Those who recall WPA projects of the 1930's and similar efforts realize the associated lack of psychological satisfaction for most workers. One problem

American society faces is that the opportunity for satisfying, meaningful work will diminish in the future for great numbers of the population. This does not mean, as it has been argued, that there will be necessarily fewer jobs because of automation. It almost certainly does mean, except perhaps for a distant utopian future, intrinsically satisfying jobs will be accessible primarily to the highly trained, highly skilled person who has the capacity and skills for growth and change.

Additionally, facing the indisputable fact of individual differences, it is also unlikely that manpower pools exist in sufficient size necessary to meet the demand in certain areas. This further restricts available, satisfactory jobs to those who are geographically mobile to more developed areas. An approach which either attempts to retrain workers for jobs which shortly will be obsolete or which do not exist in a given area is doomed to failure unless the approach stresses mobility, or is accompanied with an equal amount of economic development activities in the given area.

Summarily, what these diverse examples illustrate is that even deep caring and the best intentions aren't sufficient in the absence of hard data about the optimal conditions under which humans learn most effectively, data about effective means of dealing with problems of psychological adjustment and adaptability, and of knowledge about what kinds of skills most likely will be needed in the job structure in the next several years. Some existing programs incorporate parts of these elements into their design and operation.

SOME EFFECTIVE ELEMENTS OF CURRENT PROGRAMS

A recent national conference dealing with means by which industry can make effective use of the "hard-core unemployed" brought together over 800 key representatives from public and private agencies and industries involved in some phase of manpower development. A series of common threads in the more effective programs seemed associated with program success. (Smith, 1968) Few programs exist, however, which have done well-controlled experimental studies to determine effectiveness. Fewer still have used sufficiently sophisticated experimental procedures to enable the identification of the efficient elements antecedent to success. Additionally, manpower development projects—in common with many other organizations—have a tendency to become organizationally schizophrenic; that is, the desired image of the outcome is confirmed no matter what has occurred in reality. These factors make it difficult to get valid, nondistorted information both about how well and why programs work. One example suffices: one retraining effort reported successful job placement for 90 percent of its graduates, neglecting to mention the 90 percent constituted only half of the entering trainees, and that the "successful job placement" was with the United States Armed Services for over half of the graduates.

A few notable exceptions such as the Norfolk (Virginia) State College

Project (Brazziel, 1966), the Mobilization for Youth (New York City), the Kilmer Job Corps (New Jersey), and the Philadelphia program seem to offer some grounds for optimism regarding the feasibility of developing and replicating effective programs.

Subjective inferences about successful programs were, however, identifiable at the conference by indices such as the percentage and quality of job placements of the trainees, by trainees' attitudes, and by input characteristics. Graduates of successful programs were reported to be economically and personally productive, to have an otpimistic but realistic attitude, and those who appeared seemed to have a bearing which indicated obvious, new-found self-respect and dignity.

In general, the seemingly most effective programs all had in common the following components.

1. Programs generally contained three major structured activities: (a) specific skill training for a job where placement was imminent, (b) highly intensive, often individualized, basic education effort, and (c) a social learning and/or attitudinal change program—typically intensive group counseling or human relations training.

2. There was always a continuing effort of the project to provide help after the trainee had developed marketable skills and was employed. He was "phased in" instead of "turned out" as a finished product. This effort took many forms, but it involved primarily on-the-job counseling with the newly placed trainee. In some cases, human relations training groups were also carried on with groups of job supervisors of the trainees. The major thrust of these training efforts with supervisors was conflict resolution, usually about day-to-day problems at work.

3. In some way or another, immediate incentives or rewards, contingent upon trainee performance of some desired behavior, were designed into the system so that the rewards were available for relatively small accomplishments.[1] In contrast, "saving" all the satisfaction until after the trainee had finished long segments of work was not nearly as effective.

4. Emphasis was placed on criterion performance. Simply stated, this means training efforts were continued until the trainee could demonstrate mastery of some specific objective. One rationale for assessing criterion performance instead of traditionally comparative graduating practices is simply that there are some job tasks which are critically essential to minimum performance of any given job. For example, it would be fruitless to compare trainees in how well they know how to turn on the switch of a power lathe. The power lathe won't run unless the switch is on, and trainees either can turn it on or they can't. If they can't, there's no point in moving along to the more complex components of the job. Such an analysis can be extended to all of the acts which are required for the minimum performance of a job.

5. Long-term vocational development as a process instead of a single-event

[1] See Chapter 11.

occupational choice was a major emphasis. Conversely, a common source of conceptual and actual failure in some programs was the selection and location of initial jobs to become available to trainees. There is no particular advantage to either trainees or to society to design programs which change the status of the unemployed to that of the underemployed. Although the trainee has ordinarily the same kinds of aspirations for material and psychological satisfactions as does the employed technician, manager, and professional worker, a typical failure of some programs is the provision of training only for relatively low-level entry jobs, both in terms of skills required and economic rewards. It is no wonder that the trainee who perceives this farcical situation in a relatively accurate fashion tends to reject the somewhat onerous burden of learning a great deal of material and complex skills. He can see that his immediate economic gain is not going to be significantly greater than that which he can draw from the public coffers.

Not all trainees, of course, were placed in relatively high-paying jobs. There was, nevertheless, a subtle advantage in the long-term vocational development approach. Trainees who weren't skilled enough for higher-paying jobs were able, as one trainee put it, "to put up with the situation while they help me plan how to improve it." The approach has enjoyed success in Vocational Rehabilitation Centers, but was usually lacking in the conference retraining programs.

There were a number of other design factors[2] seemingly associated with effectiveness in some existing programs. However, a more profitable way to recapitulate may be an attempt to identify several underlying assumptions about personal and vocational developments which seem most critical to all the effective programs.

FALSE ASSUMPTIONS ABOUT VOCATIONAL DEVELOPMENT

In general, planners of effective programs designed efforts which overcame a number of common, but false assumptions about vocational development. The first of these false assumptions is that programs can deal effectively with parts of human beings. If this were true, manpower retraining programs would be analogous to bringing a car into a shop to have the transmission fixed, then putting it back on the road to run effectively. Programs which attempt solely to "fix up" deficiencies in job skills are doomed to ineffectuality. To reiterate , the most important outcome of any educational program today is the development of skills and attitudes necessary to continue adapting to and accommodating change. By any criteria, programs which included basic education skills of these kinds were more effective than ones with major emphasis on technical training for entry-level jobs. Those including some minimum technical training, more basic education, and intensive personal growth counseling seemed most

---

[2] For example, jobs were assured to trainees contingent upon their completion of the program; emphasis was placed on developing trainee initiative, independence, and responsibility.

effective. In short, the concept of manpower retraining itself is at least partially ineffectual unless it is conceived in broader terms of total and continuing human development.

A second false assumption is that some serious or unconquerable defect exists in the trainee. "These people just don't want to work," is an example of this kind of false assumption. As sociologist Marshall Jones (1969) notes, what is often mistaken for maladaption due to individual defect occurs precisely because the individual is perfectly "normal or average," and discovers the reassurances of society are unrealistic. To reintroduce the car analogy, a trainee might well be ready and able to run effectively only to find out his particular road is an Olympic obstacle course or a maze of blind alleys. Such is the case often for the black trainee. This is not to say trainees who by definition are maladaptive do not require intensive reeducative effort, or that they should shirk responsibility for themselves, but it does mean effective programs must deal effectively with the "outside system" as well as with the trainee. Examples in the successful programs surveyed earlier were (1) extended efforts with both trainees and their supervisors after the trainee was placed on the job, and (2) job-development teams emphasizing long-term vocational development.

A third false assumption is that people make decisions rationally on the basis of objective facts. The absurdity of this position is evident, yet some manpower development programs seem to assume trainees have a unique ability to thrive on decisions made for them by "objective" matching of men and jobs.

A final false assumption to be identified is that it is possible to prepare a man for a specific job. There are a number of pitfalls in this assumption. First, it implies an assembly-line model of education where a person is tooled up to fit a slot and is expected to fit there comfortably, after which the process is completed. In view of the rampart change in the United States' job structure, it is at least likely that specific lifelong career slots no longer exist. If for no other reason, it then becomes more important to develop skills of a higher order—for example, skills in making decisions, in how to continue learning, in how and where to find and make opportunities, in how to interact effectively with other human beings; in short, skills and knowledge in how to exercise humanness. Second, it is impossible to predict in the abstract all of those forces that may cause failure in future vocational development. Therefore, dealing with the immediate present while the trainee is on the job is implied. Additionally, the underlying expectation of a demand for specific-skill-trained employees is greatly exaggerated. Employability is dependent upon additional equally potent characteristics such as basic capabilities, attitudinal factors, and general personal functioning.

In conclusion, manpower retraining programs specifically, and helping efforts for the disadvantaged in general, face the same inexorable demands and complex problems as do any educational efforts. Simplistic efforts, however well-intentioned, produce none of the return legitimately expected.

EPILOGUE

There was once a monkey and a fish, sole survivors of the second Great Flood. The monkey had scampered to safety in the top of a very high tree. Looking down, he saw the fish struggling mightily against the cruel torrent. With the best of intentions, the monkey reached down and drew the poor fish tenderly to his breast.

The moral of the story is obvious.

REFERENCES

Boulding, Kenneth. "Dare We Take the Social Sciences Seriously?," *Amer. Behavioral Sci.* (June 1967), p. 313.

Brazziel, W. F. "Basic Education in Manpower Retraining Programs," in F. W. Lanning and W. A. Many, *Basic Education for the Disadvantaged Adult.* Boston: Houghton Mifflin, 1966, pp. 374-378.

Ciardi, John. "Appalachia: Again the Forgotten Land," *Saturday Rev.* (January 27, 1968), p. 16.

Diebold, John, in J. Samler et. al. (eds.) *Automation: the Threat and the Promise.* Washington, D.C.: National Vocational Guidance Association, 1964.

Homme, Lloyd. "A Behavior Technology Exists—Here and Now." Unpublished paper. Albuquerque, N. M.: Westinghouse Learning Corporation, c. 1967, pp., 1-19.

Jones, Marshall. "Some Aspects of the Sociology of Guidance," in C. E. Smith and O. G. Mink (eds.), *Foundations of Counseling and Guidance: Multidisciplinary Readings.* Philadelphia: Lippincott, 1969.

Miller, R. W., F. Zeller, and H. R. Blaine. "Implications of Social Class Differences in Beliefs Concerning Causes of Unemployment," *Research Series Z.* Office of Research and Development, Appalachian Center, University of West Virginia, Morgantown, W. Va., 1968.

Smith, C. E. National Conference on the Effective Utilization of the Hardcore Unemployed by Industry. Unpublished notes. New York State Psychological Association, New York City, March 1968.

Weisbrod, Burton A. "Investing in Human Capital," *J. Human Resources* (Summer 1966), pp. 5-21.

Wrenn, C. Gilbert. *The Counselor in a Changing World.* Washington, D.C.: American Personnel and Guidance Association, 1962.

part II

Issues

4

Innovating Educational Practice for Disadvantaged Youth

Bernard A. Kaplan

One of the most fashionable words uttered in educational circles over the last decade is *innovation*. Sometimes used synonymously with the word *change*, most educators (and the general public, in fact) are in agreement that education and the schools "need" innovation. The rub comes in terms of the answers to two critical questions:

1. What is meant by innovation?
2. Specifically, what kinds of innovation are to be permitted?

The concept of educational innovation, that of introducing something new or different, in the schools is deceptively simple. For it is such a *relative* term. As beauty exists in the eye of the beholder, so it appears, does innovation. What may be old hat in Rochester, New York, may be unheard of and untried in Phoenix, Arizona. Moreover, the same approach or activity may be old-fashioned or standard in one elementary school of a given city, but it may be completely unheard of in another elementary school of the same city only blocks away. Carrying the comparison still further, Miss Prince may use role playing and field trips consistently and extensively in her social studies classes while Mrs. King, in the classroom next door, feels these activities are unnecessary, a waste of time, and not at all advantageous in her social studies instruction— and therefore she's never attempted to apply them.

Another way of looking at innovation is to look at what appears to be the general, or traditional practice in the majority of the schools. If the practice is not prevalent in, say, 5 percent or 10 percent of the schools, then it can be characterized as innovative. Here again, however, it makes a great difference as to whether a given region, section, state, or the entire country is being addressed, or whether we're talking about rural, urban, central city, or suburban programs. Elementary school guidance programs may be innovative in rural schools or in Arkansas, but not in suburban schools or in Maryland.

Another view of educational innovation is to restrict it to practices that are clearly, indisputably untried and unknown in contemporary schools. Here we approach the realm of research and demonstration, of true experimentation and test cases. Recent educational examples of these are the Individual Programmed

Instruction (IPI) materials developed by Research for Better Schools Regional Laboratory and Computer Assisted Instruction (CAI) under development by numerous commercial firms.

The major piece of federal legislation pertaining to educational innovation, per se, is Title III of the Elementary and Secondary Education Act; Title III specifically provides for development and implementation of innovative and exemplary programs. As applied during its first few years of existence, "innovative" could be interpreted in any or all of the modes expressed above. Thus for a large number of programs funded under this legislation, the innovation applied not so much to the field as it did to the school district receiving the grant.

Recent changes in the legislation and regulations affecting Title III transferring its administration from the U.S. Office of Education to the separate states highlight an even more significant aspect of innovative educational practice. The purpose of the innovation as adjudged by statewide needs-assessment determinations is now a major consideration. In other words, innovation is no longer acceptable merely for the sake of innovation; it must be viewed in terms of realizing certain specified goals. If we adopt this qualification to innovation in education, we can immediately address key issues affecting disadvantaged youth and student populations. For example, what changes must be introduced to enable minority group pupils to achieve on a level commensurate with their counterparts in middle-class suburbia? What changes must be brought about to qualify disadvantaged students from Appalachia or the Watts area of Los Angles for admission to college and for success there at the same rate as graduates from Scarsdale, New York, or Beverly Hills, California? How can the Spanish-speaking pupil, or the migrant youth, be kept from becoming a dropout, or better yet, a potential dropout?

If we keep the above interpretation in mind, we consider the potential benefit of the innovation for the *consumer* in the system, the student. Several innovative programs that have succeeded in doing this from outside the traditional educational framework are Head Start, Upward Bound, VISTA, MDT, and the Street Academies. All of these are addressed to specific target populations. The problem, however, is how to institutionalize these successes so that they can operate both equally as successfully and routinely in the regular school program.

This latter problem brings us to the second major question—What kinds of innovation are to be permitted? This is the sensitive issue. Here the controversies emerge. For now, by suggesting change and implying adoption of alternate practices, we attack the traditional, the sacrosanct, the "time-honored," the venerable. Now the hopeful innovator risks the charge of being termed a leftist, an un-American, a revolutionary-or more colloquially, a wild-eyed fanatic or ivory-tower screwball. For if significant change or innovation in standard school practice, at least for disadvantaged pupils, is to occur, it cannot be superficial or temporary; it must be basic, comprehensive, and durable. Thus old standards (the ten-month school year), previously recognized criteria (credentials, certification), former practice (one teacher per classroom of 25-35 pupils) must be honestly reexamined for their present effectiveness and quite likely thoroughly modified if not completely rejected and replaced.

Many educators and lay persons alike are not ready to abandon the current and the traditional, in spite of their avowal that "change is needed with the changing times" and that "to stand still is to fall behind." For this group simultaneously espouses the contradictory (and usually more pronounced) view that "it must mean something if it's always been done that way," and "it was good enough for me when I was a student."

Since formal education affects everyone in some way and since it constitutes such a major proportion of local and state expenditures, the contemplation of drastic, genuine change has immediate fiscal and political repercussions. The general assumption, widely held but not validated, is that innovation—replacing a present practice with a new one—will cost more money. This may or may not be true. It may depend on the specific innovation. If CAI and teacher aides are successfully introduced, it may *reduce* the per-pupil costs of education, for the pupil may not need as many teacher hours per day as is now the case. Schools Without Walls and Storefront Academies may reduce the capital outlay required for new school construction.

Politically, however, the possibility of change is even more threatening. For the pressure groups and the vested interests of those long in power work vigorously and persistently against far-reaching innovation. The lobbies, the professional associations, the standardbearers tend to maintain the status quo as the hippies have forcibly proclaimed. Rigidity and adherence to the old standards are the results. Unless the change will also benefit the majority, or more likely, keep the majority advantaged and competitive, the proposed innovation will have considerable rough going.

Another factor that must be recognized in contemplating innovation in educational practice is that of the general fear of the unknown. Teachers and parents as a whole would much rather settle on the "tried and true" even if it is only limited in its effectiveness than to risk a different approach that might (or might not) be two or three times as effective. Part of the reason for this is the traditional lack of "departure" in education and the fear of failure by teachers (ironic in the face of so many failing students in their classes). But more importantly, parents and teachers do not trust themselves or others to gamble with variations in educational experiences for the children in their charge. Medicine, of course, provides a mechanism through hospital and clinical laboratories and field tests for research and for development of improvements in preventive and curative practice and technological application; education does not.

COMPONENTS OF SUCCESSFUL INNOVATIVE PRACTICE IN EDUCATION

If a new practice is to succeed in the public schools, the following conditions must usually accompany the activity.

Readiness

Teachers, and often students and parents, must be ready for the new program. All too frequently, a new program is initiated because the superintendent or the building principal believes it would be a good idea, or a central office staff person may draft a proposal which is subsequently funded. Project directors, or coordinators, are appointed, often on short notice and with little or no familiarity with the purpose and theoretical constructs of the original proposal. They in turn recruit or inherit teachers who will purportedly demonstrate the new approach. All too often the teachers are very vague about what is expected of them and their pupils. And, ironically, the schools having the student population requiring the most serious adjustment in educational practice usually have faculties most resistant to change.

Two principles are appropriate for would-be innovators with respect to readiness:

1. When it is possible to be selective, choose the school or staff with the personnel more likely to give the new practice a fair chance. This is not always an easy process because the more defensive staff may need the program for its school more than another. Moreover, unless those making the selection are especially astute and painstaking, the readiness of the staff may be misjudged—in either direction. Another problem may be unforeseen circumstances affecting key individuals, staff turnover being a prime consideration.

2. Provide as much information about the new program as possible. This means more than a routine one-shot announcement in the school paper. It also requires special preparation of all those who will be affected; this includes administrators, project directors, participating staff, non-participating staff, parents and students. Sometimes, of course, it is not always possible or desirable to be so all-inclusive of the various groups concerned. If control groups are a factor or if the trial would be jeopardized because of resultant pressure or attention, then adjustments should be made.

In the past, however, school experiments have suffered more as a result of exclusion of personnel in this phase rather than their excessive inclusion.

Follow-Through

Frequently, new programs are introduced with resounding fanfare and then, surprisingly, forgotten or neglected. The initial thrust, which accompanied the design of the program, search for funds and institution of the activity, is attenuated almost in direct proportion to the time the program has been underway. Ongoing programs are usually characterized by turnover in participating staff, shifts in project administration, cuts in project budgets, and departures from original plans. It is not unusual for the program not to be heard of again except at refunding periods, or in rare cases, when a controversy springs up. (The 1968 New York City teacher strike and parental confrontation over community-controlled schools and decentralization is probably the best and most recent example of such an instance.)

Several provisions should accompany the new program to avoid having it become subsequently dismissed.

1. *Ongoing evaluation* is a must. The new program must be assessed continuously and reports of its effectiveness should be made as often as possible—certainly to the participating staff and administration. The evaluation should be of two sorts, with designs for these prepared *prior* to the start of the new effort. First, the methodology and procedures utilized in conducting the new practice should be periodically examined for accuracy of translation from proposal to practice. (This is more likely to take place than the next facet of evaluation.) Secondly, the outcomes or effects on the students in the program need consistent, unbiased, and convincing appraisal. This latter phase is especially difficult in educational practice. For one thing, controlled changes in behavior in any field are extremely difficult to measure and to attribute. Furthermore, traditional educational practice has long escaped rigorous evaluation; the techniques and capability have simply not been developed. As the advocates of accountability in our public schools have submitted, we have accepted the present educational system and its product primarily on faith. Proving that a different approach will better the current one, in the light of very little concrete support for the effectiveness, one way or the other, of the present one, is not an easy matter.

Evaluation, nevertheless, which is repetitive, multipurposed, and cogent is a necessary component of the follow-through process.

2. Another aspect of follow-through is *dissemination* of information concerning either the progress or outcomes of the program. Frequent reports, responsible critiques, objective analysis should characterize information furnished about new programs. Many programs are marred by a scarcity of information or by enthusiastic descriptions of on-site "experts."

As there are several groups concerned with the successful execution of the program (see section on readiness, above) so should these same groups be kept informed of progress and results. Moreover, once the program produces significant data, such information should be shared with other educators. In the past, this has usually been limited to a journal article and a few reports at professional conventions. Now, through the creation of ERIC clearing houses and other similar efforts, new programs need not be forgotten soon after their completion. The latest turn, however, endangering meaningful sharing is the plethora of programs now starting to be reported. Such abundance bodes careful and time-consuming sifting of the literature by the innovator in order to harvest clues and suggestions in the development of his own program.

3. The third aspect of follow-through is adoption or *internalization*. If a program, or part of it—or its offshoots—warrants continuation, one would as-

sume this would naturally occur. Unfortunately, this is not usually the case. A large proportion of the programs reported in the literature are surprisingly *not* continued. Sometimes there are problems of funds, of sufficient evidence of success, of adequate staff. Sometimes the field test is highly successful, but the next step—transfer to a number of schools—meets with disappointing failure. Something happens in the transition.

The transfer of the program from a project or test phase to a regular part of the school system's operation is much more complex than the introduction of a new cleanser by Procter & Gamble; P & G does this regularly, whereas the schools thrive on tradition. When new programs are introduced in the schools on a broad scale, many of the same steps, outlined under Readiness and Follow-Through must be repeated; this customarily has not been the case in the past. Equally as important is for the new staff assigned by the schools to be familiar with the program to be introduced. This can be accomplished through in-service training or through training received by the new teachers prior to certification. Since one school system cannot influence college teacher preparation programs to any significant degree, the most realistic method must be regarded as internships provided by the school system or by school-controlled in-service education programs. Unfortunately, both of these are expensive in that they require present staff to be borrowed part-time (usually for compensation or partial substitution) while participating in the training.

A further word concerning in-service training for new programs: it appears considerably more advantageous to develop a program with both preliminary and concurrent training phases. If the staff involved receives a minimum of its training prior to the new program (summers, intersessions, etc.) during which time basic concepts, attitudes, and prerequisite skills and knowledge can be acquired, then the major portion of the training can be provided while the program is in process (during the term—Saturdays, evenings, late afternoons). In this way the teacher will be much more motivated and alert to the nuances of satisfactory introduction of the program.

A further corollary is that as teachers start a new program, responsive and sensitive supervision should be provided. Such supervision should convey to the staff a climate of assistance and support, not personal evaluation or censure. Rather than a threat, it should be viewed as a genuine source of help. Again, provision for such supervision must be included in both the program design and the program budget.

Community Involvement

The more significant and far-reaching the proposed innovation, the more necessary it is for broad segments of the community to become involved in its introduction. As in the Model Cities, the community affected should be involved not only in the decision to adopt or attempt a new program but in its conception, design, and detailed planning as well. Such participation will certainly assure a more likely degree of success. This is especially important in schools with large numbers of disadvantaged pupils. Advisory councils and ad hoc committees have been suggested as one means of accomplishing this evaluation. Such councils are effective if given a genuine role and not a paper one. Paraprofessionals selected from the community are another means of furthering participation and involvement. Student groups are still another method—and one usually neglected—in reaching greater community understanding and support. Volunteers for tutoring and assistance with school-supported or school-related activities can also draw local representatives into a closer relationship with the school system.

In conclusion, the foregoing points up the need for considerably more than the conception of a new program by educators to bring about its successful transfer to the schools. No matter how sterling the idea, it must be nourished by a considerable amount of careful planning. Such planning must cover both preliminary and operational aspects—the step-by-step development of the new program. It must take into account the readiness of the school staff, follow-through provisions, and adequate community representation. These latter components require extensive detailed planning and programming. The time, funds, and staff thus dictated must be incorporated in the overall program design. Without them, program innovation in the schools will likely continue to flounder and fail.

CHARACTERISTICS AND EXAMPLES OF PROMISING EDUCATIONAL INNOVATIONS FOR DISADVANTAGED YOUTH

While programs for the disadvantaged abound, particularly since the advent of Title I, ESEA and the Age of Compensatory Education, obviously not all new approaches are equally promising. There are some, however, that appear to offer some hope for upgrading and improving the education of disadvantaged youth. Some of these programs are listed below.

The Philadelphia Advancement School. An offshoot of the North Carolina Advancement School, the project of the Philadelphia Public Schools attempts to develop and dovetail (a) new patterns of teaching new curricular themes, (b) group learning cells, and (c) informal structures for junior high school level students.

The Action Bound Program of Trenton, New Jersey. This is one of the first attempts in the country to transfer to a public school an adaptation of the Outward Bound program, in which youths are subjected to a number of toughening, survival-type, wilderness experiences, which in the end produces more confident, resourceful, reliable, independent (but socially conscious) graduates.

The School Without Walls. This is another Philadelphia Public Schools program, provides curriculum and program for its students by drawing on the community's cultural, educational, and municipal resources. Museums, parks, libraries, and governmental facilities are utilized for on-site learning.

Mobile Laboratory Units. This project of Webster County, West Virginia, utilizes four mobile units equipped for reading, science or health-social studies. Staffed by a master teacher and a teacher aide, the units serve children in grades 3-12 in 13 schools throughout the year. In this rural Appalachian area, traditional school programs are supplemented and enriched by transporting materials and instruction directly to pupils (and their teachers).

Project STAY. This High School for Dropouts project in Washington, D.C., is an afternoon and evening high school for students between ages of 16-21. The school has a professional staff of 45 and enrolls 1,500 students in a complete academic curriculum. Special counseling, job placement, adjusted schedules, and a nursery-care center for mothers attending the school are provided. The school also operates during the summer and grants high school diplomas.

The Bus Counselor. This school aide program of Onslaw County (Jacksonville), North Carolina, employs 150 women from target school areas full-time as "big sister" counselors on buses transporting children to and from school and as school aides during the day. The counselor-aides are required to complete a 30-hour preservice training program and in-service training is also provided after employment has begun. The program serves 2,700 elementary and junior high school pupils.

New Jersey's Technology for Children Project. Pupils in grades 1-6 are taught to comprehend and appreciate the basic skills and rudiments through utilization of technological concepts, equipment, and techniques. Each participating teacher receives special preservice and in-service training. Classrooms are provided with tool chests and laboratories specially designed for each grade level. Emphasis is on individual and small group participation, reliance on all the senses in a learning-by-doing approach, and a continual relating of the learning activity to pertinent historical and contemporary occupational and technological applications.

Other Promising Programs. Other programs receiving national attention are computer-assisted instruction (CAI), individually prescribed instruction (IPI) and educational television (ETV). Head Start, Upward Bound and the Street Academies are additional examples. Project STEP, in New York State, is fully described in another section of this book.

The above programs were selected because, in whole or in part, they tend to meet the following criteria:

1. The program's emphasis is on reaching the pupil psychologically, directly, and vigorously assisting him in the learning experience. Failure to learn is perceived as a shortcoming of the program or its staff rather than of the student.
2. The program utilizes different media, sensitive personnel, and/or relevant experiences.
3. The program transcends traditional approaches in terms of school day, school year, school building and classroom, teacher-student role, curriculum materials, and organization of the school curriculum.

4. The program draws on the community and aspects of contemporary society for inspiration, substance, direction or posture.
5. The program tends to be adaptive, flexible, imaginative, exciting and goal-centered for the pupils it serves.
6. Program staff members are carefully selected or trained to facilitate the learning and strengthen the self-image of the students participating.

Fantini and Weinstein (1968) aptly sum up the current relationship between innovation and the education of disadvantaged youth:

> The time of national crisis is a time for new leadership, and a time when needed and effective changes in our social institutions have the best chances of being implemented and sustained. The crisis of the disadvantaged has provided educators with a unique and epoch-making opportunity for effecting true and penetrating reform; what will they do with this opportunity? Will they use it to perpetuate the unwieldy, ineffective, and deteriorating status quo? Will they adopt a policy of "wait and see," reacting only *after* the fact to societal demands? Or will they seize this opportunity to assume the roles of initiators, revising education to become the instrument of societal reconstruction and renewal, of individual and societal health, and of human progress?

Over the last decade educators have taken a number of hesitating steps toward meeting the challenge posited above. Some of the steps have been successful, too many have been fruitless; some of the attempts have been imaginative and salubrious, others routine and colorless; some efforts have made important contributions to educational practice in America, others have raised serious questions concerning the ability of the profession to effectively respond to the need for change.

The tenor of the times and the preciousness of formative impressionable years of an entire generation demand that the challenge of accomplishing innovative educational practice for the disadvantaged be more aggressively, more firmly, and more effectively resolved in the next decade than it has been during the last one. The schools cannot afford to merely keep apace with the past; indeed, they will not be permitted that course of action even if they choose it.

The choice, then, is not either/or, but how, when, and by whom. Educational innovation in the schools, and particularly for the disadvantaged, is a certainty—only the form and substance remain to be determined.

RELATED READINGS AND REFERENCES

Committee for Economic Development. *The Schools and the Challenge of Innovation*. New York: McGraw-Hill, 1969.

Elam, S., and W. P. McLure (eds.). *Educational Requirements for the 1970's*. New York: Praeger, 1967.

Fallon, Berlie J. (ed.). *Educational Innovation in the United States*. Bloomington, Ind.: Phi Delta Kappa, 1966.

Fantani, M. D., and G. Weinstein. *The Disadvantaged: Challenge to Education*. New York: Harper & Row, 1968.

Guggenheim, F., and C. Guggenheim (eds.). *New Frontiers in Education*. New York: Grune and Stratton, 1966.

Jackson, Philip W. *Life in Classrooms*. New York: Holt, 1968.

Miller, H. L., and M. B. Smiley (eds.). *Education in the Metropolis*. New York: Free Press, 1967.

Morphet, E. L., and Charles O. Ryan (eds.). *Planning and Effecting Needed Changes in Education*. New York: Citation Press, 1967.

Morse, Arthur D. *Schools of Tomorrow–Today!* Albany, N.Y.: 1960 State Education Department.

National School Public Relations Association. *The Shape of Education for 1967-68*. Vol. 9. Washington, D.C.: National Education Association. 1967.

Schroder, H. M., and R. W. Lee. *Effects of Outward Bound Training on Urban Youth*. Mimeo. Princeton, N.J.: Princeton University, 1967.

U. S. Office of Education. *Profiles in Quality Education*: *150 Outstanding Title I, ESEA Projects*. Washington, D.C.: Government Printing Office, 1968.

5

Implications of Integration for Educational Practice *

Nida E. Thomas

One of the most challenging opportunities facing public school administrators today is how to achieve equal educational opportunity for all children. In a recent[1] address, Dr. James E. Allen, Jr. (1965), New York State Commissioner of Education, said,

> One of the greatest barriers to the achievement of equality of educational opportunity is the existence of racially segregated schools. The elimination of such schools in our urban centers or wherever else they exist is the imperative of our day. Our children have no choice but to live in a multiracial society. The schools must prepare them to live well in that society.

In this connection it seems that the implications of integration for educational practice require that every school administrator accept leadership, as far as it is necessary, to remove the barriers.

> In short, school integration demands that, on the basis of comprehensive desegregation, there be sustained and serious efforts to develop scholastic competence and democratic values and relationships in all aspects of a school's program. (Commission on School Integration, 1963)

What are some of the areas in which a school system can assume a responsibility for promoting integration? While there are many facets of integration, discussion of some practical activities in which teachers and administrators can engage immediately seems most urgent. Three areas are examined in this presentation: (1) How the curriculum can promote integration. (2) Teacher in-service training for utilizing various teaching materials. (3) The use of intergroup relations information in standard classroom subjects.

*In this chapter the term "Negro" is used by the author who is herself Negro. "Black," however, seems to be the more current term and reflects a definite pride of racial origin. (Ed.)
[1]Original manuscript prepared in 1966. Revised for publication in 1969.

41

HOW THE CURRICULUM CAN PROMOTE INTEGRATION

Joseph O. Loretan[2] (1960) offered the following guidelines on how to achieve the goal of curriculum integration:

1. Bring all children up to the level of experience and opportunity that will enable them to function with equal chance of success.
2. Give all children an understanding of their civil rights and liberties.
3. Give all children an awareness of their roles as citizens of this country.
4. Give all children a pride in their heritage and the accomplishments of those in their ethnic group.
5. Give all children the core of common learnings that are essential to effective participation in the present-day world.
6. Give all children the opportunity to be of service to their communities.
7. Help all children examine and create spiritual as well as economic values by which to live.

In concluding his address, Dr. Loretan said:

> I believe that the New York City school system is leading the nation in striving to rectify in one generation the mistakes and short-sightedness of many generations. I believe that we have the talent, we have the motivation, and we have the commitment to turn the American Dilemma into the American Dream.

TEACHER IN-SERVICE TRAINING

Where integration is to take place everything should be done to give the teacher helpful guides to intergroup understanding. Perhaps the statement quoted below gives ample warning for the need for vital in-service programs designed to develop democratic understanding and attitudes and a "climate of acceptance" in the classroom.

One of the most fundamental requirements for integration in Northern public schools is the education of teachers for the development of democratic values and relationships in the classroom. Far too many teachers lack the insights, the skills, and sometimes the motivations essential for this task. Generally speaking, their college and university education has not equipped them to overcome the prejudices of the society of which they are a part and to guide the development of democratic values and cooperative relationships among pupils with varying ethnic and social-class backgrounds.

In situations where integration is not an issue there is an obligation to prepare students to live in an integrated society.

During the past year the staff of the New York State Education Depart-

[2] Deputy Superintendent of New York City Schools presented this material at the 16th Annual Curriculum Conference of the Board of Education, New York City, Spring 1964.

ment has been involved in a number of teacher in-service training workshops throughout the state where attention has been focused on a number of "how to" questions. The questions embrace such areas as

1. Motivating desirable attitudes in all teachers.
2. Reaching preschoolers before they have acquired prejudices.
3. Drawing on experiences of the child in order to motivate him.
4. Providing opportunities for the student to meet people from other countries.
5. Planning conferences and workshops for teachers to discuss ways to improve intercultural relations.
6. Arranging exchange visits with schools where the students are racially and culturally different.
7. Helping students plan to get together and to learn to know and respect each other.
8. Developing and carrying out programs which provide opportunities for students to learn the meaning of teamwork and good sportsmanship such as play days between schools, sporting events, school trips, camping experiences, school plays, assembly programs, and committee work.

Hundreds of colleges and universities are now conducting summer human relations workshops. Many are "living-in" workshops, in which participants have the advantages of informal discussions and associations. Some are specifically concerned with how administrators and teachers can deal effectively with special educational problems occasioned by desegregation.

There seems to be a trend toward holding similar workshops during the school year in local school districts. Through this effort all school personnel will have an opportunity to become involved in a wide range of program activities required for successful integration.

USING INTERGROUP RELATIONS INFORMATION

Starting a few years ago, letters from teachers, letters to the Commissioner of Education and to the Governor, and out-of-state inquiries came to the attention of the New York State Educational Division of Intercultural Relations (DIR)—all complaining about the exclusion of textbook information about the contributions of minority groups and of the Negro in particular. Some wanted information to help motivate Negro children and to enrich classroom materials.

Since DIR is not a curriculum development division, its concern was to discover how to give some assistance to teachers and to suggest how to integrate the contributions of the Negro into classroom subjects in a meaningful way.

It was decided to begin with a publication of information appropriate for upper elementary grades where *one* teacher had the responsibility of teaching all subjects. The resultant publication was entitled *Intergroup Relations: A Resource Handbook for Elementary School Teachers, Grades 4, 5 and 6.* It soon became obvious that there were few subject areas where the integration of information was not possible. It also became obvious that to make the information meaningful as it related to the subject being taught, it had to fit into the normal pattern a teacher uses in preparing material for subjects or club activities.

DIR recognized also that the material had to be presented in such a way as to make teachers feel comfortable in using it. This was especially necessary for those teachers who had never worked in an integrated school system. It was equally as important for the teachers in an integrated school. In attempting to encourage teachers to utilize this information several suggestions were made. Teachers were asked:

1. To be willing and motivated to do something in this general area.
2. To plan ahead for classroom activities that would result in meaningful learning experiences.
3. To obtain background information about the group to be studied before the subject is introduced.

This publication has been distributed to every public school district in New York State, Diocesan Superintendents of Schools, several teacher-training institutions, and 38 State Departments of Education. Reactions to the usefulness of the information and the approach have been very favorable.

DIR has also developed and distributed a new publication entitled: *Intergroup Relations: A Resource Handbook for 12th Grade Social Studies*. The approach suggested here is to include a discussion of some areas of inequality of opportunity which prevent the Negro and other minority groups from finding their rightful place in the mainstream of American Society.

A large number of schools across the country are beginning to set up programs designed to build a core of common learning experiences to better prepare students for participation in the present-day world. This action required vision and imagination on the part of every school official to achieve equality through integration. The challenge here is to bring the community along in this undertaking and to obtain a total commitment by superintendents, board members, and teachers.

A school district frequently talked about when discussion is centered on a school district's efforts to maintain an integrated system and provide quality education is Greenburgh District 8 in New York State's Westchester County. Some of the positive factors which make it possible for Greenburgh to maintain optimum conditions for the quality of education of all children are reported in a publication, *Equality Through Integration, A Report of Greenburgh School District No. 8* (Buchheimer, 1966). Several points from the report seem pertinent to this discussion. These are:

1. A staff chosen for its commitment to integration.
2. New biracial instructional materials for every grade level.
3. Additional in-service training for all teachers.
4. A greater emphasis on individualization of instruction in each classroom.

5. Evaluation and revision of the curriculum.
6. Encouragement of academic excellence for all pupils.
7. More communication between parents and teachers.
8. A continuation of heterogeneous grouping.

At this point it is clear that the implications of integration for educational practice seem to be unlimited. There are several key areas which must be recognized and in which solutions must be found to meet the changing temper of today's educational and social-political scene. Among some of these are:

1. The creation of a student body in each school which will reflect as nearly as possible a cross section of the population of the entire school district.
2. The creation of opportunities for representatives of minority groups to hold teaching and administrative positions which reflect a cross section of the population of school districts.
3. A clear statement of policy for the school system which seeks ways to give to each student meaningful learning experiences in an ethnically integrated school system.
4. Curriculum materials which help each child develop a respect for himself and respect for the rights of others.
5. Integrating teaching materials which give credit to the contributions minority groups have made to the mainstream of American life.
6. Continuous opportunities for professional development by school personnel on how to meet the challenges required to teach effectively in an integrated community.
7. Provision by teacher training institutions to provide meaningful learning experiences in intergroup relations in preparation for classroom experiences.
8. A commitment by school officials to provide the leadership in interpreting educational needs and in affecting policies to achieve those goals.
9. An opportunity for students, Negro and white, to become involved in worthwhile community activities designed to help bring about better human relations understanding.

The implications of integration for educational practice are everybody's business. It is important for our society to recognize and accept that integrated education will benefit the nation as a whole and not only its minorities.

REFERENCES

Allen, James E. Address presented at Inaugural Dinner, Center for New York City Affairs, New School for Social Research, New York, May 1965.

Buchheimer, Naomi, and Arnold Buchheimer. *Equality Through Integration.* New York: Anti-Defamation League of B'Nai Brith, 1966.

Commission on School Integration, National Association of Intergroup Relations Officials. "Public School Segregation and Integration in the North," *J. Intergroup Relations* (November 1963).

6

*Integrating the School Curriculum**

Nida E. Thomas

About six years ago[1] the New York State Education Department's Division of Intercultural Relations (DIR) was approached by teachers who wanted to help raise the image which minority group children have of themselves. The teachers felt some children were not contributing to classroom activity. They really wanted to know how to reach these children.

DIR began to explore what was being done to help the minority group youngster acquire a better image of himself and quickly came to the conclusion that perhaps the classroom was not as exciting as it should be. DIR hoped that the minority group child could get a feeling that he really belonged, that he could be reached at a learning level, and that he would become less of a classroom problem.

DIR experimented with a resource handbook which gave some information as to how a teacher might better integrate classroom activities on a day-to-day basis where all groups would benefit. It was felt that this idea would be helpful because it is important for Negro children and white children to learn certain things together. The Negro frequently feels that he doesn't belong. He thinks the important contributions were made by whites and that the Negro has done very little to add to the background of America. It was agreed that some of the contributions Negroes have made to our society should be conveyed to Negro children.

In the twelfth-grade social studies program DIR tried to relate the Negro contributions to the important issues of the day. This developed when DIR was asked to send a unit on Negro history to a high school in Rochester, New York, which is predominantly Negro. They thought they'd like to do something on Negro history. DIR had not developed any such unit, and therefore it asked for a list of all the social studies textbooks that were being used in a particular school. It was felt that, in the initial stages, a textbook approach would aid DIR to

*In this chapter the term "Negro" is used by the author who is herself Negro. "Black," however, seems to be the more current term and reflects a definite pride of racial origin. (Ed.)

[1] Written in 1969.

collate some information which the youngsters could discuss in more meaningful terms. This information would give a total picture of a community.

Areas selected as challenges in a democracy were personality growth and development, group life and social processes, culture and social heritage, improving intergroup relations, population trends, labor relations, planning one's career, education for all, public opinion, leisure and sports, housing and civic responsibilities, political and civil rights. It was thought that these issues were sufficiently broad to effect stimulating and worthwhile discussions.

However, in reading through the various textbook chapters it was found that a great deal of pertinent information was omitted despite the fact that some texts have been published in the last few years. Many important issues such as the Supreme Court and democracy were completely overlooked. The concept of the courts was simply explained by saying the courts were set up to protect the rights of the minority from the majority. In order that students might obtain a real understanding of the significance of the courts in this country, DIR suggested that in a discussion of the courts, it is pertinent that the student be presented material explaining *exactly how* the courts protect the rights of the minority from the majority.

Following the DIR textbook outline, there are research questions, suggestions for a film, a field trip, or a speaker to further develop the topic. Five of the very outstanding Supreme Court cases were chosen and suggested as possible research projects. Selected references were given, so a student could find the information he wished. Care was used in selecting the references so that a student would not get lost and we could be sure that the information he received was adequate. Some of the references to the first question on the Supreme Court were the *Villanova Law Review* (Maslow, 1961), the *Race Relations Law Reporter* (1956) and the *U.S. Commission on Civil Rights Reports* (1959).

The reports of the teachers who have used the unit have been gratifying. These teachers have been able to discern in this field test whether the references were readily available, and if the students reacted favorably. The teachers that tried the unit said that some of the youngsters asked why this kind of information had not been included in their textbooks. The teachers felt they had been able to involve the students in what they call depth research for a greater understanding of some of the basic issues of the day. Prior to this unit some of the students had been very opinionated in the wrong direction.

The writer was in one classroom in Long Island where the lesson was about the Southern States' rejection of an order from the federal government in the nineteenth century. When asked why he did not relate that particular period of history to what was happening to the Supreme Court decision of 1954 the teacher said the class he was working with was too slow and that he didn't think they'd be able to "pick this up." He thought he would be able to do this with a faster class, however.

With the "then and now" approach advocated by these materials it is possible to use current data to make historical information more meaningful. It helps youngsters to realize that some of the things being talked about now didn't just begin to happen today; they have been in existence for a long time.

DIR developed a bibliography that would be helpful to the teacher by listing organizations in the appendix so that a teacher could write to these resources if he needed additional information (1965). It is most important to integrate the information in the right place because people now have to think about the whole civil rights issue, and they do not really understand what equality of housing, employment, or education mean. Many people, including teachers, think housing equality to the Negro means a right to move into a white neighborhood. This is not the issue. Instead, the issue is to be able to make a decision to move into a neighborhood that happens to have a house that meets one's particular needs.

It seems inappropriate that in most of our school systems youngsters cannot discover someone or something with which they can identify. Washington, D.C., public schools have developed a series called "The Contributions of the Negro in American History." (1964) It is a very interesting publication that has drawn together all phases of Negro life, and it can be used as a supplement to other materials. The Detroit public schools has prepared "A Struggle for Freedom," which centers on the background of the Negro in slavery. While these publications represent some of the specialized things that help, what is critically needed are the knowledge and ability to integrate such fare into everyday teaching. For instance, if a teacher is planning a lesson on inventors, he should include the names of people other than white Americans who have made significant inventions. This should become a routine part of the educational program. For example, a group in New York, The Negro History Associates, have published a little brochure on "inventors." A filmstrip that goes with the brochure discusses the inventors in the eighteenth and nineteenth centuries and lists the people, including blacks, who have made outstanding contributions to the field of inventions for this period.

Let us now consider another area of the school curriculum relating to self-image and identification figures. Some of the youngsters who are potential dropouts could be held a little longer if they felt there was something or someone associated with the school program with whom or which they could identify. If in our guidance programs there are jobs, people, and/or places with which the youngsters can identify, then schools might be able to reach young people at a more effective level then previously.

The writer has observed that when it is announced in the Negro schools she has visited that she is from the State Department of Education [Nida Thomas is a Negro] the children sit up straight, grin, and start looking as if they want her approval. It is really something for some of the youngsters to see a real live person of their race from "outside" that they can touch who represents them. Here they can identify.

Perhaps children have been cheated because they have not been provided with realistic aspects of life. One Negro girl, being urged to enter a particular vocational area, replied that she had not seen any Negroes there so there most probably were none. This girl, like many other American children, relies heavily on what she sees. And if we don't provide opportunities for children to *see* certain things, they are not going to see them.

Because one can't identify with something one is not aware of, educators have to provide for such identification. The schools must work with children who do not want to achieve. Educators must convince dropouts that if they are going to compete, then they must bring to the job something salable. It is disturbing to find Negro children whose guidance counselors have told them that there is no place for them in some specific field.

The attitudes and behavior of some school counselors came to the attention of the writer in a guidance seminar at which she spoke at New York University. Some of the statements made by the guidance counselors went like this: "Well you know it isn't possible to get into an electrical union." "Do you advise us to encourage youngsters to go in this direction even if the jobs are limited?" Of course! The world is changing. If one does not have some people prepared, the present process of minority groups being eliminated from job opportunities because they lack appropriate skills will be repeated.

Many people have been deciding for the Negro and other minorities in America that there is no place for them. They base their opinion on what they are looking at today, and this is not right. Assuming that guidance counselors have knowledge about job opportunities, they may not *believe* that the Negro youngster can be successful; therefore, the Negro youngster isn't encouraged to prepare for a particular field. To succeed, the youngster needs to be given encouragement by one with whom he can identify.

Many times parents who are discouraged create the same problem. What can one advise a mother to say to her youngsters when their older brother or sister can't get a job? This is the sixty-four-dollar question.

Several approaches might be possible. In the Urban League when parents have this attitude, parent conferences are held. A collection of pictures from the Phelps Stokes Fund which show Negro people in various skilled occupations can be used to prove that there really are some people who are Negro and who have succeeded in the world of work. Naming successful people within the community can also be of help to parents.

Some schools hold career-conference nights for parents. Resource people from the community come to a PTA meeting to discuss specific careers about which these parents might want to know more. Some people by the time they get home from work are too tired to care about such occupation conferences, so then one must go to them. If there is an agency in the community, such as the Settlement House, an Urban League, some other group-work agency, or even YWCA's which have mothers' programs, they can be used to acquaint the family and children with occupational information.

Career clinics within the churches have proven successful. The ministers are asked, as a part of their youth program, to have career nights. Career church programs have worked with parents when PTA programs would not. There have been a few television programs for which notes were sent home or parents were called and asked to watch. School personnel can advantageously incorporate the efforts of everyone who is doing anything to help with the job. All resources should be used to help reach the parents and the children. Some parents are bitter and really feel that there are no opportunities. Also, parents should be encouraged to allow their children to find employment in another town if there is none in the neighborhoods where they live.

In conclusion, teachers, counselors and administrators must provide their students the opportunity to identify. Identifying is different from assigning all Negro teachers in a Negro school. One can identify with people one likes and with people to whom one can relate, whether they are white or Negro. In terms of raising the image of the Negro youngster, many people with whom he can identify are sorely needed.

There should not be white schools without Negro teachers in them either. It works both ways. Some people say that a Negro teacher should not be assigned to a white school when there are no Negro children there. But in teacher-training institutions do they say to the future teachers, "If you're teaching white children you must use this approach and if you're teaching Negro children you must use another approach"? No, they say, "This is the way you should work with the pupils in your classroom." When we begin to look at Negro children as being first of all pupils and second of all Negroes, the problems of school integration and appropriate curriculum and staff development will be much nearer solution.

REFERENCES

Division of Intercultural Relations. *Intergroup Relations*—A Resource Handbook for Twelfth-Grade Social Studies. Albany: University of the State of New York, 1965.

Maslow, Will. "Defacto Public Schools Segregation," *Villanova Law Review*, Vol. 6, No. 3 (Spring 1961).

The Contributions of The Negro in American History, Washington, D.C.: Public Schools of the District of Columbia, 1964. A series of booklets provided by the District of Columbia to aid teachers of blacks.

Race Relations Law Reporter, Vol. 1, No. 1 (1956).

United States Commission of Civil Rights, 1959, Part 3, Public Education.

part III

Dropouts

7

School Dropouts—The Persistent Problem and the Search for Solutions

Daniel Schreiber*

The school dropout problem has always been with us, for when an educational system permits children to leave at a specific age there will be students who will quit before graduation. In the United States, where the problem is of considerable concern, three major factors contribute to the school dropout problem. (Conference on Unemployed, 1961)

The first factor is unemployment. The unemployment rate in our country did not fall below 5 percent from the recession in 1958 through 1964.[1] It is true that more workers are working, and that more new workers are entering the labor market. Yet at the same time more young workers are unemployed.

Among the unemployed, it is estimated that approximately 750,000 to 1,000,000 are under 21. The danger, of course, is that if those under 21 remain unemployed for too long they will become unemployable.

The second factor that contributes to the school dropout problem was noted by Conant (1961). That year the National Conference for Children and Youth predicted that there would be riots in major cities. The potential rioting was related to the problem of the unemployed young people in slum neighborhoods. While the riots might begin with civil rights demonstrations, young hoodlums could prevail after the rioting began by wanton destruction of life and property. The prediction of the riots was accurate, and so too was the prediction that unemployed youths would participate and intensify the problems. It is as if the civil rights demonstrations served as catalysts for the explosive expression of destructive despair usually ignored in the slums.

It is not surprising, then, to find that the crime rate of young people has steadily increased. In slum neighborhoods the rate may be as high as 100 young

---

*Dan Schreiber edited the NEA-APGA work titled *Guidance and the School Dropout*, published in 1964 (see reference list). This chapter has been abridged from a typescript of a magnetic tape recording of a speech given at Cornell University during one of the summer workshops on the disadvantaged. Most references and greater details are to be found in the aforementioned work. (Ed.)

[1]Unemployment dropped below 5 percent in 1965 and has been between 3.5 and 3.8 percent from 1966 through 1969. (National Industrial Conference Board, 1967)

people for every 1,000 people—that is, one out of every ten youngsters in these neighborhoods has had some type of police contact.

The third factor contributing to the dropout problem is the migration of both whites and Negroes from rural areas into urban centers. Technological improvement in the rural areas or farmlands has been forcing people off the land and into urban centers. The problem becomes dual, since the migrating population is unprepared for the conditions of the urban centers and the urban centers are poorly equipped to handle them.

While the migrants are interested, willing, and diligent workers, they are unable to meet the demands of the work available to them in the urban centers. Unfortunately in many cases the children of the migrants follow the same pattern, so that in some cities there have been three successive generations of unemployables on public assistance.

Such then are the factors that contribute to the school dropout problem: unemployment, social unrest, and migration. But who or what is the dropout; what does he look like?

Most likely he will be sixteen years old, because after that age education is no longer compulsory in most states. The fact that the dropping out occurs during the youth's attendance in secondary school does not minimize the role of the elementary school in creating a potential dropout. The youngster develops into a dropout over a period of time. He tends to become truant before he drops out. He usually realizes that the attendance officer may ignore him because he is close to the age when he may legally drop out. The officer sometimes will not bother to take the youth to court as an habitual truant since he will be over sixteen before his case comes up.

The youth probably has begun to drop out mentally by the time he is fifteen. He generally has a lower intelligence than the graduate, but various studies have shown that anywhere from 50 to 70 percent of the dropouts have IQ's in the normal range. Even if we take the smaller range, the 50 percent one, approximately 500,000 youngsters who will drop out this year have enough intelligence not only to graduate from high school but also to benefit from a high school diploma.

One study in New York State (Woolatt, 1961) found that approximately 13 percent of the dropouts had IQ's over 110. Hoyt (1962) found the same to be true in Iowa. It is not safe to assume that when a youngster drops out from school he has low intelligence.

The dropout usually comes from a family where his older brothers or sisters have already dropped out of school. It has become a family pattern if the youngster is not doing well in school, the family encourages him to leave. In studies of school discipline and school referral, the dropout is usually found to be both a discipline and a behavior problem. He no doubt takes a disproportionate amount of administrative time.

His characteristics as a discipline and behavior problem do not disappear, though, after he drops out. Statistically (Schreiber, 1964), one out of three dropouts will have some type of police contact, which is a high percentage since the national average for high-school dropouts is 3 percent. Yet we must also remind ourselves that two-thirds of the dropouts—a larger fraction—are decent, law-abiding citizens.

The dropout thus far may be identified as average or below average in intelligence and a potential police problem. Another characteristic that seems common to all dropouts is a retarded level of reading. Dropouts are usually a minimum of two years behind grade level in reading. (Findley, 1964) Obviously reading retardation frequently leads to grade retention. Again we find that if a youngster has been retained once in the elementary grades and once in the junior high school grades, he will not graduate; rather, he will become a dropout.

He is two years older than his classmates, yet he does not read as well as they do and he is aware that he will not answer properly. Therefore, rather than remain in an environment that preordains failure, he leaves. He feels alienated from the school and seldom participates in extracurricular activities. To this extent, he says, "You don't like me; you don't want me; I will reject you too."

In a study undertaken in Ohio (1961-62) concerning emotional and social maturity, it was found that the dropout was less emotionally and socially mature than most graduates. The saddest part of all is that the dropout's parents, by and large, are themselves dropouts. In a Maryland study (Schreiber, 1964, p. 15), more than 80 percent of the dropouts came from homes where the parents were dropouts. In Ohio, it was over 70 percent. When a dropout is asked why he is leaving school, he usually says he is going to go to work. However, where studies have been undertaken on a follow-up of such intentions, as in Atlanta (Schreiber, 1964), it was found that fewer than one out of four were able to find jobs. The dropout gives this explanation to the counselor usually to save face. It is not the real reason. If pressed further, he'll say he's not interested in school. He is not interested in school because he knows he cannot succeed there.

Another important factor associated with dropouts are the attitudes of teachers. While not all teachers can be considered problems, the dropout's frequent confrontations with them are less than encouraging. For example, there is the teacher who says, "What? Are you still here? Well, aren't you better off working and helping to support your mother?" Then there is the teacher who says, "If you don't do your homework, you're going to fail." The problem should be obvious—the youngster cannot read the book. He may be in the ninth grade, having failed once in elementary school and once in secondary school, but he is probably reading at the sixth-grade level. His textbooks are written at the level of the ninth, tenth, or eleventh grade. Obviously, he will be unable to do his homework and it will be clear to him that he will surely fail. Then the school calls the parent in and tells him that his child must improve, and this goes on until the end of the year, when the student is failed.

Now if a teacher knows that a student is failing, should he not do more than tell him that if he does not improve he is going to fail? He knows that already. He has been told it year after year. In fact, he knows that he can receive a passing mark sometimes if he exerts some little effort and if he keeps quiet. Some schools have developed this system. One school has the numerical basis of 65 as passing. The student receives a 65_W, which means that he has tried hard. He really does not pass but he has been a good kid, and since there is no reason to fail him, he receives a passing grade.

Are teachers willing to say at the end of the second marking period or even the first marking period that they will take those youngsters who are failing and put them out of the class with the intention of setting up a smaller class? Is there any justifiable reason why the secondary school youngster must be scheduled for four or five major subjects? Why can't he take three and possibly take a double period in the subject in which he is having the most difficulty? Not everybody is graduated in four years. Many people need five years to be graduated. Why cannot a student use five years without being degraded by failure?

What must it do to a child to be told at the age of seven that he does not have what it takes—that he is going to be left behind? What do we do after we fail him in grade 1 or in grade 2? At the beginning of his educational life, he is told already that he is not equipped for this world. And what do we do after we fail him? Do we make any special provision for him? Or does the teacher treat him as if he were entering the class for the first time again? By and large neither happens. The child is left to fend for himself, as a failure.

A good example and description of this situation can be found in Harper Lee's *To Kill a Mockingbird* (1960), which describes a youngster's first day in school with a young, new teacher who goes to the blackboard and writes the alphabet. Then she turns to the class with a big smile and says, "Who knows what this is?" The author of the book says properly, "Ninety percent of the class knew what that was because 90 percent of the class were repeating the grade." Since this incident relates a situation common in a school system that fails many of its students, it might be worthwhile to think in terms of a non-graded primary, at least for the first three years. In such a situation, youngsters progress through the first three years. The first opportunity for failure could not occur for four years for some youngsters and thus it is put off until the child reaches age 10. Psychologically the impact would be greater at age 7 than at age 10.

Dr. Robert Hess, at the University of Chicago, (unpublished) has studied the attitudes of young parents toward school. He defined four economic groups: upper-middle-class, middle-class, low-income, and welfare. He limited his study to one ethnic group. The parents were asked, "What would you tell your child on the first day he was going to school?" The upper- and middle-income parents said, "I would tell my child that he was going to school to learn, the teacher is there to help him, and he is to ask the teacher for help whenever he needs it." The welfare and lower-income parents said, "I would tell my child to behave, not to get into trouble, and to come right home from school."

When Hess showed the parents a picture of a parent and a teacher holding a conference, the upper- and middle-income parents said, "This is a teacher-parent conference and they're discussing information about the child which will help the teacher do a better job." The lower-income and welfare parents said, "The parent was sent for because the child was bad; and the teacher is saying that the child better behave."

From this study, then, it would appear that the middle-class child and his parents view the teacher as a person who helps. The pupil can feel free to ask questions because the teacher will give him a proper answer; empathy exists from the start. The teacher, then, is seen as a friend, and one goes to a friend for help. The welfare child and the lower-income child come to view the teacher as an enemy. "Don't get into trouble or you will be punished. The teacher grades you, so behave, keep quiet, and don't volunteer. As soon as school is over, leave immediately and don't stay around."

If these attitudes prevail, what can be done to change them? They can be changed only if the parent becomes involved in education, because it is the parent who must accept the teachers and transmit that acceptance to the child. Unless the parent views the teacher positively, the child will come to school reflecting fears and hostility. Deutch (1963) and associates have demonstrated the value of parental involvement in their preschool nursery programs operated by the Institute for Developmental Studies. They have concluded that parental involvement in the child's school program is critical to both socialization and language development. They have been quite successful—taking preschool children, working with them, and involving their parents.

An experiment has been conducted in Portland, Oregon (Schreiber, 1964, p. 5), where efforts were made to involve parents as well as students in education. A class for 18 four-year-old children was established in a slum neighborhood. Thirteen parents were persuaded to attend a workshop at the University of Oregon for one full day each week and to spend the remaining four days in the kindergarten with the teacher. The purpose was ostensibly to have them learn about the interaction of children and child development. Of course, as participants and aides they also began to feel useful to the teacher and the school.

Baltimore (Schreiber, 1964, p. 15) also set up a prekindergarten program which involved parents as well as volunteers. Both of the programs in Oregon and Baltimore presented the concept, relatively new in education, that schools could begin educating youngsters at the age of three or four. And while it may be desirable for all children, it may be essential for the slum child.

Studies have proven that the gap in academic achievement between the successful middle-class student and the unsuccessful slum child is smallest when the children are young. But when they are age 14, 15, or 16 the gap between them is larger. Assuming that our objective is to reduce the gap, then the time to make the most significant gain is when the child is young. Although many changes will need to be effected during the early education stages, the first change must come in attitude. Without a change in the attitude of both educators and parents, dropouts will continue to occur despite such early efforts.

Edgar Friedenburg (1963) succinctly says that these youngsters, with their history of school failure, cannot find out what they are good at and therefore do not know what they can be. It means, in effect, that educators must establish programs that will insure some degree of success. Educators must provide the child with the possibility of discovering what he *can* do, not what he *cannot* do. In knowing what he can do, the child is better equipped to enter adult life, since he will already have had a considerable amount of achievement.

There is yet another area where schools are not facing up to the dropout problem. Many school systems, because of their size, do not offer a sufficient variety of courses; this is the case in schools with a student population of approximately 100—and there are many of these. Twenty-five percent of all the high schools in Vermont have a pupil population of less than 100. (Keim, 1962) It is obvious to most educators that if a school has 100 students, the number of teachers it will generally be able to sustain is four.

What type of curriculum can be offered these students? The four teachers will each teach two subjects. There will be no choice for the student. Under such impoverished circumstances, it is hardly surprising to find that the dropout rate in rural areas is usually as high as the dropout rate in urban centers.

The problems of vocational training are not confined to rural areas. In a recent report of holding power in large city school systems, it was found that the dropout rate in vocational schools was higher than the dropout rate in general schools. One reason is that some of our counselors have taken the attitude that if a boy is not intellectually gifted, he must have manual dexterity. Therefore, he is guided into vocational education.

However, most vocational education programs are basically oriented toward a craft type of training which demands reading and intellectual ability; consequently youngsters who are blindly directed into these courses drop out in great numbers. Studies have shown that in the traditional vocational high schools most of the dropouts occurred at grade 10. It is probably one of the most expensive miscalculations in education because vocational education costs on a pro rate basis about one and one-half times as much as education in a general high school. The reasons are quite obvious: class size is smaller, making vocational-education teaching more expensive; and the cost of the machines and possibly the cost of the equipment is higher. Unless the vocational school curriculum changes, and it now appears to be doing so, the program will continue to be inefficient and expensive, and deficient students will continue to drop out.

Programs initiated throughout the country to curb dropouts have assumed a three-pronged attack: to work with youngsters who have dropped out of school in an attempt to give them employment skills; to work with the potential dropout at the secondary level; and to work with very young children, especially the preschool child. Since the latter approach has been mentioned earlier, we will consider the first two kinds of programs at this point.

The most impressive program to train dropouts and have them reenter the job market has been instituted by the Department of Labor through the Manpower Defense and Training Act, in which funds are allocated to establish courses. In many cases the training is undertaken outside the public school system. In some cases, the school is part of the contract. Under MDTA programs many dropouts receive training and skills which permit them to successfully enter the labor market. In some cases those chosen have had neither the experience nor the training necessary for the job. Part of this is occurring because educators have in the past defaulted in their responsibility. They have in effect said that we do not want these youngsters; they cannot learn in our setting; let somebody else worry about them. Yet there is a danger that educators will be developing a third educational system in the country—public, private, and now, this particular type, which is a separate governmental enterprise.

Industry is much concerned about the dropout. Because of its changing technology, industry is reticent to hire anyone unless the employee can be trained and can be worthy of promotion in the job. Such policies have caused much controversy between educators and management. Usually the job requirements and the job specifications are overwritten; the reason given is that management does not want somebody to remain frozen to the entry job. It wants someone who will be promoted as he grows older.

A classic example is the young man who applies for the lowly job of sweeper at any one of the large companies. Unless he has a high school diploma, he will not get beyond filling out the application. Everyone knows a high school diploma is not essential to sweep a floor, but the company does not want to take the risk. In recent years, it has come to the point that if an applicant does not have a diploma, companies do not want him.

When Western Electric Company in Indianapolis (Schreiber, 1964, p. 7) checked through its workers' records, it found that a fairly large percentage of workers were school dropouts. The company then offered to loan the area school system space at the Western Electric plant if the school system would send teachers to educate the "dropout" workers. Classes were undertaken in the plant and many of the dropouts are now earning a high school diploma—their certificate of future employability. This approach is a good idea because workers in a large plant do not need to go downtown to the evening adult high school. It is also interesting that the school system is willing to send the teachers to the plant rather than have all the workers go to the school. Incidentally, the plan saved the school system money because the plant paid the maintenance costs, paid for electricity, and donated the space.

Another example of an industry that became involved in education can be found in the Double-E-Program in Chicago (Schreiber, 1964, p. 8) in which youngsters who had dropped out of school were hired by a local business firm after they had been recommended by the school system. This particular system took youngsters from various sections of the city. Some of the youngsters did not meet the entrance eligibility requirements for a beginning worker; yet they were accepted. The youngsters were not placed in menial jobs. Some were placed as sales clerks, others as bookkeepers or as bill posters, while others were placed as stock boys and maintenance men. They worked three days a week and went to school two days a week. The classes were held not in a school building but in rented office space near the company. The dropouts were thus relieved of the feeling that they were returning to failure.

The business firm learned that some of these youngsters would like to talk to somebody, so a Junior Executive was assigned to every two youngsters. He was described as the "listening counselor." The function of the Junior Executive was not to give commands to the youngster, but to *listen* to his trouble and to answer any questions the youngster might have. Of the 60 youngsters who were brought into the first program, more than 50 remained. The program is still in effect.

Another outstanding program ties work-study in with Civil Service. It promises the youngster that he can obtain a job eventually in Civil Service if he can pass an examination. As work-study programs multiply and expand, one of the problems the educators will be facing in the next four years is the scarcity of jobs in private industry. A possible source will be in areas such as civil service and government jobs.

In San Francisco (Schreiber, 1964, p. 10) there is a similar program for youngsters who live in public housing. These youngsters are usually from low-income families. They work in the public housing offices where they live under a unique work-study program; they work for four hours in the office and attend classes for four hours in school. The work assigned includes office work, book-keeping work, grounds work, and repair work. The youngster not only becomes exposed to a variety of tasks he can accomplish but at the same time he gains a feeling of job satisfaction.

Also of note is the Kansas City (Schreiber, 1964, p. 10) experiment that Dr. Robert Havinghurst proposed. The purpose was to see if the program would be a deterrent to delinquency. One hundred delinquent boys in grade 7 were given a work-study program. The work at the seventh-grade level was in-school work. The boys performed minor repairs in carpentry and in painting. By the time the youngster reached grade 10, he was assigned to work-study with paint jobs outside the school.

In the last appraisal, the program proved not to have had any large impact on reducing delinquency. It has increased school attendance and it has improved attitudes toward school, but the police contacts that are occurring outside of school are occurring to the same extent as they were before the program began.

These are examples of the kinds of programs being offered the school dropout and potential dropout. Yet, good as they are, unless educators do something radically different than they have been doing the rate of one million youngsters who drop out of school every year will continue unabated. This, then, is the challenge.

REFERENCES

Conant, J. B. *Slums and Suburbs.* New York: McGraw-Hill, 1961.

Conference on Unemployed. "Out of School Youth in Urban Areas," sponsored by the National Committee for Children and Youth, Washington, D.C., May 24-26, 1961.

Deutsch, Martin. "Nursery Education: The Influence of Social Programming on Early Development," *J. of Nursery Educ.*, Vol. 18, No. 3 (April 1963).

Division of Research and Division of Guidance and Testing. *Pilot Study of Ohio High School Dropouts, 1961-62.* Columbus: State Department of Education, 1963, p. 23.

Friedenburg, Edgar Z. *Coming of Age in America.* New York: Random House, 1963.

Fundley, Warren G. "Language Development and Dropouts," in Daniel Schreiber (ed.), *The School Dropouts.* Washington, D.C.: National Education Association, 1964, pp. 160-169.

Hoyt, Kenneth B. "The Counselor and the Dropout," *Clearing House*, Vol. 36 (May 1962), pp. 515-522.

Lambert, Nadine. "High School Dropout in Elementary School," in D. Schreiber, (ed.), *Guidance and the School Dropout.* Washington, D.C.: National Education Association/American Personnel and Guidance Association, 1964, pp. 52-53.

Lee, Harper. *To Kill a Mockingbird.* Philadelphia: Lippincott, 1960.

National Industrial Conference Board. *Economic Almanac: 1967–68 Business Fact Book.* New York: Macmillan, 1967, p. 33.

Schreiber, Daniel. *Guidance and the School Dropout.* Washington, D.C.: National Education Association/American Personnel and Guidance Association, 1964.

Woolatt, Lorne H. "Why Capable Students Drop Out of High School," *Bull. N.E.A. Sec. School Principals*, Vol. 45 (November 1961).

8

Characteristics of and Programs for the School Dropout: Some Research Findings

John A. Meacham
Ellen Britz Mink*

INTRODUCTION

A variety of forces—cultural and intrapsychic—combine to force America's problem youth from their middle-class schoolrooms to our nation's streets. There youth, victims of a rapidly changing socioeconomic world, are little or rarely understood. Most attempts at understanding focus themselves into roughly four major areas: (1) home; (2) school; (3) socioeconomic stress; (4) intrapsychic phenomena. However, society tends to act as if the major source or sources of difficulty are intrapsychic. Hence, scales to identify potential dropouts and programs of remedy seem to focus primarily upon the individual, with little or no attention being paid to the ills of a socioeconomic system in need of change.

The reader needs to keep in mind, as he searches through the many research findings reported on the following pages, that the results tend to represent the intrapsychic bias. But the blatant inefficiency of our public schools is also represented by the data, and the alert reader will examine the reported findings in the light of the interaction between a changing social structure and the human members functioning within the many discontinuities that exist. Those people caught in the conflicts of the broken system suffer a kind of destructive anxiety which the following pages describe in the coldness of scientific fact.

CHARACTERISTICS

Research contradicts the theory idea that all dropouts are slow learners or functional illiterates. One study revealed that 63 percent of dropouts are capable of

*Many persons made research contributions to this chapter including Loretta Culiz, M.S., John A. Smith, Ed.D., Lawrence Barker, Ed.D., Margaret Becker, M.S., and the editors.

graduating. Rombouts (1963) thinks that they mainly have emotional problems derived from home and school environment. He notes that if each teacher concentrated on one potential dropout, the cumulative effect over the years would eliminate the problem.

Bowman and Matthews (1960) found a range of 60-115 in IQ scores with a mean of 83. Their results were twofold: (1) 75 percent of the dropouts fell in the lower half of the distribution, and (2) 55 percent of those who stayed in school also fell with the lower half of the distribution. Two notations should be made with the foregoing research. First, the investigation is reporting data on two separate populations, and second, a significant number of young people who remain in school fall in the lower half of the intelligence distribution. (It should also be noted that 25 percent who drop out fall in the upper half of the intelligence distribution).

Liddle (1962) found that dropouts, as a group, have below average intellectual ability, are average or below for their grade, are often absent, and are failing one or more courses.

The NEA Research Division (1963) reports conflicting findings as to the importance of the intelligence quotient as a factor contributing to school dropouts. Some researchers find that intelligence is of minor importance while others find it is significant.

Several studies interestingly indicate the flexibility of IQ scores with environmental change. Among the most significant of these studies was one conducted by Skodak (1949), who placed one hundred children, all under the age of six months, into adoptive homes, all of which were in the higher socioeconomic levels. All the foster parents were in managerial occupations. The intellectual development of these children was followed by periodic testing over a thirteen-year period. The mean IQ score of the children at age 13 was 106 as compared with a mean of 85.7 for 63 of the true mothers, who were mostly from the lower socioeconomic levels. The difference of 20 IQ points was highly significant.

Woollatt (1961) reported that in the New York State Holding Power Project, 12.1 percent of the dropouts had IQ's of 110 and above and 30.4 percent had IQ's below 90.

In the Illinois Dropout Study (1962) all of the following background items helped identify dropouts:

1. Low educational attainment of parents, stepparents, or grandparents.
2. Low educational attainment of brothers and sisters.
3. Low occupational level of father.
4. Early marriages.
5. High physical mobility of the family.

Any item that one would choose as indicating, with reasonable accuracy, the extent of the family's interest in education is an item likely to discriminate between dropouts and graduates. In the analysis of the data in the Illinois study, such items were found always to be related, often quite highly.

Allen (1956) found that the families who produce the majority of drop-outs are low-income families whose social status in the community reflects poor cultural environment. What is not known in behavioral terms is how a poor cultural environment is dysfunctional to academic pursuits. Do children avoid school simply because they don't have nickels for the extra ice cream at lunch or party time? Or is there some really significant value clashes or both?

Bledsoe (1959) found that those students whose parents were employed in professional, managerial, agricultural, clerical, and saleswork dropped out in proportions less than expected by chance. Those parents who were unskilled laborers, retired, or unemployed had children who dropped out in proportions greater than expected by chance. Achieved educational level of children is also closely related to educational status of parents. Bledsoe asserted that students whose parents had some college education did not drop out; those whose parents had completed high school dropped out to a lesser extent than those whose parents had less than a high school education. Parents with five or six years of school had the highest dropout rate among their children.

Findley (1964) found students from lower-class homes are at a disadvantage because language is often used improperly and the importance of language development is not stressed.

Findley (1964) stressed the importance of both language and mathematical skills in our technical world. He suggest that an overemphasis is placed on reading and that many students fall behind early and become discouraged with school in general when they may be deficient only in reading. Failure then becomes forced, is a negative experience associated with school, and breeds discouragement.

Students are principally influenced by the attitudes of their parents and other adults in their environment. The lower-class child does not have the importance of school impressed upon him by his family and community (Findley, 1964). Allen (1956) states that their social status is related to their values, goals, income, and general way of life. He also notes the family's inability to meet school costs which influences a child's dropping out of school.

Penty (1956) found a relationship between reading ability and withdrawal from high school:

> Three times as many poor readers as good readers dropped out of school, and the likelihood of a poor reader's dropping out was greater when other factors pressuring a student toward withdrawal were present.

As would be expected, failure in school is closely related to dropping out. Dropouts are often grade repeaters; they fail early, most often in the first, third, and fourth grades, and they show a general decline in scholarship from the elementary to the senior high school. Cook (1954) found that dropouts in the school he studied averaged D grades, while the stay-ins averaged a high C.

Dresher (1954) considers failure in elementary and in high school a very important factor in withdrawal.

As a result of a dropout study in a high school district (Identifying Potential Dropouts, 1965), a committee of teachers and the administration developed the following guide to identify dropouts: (1) Children—especially boys—who start school before being ready for such an experience. (2) A bad or irregular first-grade experience which may have been caused by moving, illness requiring frequent long periods of absence, or a traumatic experience such as a death or a broken home. (3) An irregularity in standardized tests and testing procedures which results in a considerable difference between language and nonlanguage intelligence scores, test scores and actual classroom achievement (especially reading); obtained grade placement and average anticipated grade placement in verbal facts. (4) Youngsters who change schools frequently. (5) Tense overachievers who may "burn out" or become negative toward academic achievement as they grow older and become more independent. (6) An obvious bad attitude evidenced toward the school and the teacher. (7) Irregular attendance and frequent tardiness which are without known physical cause. (8) Awareness of marked traits which differ from classmates such as interests, physique, social class, nationality, dress, and personality development. (9) Marked disinterest identified in school with a feeling of "not belonging." (10) Negative attitudes parents have toward formal education.

Several characteristics were discussed by Roberts (1959), and among them the idea that dropouts seem to develop an inadequate and ineffective personality structure was predominant. The dropouts come from families that lack consistency and stability; the family is usually large and has a low income. At school these children find themselves in difficulty educationally, emotionally, and socially. They express their frustrations by withdrawal or by aggressiveness, hostility, and absence. When the law permits or when they find a way, they become dropouts.

In a pilot program to aid returning school dropouts, Honn (1965) cited the following reasons as given for dropping out of school: lack of interest, unsatisfactory school situation, pregnancy, marriage, personality, economic necessity, home difficulty, and military service. Reasons noted by the field counselor through home visits plus individual and group counseling were unsatisfactory school situation, lack of interest, pregnancy, economic necessity, health, marriage, and home difficulty. Both studies indicate that the majority of the students fell in the categories of lack of interest and of an unsatisfactory school situation. However, the latter is not clearly defined.

A study of Minneapolis vocational high school students (Martin, 1964) compared dropouts and graduates by using intelligence tests, occupational interest tests, work in various courses, and such background material as occupation of father, junior high school attended, absence record in junior high, and personality ratings by teachers. High school achievement was measured by courses in

English and technical and related subjects. The study found a graduate more likely to come from a normal family background, and that those who come from schools away from a downtown area do have a better attendance record, are better liked by classmates, are more reliable, have more initiative and have a slightly higher tested intelligence. The graduate did better work in English, related courses and shop; however, the graduate did *not* differ from the dropout in occupation of father, sex, or eighth-grade achievement in reading and arithmetic tests.

Mental retardation (lack of genetically determined potential) is so closely bound up with grade and subject failure and attendance that it is difficult to consider these topics separately. The pupil who has failed his grade and who is retarded will often lose interest in school and skip classes. Of course, absence results in loss of skill and knowledge, and contributes to continued failure; thus, the vicious circle remains unbroken. Retardation is considered one of the most reliable measures of the probability that a pupil will not finish high school. Any pupil retarded two years by the time he reaches the seventh grade is unlikely to finish the tenth grade and has only a negligible chance of finishing high school. If a pupil is retarded as much as three years, he is not likely even to enter the ninth grade. (Schreiber, 1961)

In the Ohio Pilot Study of Dropouts (Division of Research, 1963), it was found that attendance and discipline problems, although related to dropping out of school, could not be identified as causative factors. Reducing attendance and discipline problems can however be successfully achieved only by attacking the basic problems of which they are symptomatic.

NEA (1963) also reports that dropouts were more dissatisfied with their social relationships in school than were the stay-ins. They considered themselves to be poorly treated by students and teachers alike. NEA also found that the students who eventually dropped out do not take part in extracurricular activities. The reasons given were lack of money and rejection by their classmates. Apparently, dropouts are not active in the extracurricular life of the school. However, students who remain in school often avoid extracurricular life. Even though some efforts have demonstrated that dropouts can be reclaimed through sports involvement, lack of such involvement as a single criterion of dropout proneness is not very useful.

Allen (1956) outlined a number of characteristics of dropouts. He asserted that the dropout does not participate in extracurricular activities and is not socially drawn to the school; he is not in an accepted group of fellow students and is ignored by his teachers.

To recognize the factors over which the school has had little or no control is not to say that the school can do nothing; it is only to define the area within which the school must expand its effort. There is no simple explanation for the behavior of the dropout, and there is no simple or single solution to the problem, but one of the first steps the school can take is to recognize the potential dropout as early as possible. (Schreiber, 1961) (30) One conclusion is evident—

the factors that alienate a student from school are at least partially contributed by the school. Many "would be" students are "force-outs" due to school policy, personnel, and curriculum.

Significant characteristics were gathered on 2,407 dropouts in Colorado High School districts (Colorado Dropout Project, 1965) with a 25 percent dropout rate. A questionnaire completed on each known dropout, 116 former students, revealed the following: (1) 60 percent were of average or above average intelligence; (2) 67 percent were below average in achievement; (3) 41 percent were retained at one or more levels; (4) of the 13 percent of males who were expelled due to behavior, two-thirds were average or better in intelligence; (5) marriage and pregnancy accounted for 35 percent of the female dropout, and three-fourths of the girls were average or better scholastically; (6) one-fourth of the male dropouts and one-tenth of the females had previously been expelled or suspended; (7) 20 percent had a serious emotional problem; (8) three-fourths of the males and two-thirds of the females did not participate in extracurricular or community activities; (9) 31 percent were not accepted by other pupils; only 5 percent were rated as being popular or being a leader; (10) 20 percent had less than adequate ability to pay normal school expenses; (11) 42 percent of the parents had an unsatisfactory attitude toward school; (12) 5 percent of the dropouts had physical disabilities.

Tuel (1966) investigated reasons given by pupils for quitting school. The results indicated: (1) dissatisfaction with school, 57 percent; (2) marriage, 25 percent; (3) financial, 13 percent; (4) military, 5 percent. Tuel also reported the following characteristics as being related to dropouts: (1) a strong correlation between dropping out and a proximity to the lower end of the socioeconomic scale; (2) a greater incidence of homes broken by death, divorce, or separation; (3) a significant degree of academic retardation (one study showed 54 percent of dropouts to be retarded one or more grades). (4) Although the mean IQ of dropouts has been found to be only ten points lower than graduates, a large proportion of dropouts scored within the normal range of intelligence. (5) A greater part of the dropouts had the mental capacity to complete high school despite the fact that they fared worse than three-fourths of the graduates in grades. (6) Boys quit at an earlier age than girls. (7) Teachers rated graduates superior to dropouts in industry, leadership, resourcefulness, and social acceptability. (8) Dropouts reported a lesser degree of participation in extracurricular activities.

Many studies list early school failures as characteristic of dropouts. Allen (1956) stated that most dropouts are unsuccessful in school and are retained one or more grades. Therefore, many potential dropouts are average in academic ability. He reported also that dropouts tend to be low in their abilities in mathematics and reading.

As symptoms of a dropout, Tuel (1966) described the following: (1) grade failure, especially in the elementary school; (2) low verbal intelligence (placement in the lowest decile on mental abilities or reading test); (3) low socioeconomic background, minimal family education, low level of parental occupation, or a broken home; (4) frequency of absence, and (5) lack of participation, general maladjustment and insecurity.

West Texas School Study Council (Barclay, 1966) compiled interview and questionnaire data with the help of 501 former students (now adults) in 13 West Texas communities. Results showed that the urge to quit school accelerated when the student felt that the teacher was not sensitive to his needs as a person. Dropouts not only blamed the school, they also suggested self-blame. Sixty-five of the respondents were parents who suggested the importance of teaching home and family life in the curriculum. They also noted that the vocational courses they had taken were generally most helpful when they left school. One interesting implication pointed toward placing greater stress upon responsibilities of home and family living.

Hollingshead (1941) found that eight out of nine dropouts come from the lowest social class. In Chicago, studies of 70 secondary schools showed that 72 percent of all dropouts were from families of low socioeconomic background (Tesseneer, 1958).

The reasons a student stays in or drops out of school are usually multiple and complex. The characteristics resulting from these reasons or causes are equally multiple in nature. There is no single characteristic or pattern of characteristics that will describe all dropouts or identify all potential dropouts. However, varying combinations of a number of identifiable factors do appear to be related to dropping out of school. The significant variables are family background, which includes below-average socioeconomic and cultural status; employment of the father as an unskilled or semiskilled worker, and failure of parents to complete high school; low intelligence quotients of dropouts, little or no social relationships in school, little participation in extracurricular activities, early school failures, failing at least one subject, low marks, grade retention of a year or more, overage for grade, low reading and mathematical ability, language difficulties, inadequate personality structure, high absenteeism in school, and improper, inadequate, or changing school curricula.

Many previous studies have been hampered by the fact that relevant data were incomplete and unrecorded. Probably one of the least satisfactory of the items usually recorded is the one regarding leaving school. Schools often know little about why the student left school or what happened to him after he left.

It is apparent that causes of dropouts have both common and alien themes as studies move from one geographic and subcultural region to another within the bounds of the great diversity that is the United States of America.

DROPOUT PROGRAMS

The dropout rate in the total Illinois school population decreased from 36 percent in a 1962 study to 27 percent in 1964, while the national average was constant at 36 percent. Eighty-three school districts in Illinois initiated research (O'Neill, 1965) into the dropout problem which result in certain modifications of school policies. Among them were the following: (1) slow learner program; (2) work-study programs, distributive education and occupation courses (allows for credit for work experience on a part-time basis); (3) remedial and/or developmental reading program designed to fit the needs of all; (4) occupational information units of study relative to occupation trends, job requirements, job placement, and local employment opportunities.

Changes in the curriculum were supplemented by existing guidance and counseling programs with unique innovations in these areas: group counseling, parent-student-counselor conferences, referral agencies, in-service education for teachers, workshops, and related programs. The department of guidance also initiated a pilot program in 30 elementary school districts anticipating this would aid in the early identification and prevention of dropouts.

Arnold Cheyney (1965) suggests ten criteria for evaluating programs for dropouts.

1. Since the dropout problem is only one among many facing public schools, no curricular innovation should be broadly established for the early school leaver at the expense of the entire school program.
2. A program should be developed and maintained for potential dropouts which will be concerned with his optimum growth and development.
3. Develop a comprehensive program should be developed which will deal with elementary causes in the early elementary school years.
4. Only a cooperative school, home, and community wide effort will bring lasting results.
5. Financial resources at the program's inception should not prohibit future continuation of a program.
6. School staff must be involved in the formulation of the program and be ready to accept the responsibilities in adequately carrying on the program's objective.
7. Take stock (before programming) of present resources, services and facilities geared or related to the program.
8. Specific objectives must be stated in terms of behavioral goals.
9. Adopt an evaluation procedure that will indicate continuous status of the program.
10. The dropout program must include a change variable.

In a symposium on the dropout (*The Dropout*, 1964), six prominent Philadelphians discussed dropout problems and solutions pertaining to their individual fields. It was suggested that family service and community resources be made available to prevent dropouts, and that urban league in Philadelphia should continue to serve youth withdrawn from education. Urban projects under way include a tutorial project in which volunteer college and high school students give help to culturally deprived, slow students after school hours, and a Friends Neighborhood Guild Work Program in which fifteen- and sixteen-year-old students (in school) earn money during the summer. Counseling, tutorial services, school-work programs, and remedial reading clinics should be expanded. To provide adequate counseling, the staff would have to be doubled. Other programs referred to for possible cooperation were vocational rehabilitation, the armed forces, and juvenile court.

A survey of programs in Texas which described several school dropout projects is described by Brechtel (1965). The programs were classified into four areas.

1. *Special Classes.* New curriculum plans were made for grades 7-12 with flexible course sequence selections at four ability levels at Corpus Christi. An ability grouping program, by subject, at San Antonio provided accelerated, average, and special sections in English, math, science, and social studies. The Houston Talent Preservation Project initiated special classes for underachievers two or more years retarded in reading and math and having poor school adjustment on entering the seventh grade. They were grouped for two hours of language instruction and one hour of math taught daily at their level in classes limited to twenty.

2. *Vocational Courses.* Distributive education programs and industrial cooperation training were especially popular since the pupil was paid. Pupils in the program attended school three hours in the mornings and received school-supervised on-the-job training in the afternoon. The Weslaw School District also opened a vocational school for grades 7, 8, and 9. The youngsters were at least fourteen years of age and two years retarded in the academic program. In addition to academic course work, the pupils received training in trades with only 2 percent of the pupils dropping out during the school year when normally the expected dropout rate was 20 percent. The Dallas Vocational School initiated a training program for dropouts age 15 or older who could not be returned to a regular school program. Pupils were allowed to enter any time and remain as long as required to prepare them for trades.

At Weslaco, Texas, the effectiveness of a vocational program for average junior high school pupils was evaluated. Students referred to as "bad-apples" and slow learners from the elementary and junior high schools were invited to enroll if they were two or more years below average in grade and the parents had given consent. During the first year, teachers worked out programs to fit the student's abilities. Teachers noted change in morale with improvement in initiative and cooperation in the trade setting rather than in the academic setting. All of these students were potential dropouts, and yet with two or three years of vocational training more than one-half were high school graduates. The most important factors in the success of the program may be attributed to the philosophy and personality of the principal who insisted on stressing the positive and treating students with respect.

(3) *Financial Assistance.* Fifteen- and sixteen-year-olds inclusive were eligible for the Extension of Texas Aid for Dependent Children.

4. *Study Centers.* Personal and continuing encouragement was offered to the potential dropout through the study center. A center in Victoria Courts Housing Project, San Antonio, sent letters to parents of students in grades 5-9 who were failing or nearly so, inviting them to study in the center.

Chamberlin (1964) conducted a study of average seventh-graders who were thought to be dull and lazy. An average IQ of 96, a few points below the average for the entire school, was reported for 21 boys and for 13 girls, but the achievement test scores of the group fell below their mental age. It was questioned whether underachievement was related to difference in age between the average group and their peers. Thirty-three of the thirty-four had repeated a grade at least once. All displayed a common pattern of being embarrassed when asked why they were older than other students in their class. The group used rationalizations to deny the value of school. They revealed a deficit in self-esteem and marginal school adjustment.

The students were enthusiastic when the faculty posed the possibility of gaining back the year they had lost. Each volunteer needed parental assent and had to work up to his ability. All thirty-four were transferred into an experimental group. After the group had been placed under a new "core" teacher and after the counselor had introduced them to daily visits by the principal, teacher, and district officer, the number of underachievers shrank to twenty-five. The curricula generally followed an eighth-grade plan with all possible materials gathered for individualizing work into a personal contact basis.

The youngsters were pre- and posttested with the *Metropolitan Achievement Test.* Results indicated a median growth ranging from 100-525 percent of the usually expected growth. In a writing assignment on "What Happened to You in Core 87?", the students revealed an improved attitude toward school. When the original seventh-grade group reached grade 11, eight were still in school, fifteen were rated as making average or better adjustment, and three were rated as poorly adjusted.

Chamberlin (1964) concluded that an average underachiever had clearly sprinted ahead under the effect of a contrived motivating environment. Skipping a year seemed to have had a positive effect on the majority of the youngsters.

Houston, Texas has a Talent Preservation Program (Helping the Potential Dropout, 1964) for the academically retarded and socially maladjusted in seventeen junior high schools. Instruction is geared to learning and cultural enrichment; reading is emphasized, and a special effort is given to show the practical value of school subjects.

Some of the features initiated in Los Angeles senior high school (Honn, 1965) to determine whether or not the dropouts, if encouraged, would return were to have the field counselors establish and maintain continuous contact with the dropout and his family and to assist in developing and following through on a planned program leading to further training and employment.

Techniques and resources used by field counselors were home visits, individual and group counseling, individual testing, referrals, field trips to businesses, and cooperation with community agencies offering services. The principal objective was to place the counselee in a program in which he could learn a skill or graduate. Counseling procedures were based mainly on a one-to-one relationship; group guidance was used only to complement. After a group session introducing the project, the students met with field counselors to select a school, choose subjects, make arrangements for permits and transportation, and direct a letter of introduction to the school counselor. Returnees were allowed to select their course of study but most chose required subjects.

There was a considerable change between goals listed by the returning dropout at the beginning of the project and those listed at termination—vocational goals were more reasonable in light of ability. At the end, field counselors reported giving service to 64 counselees of whom 35 were still in school.

At Ithaca, New York, the dropout rate was cut 25 percent when 8,400 pupils followed ten programs (Ten Programs to Prevent Dropout, 1966) to aid actual and potential dropouts. The programs are:

1. *School to employment.* A work study program limited to fifteen-year olds, identified as potential dropouts, which prepares students for full-time employment when they leave school and works to keep students in school. One half of the day is spent in class, the other half on the job. Each individual is assigned to regular subjects in specific areas of his strongest interest, while the jobs are selected to match student aptitudes. A teacher-coordinator meets with the group daily, works closely with each student, attempts to define individual problems, helps develop attitudes, habits, and skills which aid the student in solving his problems.

2. *Distributive education.* The program is designed for those who have taken courses in retailing, show an interest, and who may quit school. Students are placed in outside jobs wherein the employer agrees to actually supervise and teach youngsters. The student is paid and earns credit.

3. *Neighborhood Youth Corps.* Under the provisions of the Economic Opportunity Act, the program is run by the Ithaca schools and state employment office. It is designed for actual and potential dropouts, and for graduates who can't find a job. Students ages 16-21 are placed in jobs where they will receive special supervision and training.

4. *Evening extension school.* Correspondence courses for dropouts are paid by the district.

5. *Terminal counseling program.* The guidance counselor specializes in terminal students and maintains close contact with auxiliary services with state employment service and local employers.

6. *Vocational education.* Technical courses plus part-time jobs provide marketable skill for the students.

7. *Career fair.* A two-day introduction to the world of work with speeches, interviews, exhibits, emphasizing nonprofessional occupations.
8. *Tutorial program.* Volunteer college students provide effective remedial instruction.
9. *Remedial summer school.* Designed to help junior high students overcome deficiencies in reading and math.
10. *High school equivalency exam.* A certificate provided upon passing the test qualifies the students for further trade, technical school training, and civil service jobs.

In another study by Michael L. Thompson (1963) twelve approaches were proposed as being necessary to remedy the dropout problem.

1. Compulsory school attendance should be eliminated. Studies have indicated that it would be better to eliminate age requirement and provide curricular study encouraging them to stay.
2. There should be a cooperative relationship between the planner of the school curriculum and industry which would keep schools up to date on technological changes.
3. There should be an increase in special services such as counseling, speech therapy, and health available to all students at every age.
4. Urban renewal is necessary: 70 percent of the increased dropout rate occurs in slum areas.
5. Greater emphasis needs to be placed on adult education.
6. Teachers must have adequate training.
7. School facilities must be up to date.
8. The school should make studies of its holding power and act accordingly.
9. Pupil involvement in activities should be maintained.
10. All community agencies should cooperate with the school.
11. Hidden costs of education should be removed.
12. One of the chief causes of dropouts is the lack of financial resources for texts, tickets, dances, yearbooks, and the like.

A study by Strom (1964) suggested that the determination of curriculum for the potential dropouts should be on the basis of: (1) what is known about why the pupil rejects school, (2) unique characteristics of the pupil, and (3) the pupil's occupational outlook for the future. Strom indicated that we should note the subject areas designated by the dropout as being their most difficult courses of study. Researchers have identified reading—language art—as being a specific problem for the dropout. Strom stated that a readiness program which gives the student many experiences with words including visual and auditory discrimination should be used.

According to dropouts, social studies is considered the most difficult course of study. It is necessary for the teacher to provide an excess of ready-made explanations so that the student will develop abilities in independently gaining insight into concepts. In math where learning is cumulative, slow learners may fall hopelessly behind if pressured to keep up with the average. Studies have shown that slow learners go through substantially the same mental processes except at a slower pace.

CONCLUSION

From a reading of the foregoing research findings two or three different aspects stand out clearly. First, by and large, most of the studies dealing with dropouts deal with descriptive items or "symptoms" of the dropout as opposed to the actual causes. For instance, reading level below grade level is traceable to a deeper cause which could stem from different sources or a combination of the sources. Remedial procedures cannot be built from knowledge of symptoms only. Causes must be dealt with in establishing a sound program of dropout prevention. On this point, one of the most prevalent symptoms of the dropout is that he comes from a low socioeconomic group. However, all students from this group do not drop out. A very important question might be, Why is it that other students in the lower socioeconomic group did not drop out? The problem seems to lie not in being a member of the lower socioeconomic group, but in what would appear to be the association with the attitudes and life style which have been developed in and are commensurate with the lower socioeconomic group.

The above review should cause the reader to become poignantly aware of the multitude of community forces which need to be brought to bear to remedy the spectrum of problems presented to schools by the student who shows signs of alienation from the conventional school program. Perhaps counseling programs should serve to (1) process students through diagnosis and remedy, and (2) provide an impetus toward mobilization of the community's resources on behalf of the school alienated student.

REFERENCES

Allen, C. M. *Combating the Dropout Problem*. Chicago: Science Research Associates, 1956.

Barclay, J. R. "Sociometric Choices and Teacher Ratings as Predictors of School Dropout," *J. School Psychol.*, Vol. 4 (Winter 1966), pp. 40-44.

Bledsoe, J. C. "An Investigation of Six Correlates of Student Withdrawal from High School," *J. Ed. Res.*, Vol. 53 (1959) pp. 3-6.

Bowman, P. H. and C. V. Matthews. *Motivations of Youth for Leaving School*. U.S. Department of Health, Education, and Welfare, Office of Education Cooperative Research Program, Project 200. Quincy, Mass.: Quincy Youth Development Project and U. of Chicago Press, 1960.

Brechtol, Helen. "A Sampling of School Dropout Project in Texas," *Texas J. Sec. Educ.*, Vol. 18 (Spring 1965), pp. 13–18.

Chamberlin, G. L. Calvin, "Acceleration for Average Potential Dropout," *Educ. Digest*, Vol. 29 (January 1964), pp. 11–13.

Cheyney, A. "Ten Criteria for Evaluating Programming for Dropout," *Peabody J. Educ.*, Vol. 42 (January 1965), pp. 216–218.

Cook, E. S., Jr. "How I.Q. Figures in the Dropout Problem," *Sch. Exec.*, Vol. 74 (1954), pp. 56–57.

Deutsch, M. "Early Social Environment: Its Influence on School Adaptation," in D. Schreiber (ed.), *The School Dropout*. Papers Presented at N.E.A. Symposium on School Dropouts, Dec. 2-4, 1962. Washington, D.C.: National Education Association, 1964.

Division of Research and Division of Guidance and Testing. *Pilot Study of Ohio High School Dropouts, 1961-62*. Columbus: State Department of Education, 1963.

Dresher, R. H. "Factors in Voluntary Dropouts," *Personnel & Guidance J.*, Vol. 32 (1954), pp. 287–289.

"The Dropout: A Symposium," *Education*, Vol. 85 (December 1964), pp. 195–198.

Epps, Margaret W., and W. C. Cottle. "Further Validation of a Dropout Scale," *Voc. Guidance Quart.*, Vol. 7 (1958-59).

Findley, W. G. "Language Development and Dropouts," in D. Schreiber (ed.), *The School Dropout*. Washington, D.C.: National Education Association, 1964.

"Helping the Potential Dropout," *P.T.A. Mag. Educ. Digest* (January 1964).

Honn, F. R. "A Pilot Program to Aid Returning School Dropouts," *J. Sec. Educ.*, Vol. 40, No. 94 (April 1965), pp. 177-183.

Kennedy, Lorraine. "Weslaco Attacks its Dropout Problem," *Texas Outlook*, Vol. 50 (January 1966), pp. 19–21.

Liddle, G. P. "Psychological Factors Involved in Dropping Out of School," *High School J.*, Vol. 45 (April 1962), pp. 276–280.

Martin H. W. "Dropouts and Agricultural Education," *Education*, Vol. 85 (December 1964), pp. 217–220.

National Education Association Research Division. *School Dropouts*, Memo No. 10. Washington, D.C.: National Education Association, 1963.

Nerrman, W. L., and W. C. Cottle. "An Inventory to Identify High School Dropouts," *Voc. Guidance Quart.*, Vol. 6 (1957–58).

"Procedures for the Identification of Potential High School Dropouts," Office of Superintendent of Public Instruction. Springfield: State of Illinois, 1962.

O'Neill, J. H. "Illinois Dropouts or Pushouts—What Has Been Done—What Can Be Done," *Ill. J. Educ.* (January 1965).

Penty, Ruth C. *Reading Ability and High School Dropouts*. New York: Teachers College Press, 1956.

Roberts, J. L. "Let's Keep them in School." *Calif. J. Sec. Educ.*, Vol. 33 (February 1959), pp. 115–118.

Rombouts, J. R. "Reaching the Drop In Before He Drops Out," *Mich. Educ. J.*, Vol. 41 (November 1, 1963), pp. 24–25.

"School Dropouts," N.E.A. Res. Memo No. 10. Washington, D.C.: National Education Association, 1963, cited in A. B. Hollingshead, *Elmtown's Youth*, New York: Wiley, 1941.

Schreiber, D. *School Dropouts*. N.E.A. Res. Memo 1901-36. Washington, D.C.: National Education Association, 1961.

Skodak, Marie, and H. M. Skeels. "A Final Follow-up Study of One Hundred Adopted Children," *J. Genet. Psychol.*, Vol. 75 (November 1949), pp. 85–125.

"Identifying Potential Dropouts," *News & Notes on Calif. Educ.*, State Department Public Instruction, Vol. 3 (September 1965), p. 31.

State Department of Education. "Colorado Dropout Project," *Colorado Sch. J.* (February 1965).

Strom, R. D. "A Realistic Curriculum for Predictive Dropout," *Clearing House*, Vol. 39 (October 1964), pp. 101–106.

"Ten Proven Programs to Prevent Dropout," *Sch. Mgmt. Educ. Digest*, Vol. 31 (January 1966), pp. 1–4.

Tesseneer, R. A., and L. M. Tesseneer. "Review of the Literature of School Dropouts," *Nat. Assoc. Sec. School Prin. Bull.*, Vol. 42 (May 1958), pp. 141–153.

Thompson, M. L., and R. H. Nelson. "Twelve Approaches to Remedy Dropout Problem," *Clearing House*, Vol. 38 (November 1963), pp. 200–204.

Tuel, J. K. "Dropout Dynamics," *Calif. J. Educ. Res.*, Vol. 17 (January 1966), pp. 5–11.

Woollatt, Lorne H. "Why Capable Students Drop Out of High School," *Bull. NEA Sec. School Prin.*, Vol. 45 (November 1961), pp. 1–8.

part IV

Counseling

9

Group Counseling with Disadvantaged Youth

Oscar G. Mink

Gesellschaft communities typify the American way of life in the 1960's and show every promise of increasing in size, number, and degree. Urban migration continues. Citizens multiply by the tens of thousands. Daily, people trade more freedom to make subjective, free choices for the less meaningful securities like federal and state benevolence and controls on every conceivable item from milk products to contraceptives. The *Zeitgeist*, entangling human struggles as a rampaging flood engulfs an army of floundering ants, appears in the guise of human understanding. Rising like a specter on Egdon Heath, it calls itself the champion of truth.

The truth expounded by this nightmare is a creature that permeates human thought and social action with concepts like psychic determinism, irresistible impulses, nonaffectivity (not caring), and some sort of maudlin, passive (romantic) "love" for one's fellow-man which justifies almost any action from buying a new convertible to deserting a family. Individual responsibility fades into the past in deference to inadequate family life, poverty stricken, subcultural, victim of prejudice. Indeed, we live in a setting designed for neglect of humaneness and in particular human neglect.

The reader can find numerous examples of social irresponsibility in his day-to-day life. For purposes of this discussion, it is sufficient to note that today's social world tends to encourage the extinction of a critical human quality—responsibility—or the making and keeping of commitments. Our problems are always someone else's fault, as depicted in this little verse:

> O mongoose, where were you that day
> When Mistress Eve was led astray?
> If you'd but seen the serpent first,
> Our parents would not have been cursed.

IMPERSONALIZATION

What does impersonalization in society mean to homo sapiens? Scholars do not agree, but life works of men like Howard Liddell (1958) on "experimental neurosis" and Harry Harlow (1958) on "contact comfort," to say nothing of the purely subjective experiences of people in general, describe alienation as worse than death. William Glasser, in *Reality Therapy* (1965), couples the need to be loved with the need for self-esteem (to respect one's self or to view self as worthwhile and consistent with ideals and experience) as the dyad of primary needs prepotent to all other human needs.

Total despair and flagrant self-abuse found in the wanton minds, hearts, eyes, and irresponsible behavior of the dope addict, sex offender, and alcoholic occur only in the absence of love and self-esteem and make such persons candidates for some type of incarceration. The absence of one or the other characterizes most disadvantaged youth. An impersonal, human society confounds reason. Impersonal societies dehumanize themselves, maybe even deanimalize themselves. The alert, concerned counselor will try to build client self-esteem and convey love. Groups are an able vehicle for both efforts.

JOB STRUCTURE

Two theories applied to current problems of economic involvement have been used to explain unemployment. The most popular, generally ascribed to former President John F. Kennedy's economic advisors, is the theory of total aggregate demand—not enough jobs for the people. Solution: cut taxes, pump economy, create demand for more services, hence more jobs. From 1966 through 1969, actions based on the theory have cut unemployment rates in every age bracket except the most critical age span of 16-25. Here unemployment continues to rise.

The second theory revolves around job structure. Briefly, jobs exist, but the labor force lacks appropriate skill profiles. The latter theory best describes the plight of the young, potential worker. The paradox of unfilled jobs and unemployed youth coupled with the youthful trend of the general population—by 1975 over 50 percent of the population will be under 20 years of age—suggests that a drastic unemployment problem exists just beyond the horizon. If federal-state policies continue to neglect the young worker, one can predict an unemployment rate approximating one-half of the rate following the 1929 crash, or roughly 12 percent by 1975. Educationally handicapped youth (principally culturally disadvantaged) face a bleak, if not tragic economic future.

SELF-CONCEPT, LEVEL OF ASPIRATION AND CONTROL EXPECTANCY

Brookover and Patterson (1962) found that self-report measures of a student's concept of self as an achiever are just as potent in predicting school achievement as measures of academic aptitude. Edwards and Webster (1963) identified positive self-concepts as leading to higher aspirations and greater academic achievement. Yet Wylie (1963) reported that Negro and lower-class children tend to underestimate their ability to achieve. These reports corroborate a wide variety of less objective observations on behalf of practicing clinicians and teachers. Much of the apparent failure of disadvantaged youth derives directly from self-perceptions and control expectancy. (Coleman, *et al.,* 1966).

Others (Sears, 1940, for example) have demonstrated the lack of reality in the levels aspirations set by persons subjected to consistent failure experiences. Failure begets more failure in a vicious cycle of self-feeding psychic distortions. The question is, how can one best modify self-concepts and expectancies of the disadvantaged? Perhaps through group process.

SOCIAL INTELLIGENCE

Humans faced with extreme threat develop survival techniques or yield to destruction—psychic, spiritual, or physical. The disadvantaged develop highly refined skills at manipulation. Kids survive the social injustice, fleshpots, and pot of Harlem through sheer social skill or social intelligence. They become masters at manipulating others to gain personal ends. Many termed sociopathic or psychopathic use their tactics as a means of survival. Interestingly enough, society aids and abets. How?

Joe's mom and dad are away from home at all hours of the day and night. Joe steals, gets caught, is hauled into juvenile court (usually parodies of social justice), and mom and pop get blamed. What happens to Joe? Poor boy. He couldn't help himself! The concept of psychic determinism proves again its destructive nature. Followed to its logical end, psychiatrists will replace judges on the bench.

Irresistible impulses aren't irresistible. People can be taught to make and keep simple agreements. Youth have learned that poor feelings justify poor behavior. Now they must learn that good behavior creates good feelings. The first step in rehabilitation of the socially irresponsible is to hold them socially responsible. People who make and keep simple agreements earn love of significant others and gain self-esteem. New opportunities demand new social skills. The task of the counselor working with disadvantaged youth slated for social integration is to help youth accomplish and do in place of failure and manipulation. It is my experience that groups of peers are most effective in helping each other *accomplish* and *do*.

PROBLEM SOLVING

Disadvantaged youth tend to either avoid or in general do poorly at problem solving. Deutsch ascribes these conditions to "so what" attitudes and failure to gradually cultivate problem solving skills. Again, they need to learn in an atmosphere where the importance of honesty in problem solving—providing all essential facts—emerges in daily experiences. Carryover to academic problems demands that curriculum problems be explicit, appropriate to achievement level, sequenced from simple to complex and concrete to abstract. Experience for social problem solving occurs in human groups. Large-group approaches applied by Glasser and Iverson (1966) show promise. Moving clients through a process of measured confrontation and mutual problem solving to the point where they become self-sufficient defines the task. Teachers and counselors alike must become aware of and apply the principles of problem-solving behavior in order to cause students to acquire similar skills. Skill acquisition leads to an increased sense of internal or self control over social rewards.

CULTURAL STIMULATION AND ACHIEVEMENT

Writers (Mink, 1961; Gordon, 1965; Hunt, 1961) reviewing relevant research and theory have established several creditable conclusions about the effect of cultural deprivation on subsequent performance. Viable thoughts depict:

1. There is no creditable evidence to suggest that racial differences in intelligence exist. Measured differences occur through cultural inequities.
2. Disadvantaged youth raised in middle-class homes display measured intelligence significantly higher than their biological parents.
3. Early deprivation can effect a decrement on a person's future academic or intellectual performance.
4. Remedy of effects of deprivation is at least partially possible, sometimes dramatically so. Degree of success is related to degree of deprivation, length of time deprived, and age of youth subjected to attempted remedy (Schreiber, 1962).

Cultural deprivation or variation may adversely affect response modes, perceptual styles, intellectual functions such as language development, cognition, intelligence, speech, comprehension, and vocabulary—all necessary in the middle-class classroom. Yet most authorities believe, as Schwebel (1965), that ". . . the socially deprived have the capacity to develop the cerebral functions necessary for advanced learning. Whenever our society shall want high-level, universal education, it can have it."

Recognizing that these youth lack the experiential background for learning, reading, and verbal expression in currently applied communication modes and information displays, educators wishing to help the disadvantaged overcome educational defects must be willing to restructure information displays and vary communication techniques. Maybe the classroom as we knew it is obsolete as a setting to meet the educational needs of all youth.

AUTHORITY

Authority orientation of the disadvantaged directs itself more toward peers than toward traditional authority structure like parents, school, and church. Conventional society's destruction of opportunities for the culturally variant leaves the youth of the socially deprived no choice except to rely on each other. Experience in the Job Corps and similar programs over the years has demonstrated the impotence of a conventional authority in influencing behavior of the variant youth. William Foote Whyte (1943) makes this case clear in *Street Corner Society*. On the other hand, these groups—in Whyte's case, the Nortons—have clear-cut lines of structure within their group and clearly influence each other's behavior, probably more so than anyone else in any single individual's environment. Rice (1963) points out similar conditions among girls in the Brownsville section of Brooklyn.

The case is by no means clear. Many socially deprived, ill-housed, ill-fed, ill-clothed, and ill-educated persons do respond to and live productively in conventional authority structures. In the writer's experience, the latter is particularly true of the West Virginia, rural, Appalachia village or "holler" (hollow) dweller.

The case for blatant suspicion of conventional authority structure among the disadvantaged is sufficient to avoid exclusive use of the structure in behavioral change approaches. Hence the case is made for peer-group processes.

With the foregoing discussions in mind, it is now appropriate to examine counseling in the group setting with disadvantaged youth.

GROUP COUNSELING

"Large groups work best." "No! Groups of eight or less function most effectively!" Reading the literature on group size is like tasting tonics of yesteryear—all taste like some combination of water and alcohol, but only hearsay makes the tonic work.

Clinical experience with disadvantaged youth dictates caution with setting fast rules on group size. Age of clients, verbal facility, and group purpose dictate size. Due to patience and the need to be active, there is a direct relationship between age and size. Younger students need smaller groups and more opportunities for active participation. Yet students with low verbal communication potential, as the disadvantaged tend to be, need larger groups with more opportunity for withdrawal. Leaders wishing to engage a community problem solving, with practice operate successfully with groups as large as 80 or 90. Practitioners reporting notable success with large groups, Glasser and Iverson, advocate large groups and work with 30 to 50 girls on a day-to-day basis.

In considering group size, pay your money and take your choice. If you're insight-oriented and reasonably inexperienced, groups of 12-15 may be best with the disadvantaged. This is particularly true when other staff and institutional restraints are weak, uninvolved, or nonexistent.

LEADERSHIP

Counselors should assume the role of an authority on behavior change. In short, control and lead the group, channel communications, and limit disruptive factors like individual domination, resistance, and group mores violations. Still, the counselor does not assume full responsibility for successful group operation. Every group member should become a cocounselor and assume responsibilities for maintaining ground rules. Among the disadvantaged, the peer cocounselor may well have the most impact for problem solution, planning, and subsequent control and audit of other member behavior. The peers may well provide the reinforcements, motives, and support crucial to behavioral change.

Counselors debate homogeneity and heterogeneity with respect to sex and nature of the problems. It is doubtful that any of the "experts" really know. Personal experience demands heterogeneity of sex and problems for ideal adolescent or young adult groups. Where monosexual groups are imposed by institutional structure, groups apparently function effectively. General problem areas with typical adolescents center around authority and psychosexual development. Psychosexual problems are best solved in heterosexual groups. Generally, heterogeneity with respect to problems, sex, communication skills, and intellectual and motor skills seems to enhance functional effectiveness of either task-oriented or social-problem-solving-oriented groups.

Theoretical orientation determines group process. Reality therapy practitioners differ significantly from client-centered analytical therapy practitioners. Yet I believe that the human relationship variables are reasonably universal. Counselors must become involved with clients and clients with counselors. Principles like honesty (giving or sharing all the facts), responsibility (making and keeping simple agreements), respect (the kind of love that leads one to intervene in the life of another as a helper, even if at times your help is refused or not wanted), congruence (be open and honest in expressing your feelings), positive regard (each person has worth and *you really believe it*), and acceptance (people have worth and you assist them and try to work with them even if their value systems violate yours)—all are appropriate and necessary conditions in group work. The good group leader exudes warmth but avoids being maudlin. Through his relationships with the group and individuals therein he infuses new life into effete persons. A leader is never obsequious and a group never survives anarchy. Group members are expected to support the same principles of group functioning and goals as are the leader. Individual therapeutic goals are mutually agreed upon.

MEMBERSHIP

Group members participate actively in problem-solving activities. Good group members adhere to group mores, avoid monopoly of group process, and support, accept, and confront other group members. They assume responsibility for their own behavior, accept group controls, and attempt to set and realize responsible goals. As noted, good membership means adherence to problem-solving efforts, support of others, group maintenance, and adherence to group ground rules. The latter may vary, but usually include regular attendance and active commitment to remain throughout a session, as well as other behaviors stated or implied in the concepts already outlined.

Counseling groups are never membership groups in the classical sense, but reference groups. Group members must base critical decisions on group reaction as well as individual inclinations. Most decisions must be referenced in terms of group reaction if the counseling group is to have impact on individual behavior.

Group involvement occurs in many forms. Transitions towards deepening involvement are characterized by emotional crises—tears, sobs, anger, self-disclosure, resolution of confrontation—and responsible group participation. Curiously, involvement with the counselor and specific group members occurs similarly and could probably be measured in degree by counting frequency and intensity of transitions like self-disclosure.

A final word on the responsibility of group members. Behavior change doesn't occur in a vacuum. Whether learned or instinctual, behavior is modified by learning. To be useful, learning must in some way be applied in order to yield fruits for the learner. Agreeing to behave in new ways and trying out the new ways is an essential aspect of group process. The group becomes mother, father, judge, jury, defense, prosecution, minister, teacher—an active influence with specific goals for specific people. The greatest therapeutic gain will be made by individuals who make and keep agreements.

Through group process and subsequent behavior, unloved people can become loved, self-respect restored, problems solved, contructive motives and behaviors established, and destructive behaviors dropped. Self-concepts become more realistic and lead to meaningful aspirations and mastery. Problem-solving skills are acquired, responsibility and honesty are experienced, practiced, and accepted in personal and interpersonal endeavors. These latter qualities can lead to surmounting of educational deficits, employment, stable marriages, and similar universal goods. All in all, able management of effective groups appears as an indispensable aid in the remedy of many deficiencies apparent in the disadvantaged.

GROUND RULES FOR GROUP COUNSELING[1]

1. All members should be required to attend meetings unless they are excluded medically.
2. No member will be permitted to leave the group while the meeting is in process.
3. All participants are to remain seated during the entire meeting.
4. Discussion should not be offensive to the group—that is, no personal insults or deliberate use of vulgarity will be used. Members will be warned that they will be called to account for any indiscriminate use of these terms. On the other hand, there should be no flat rule to the effect that occasional use of

[1]See Glasser and Iverson (1966).

such terms will automatically lead to expulsion from the group. Members will be asked to use language which is comfortable to them.

5. No topics are specifically forbidden. Topics which the youngsters in group counseling sessions want to talk about cover all the specifics in such areas as school (teachers and routines), personal ambitions, living in my neighborhood (from cops to church), personal problems (sex, marriage, family living), and the work area (jobs, bosses, pay). There is practically no limit to the more personalized aspects of such questions that the alert counselor can draw out for beneficial discussion for the group.

6. Disciplinary action will NOT be taken for material revealed in the meeting unless this material has to do with security of person or property.

7. Extra activities during group meetings, such as side conversations or reading, are not permitted.

8. No gross physical movement will be allowed.

9. Members presenting unacceptable behavior in the group will be asked to leave the meeting.

10. Neither staff nor members should make retribution later for material revealed in the group meeting. All members should understand that problems started in the group meeting should be completed in the group meeting. Subgroup planning is acceptable.

11. Staff members do not need to discuss their personal lives.

12. In general, the meeting should end when it is scheduled to end. Sometimes, however, the leader may be convinced that the meeting should continue until certain material is resolved. In these cases, the meeting could be continued for a reasonable length of time, or until the time that is scheduled for the evaluation critique.

13. All staff observers and visitors (if any) will be required to attend postmeeting critique.

14. Other rules may be devised as appropriate to the group and its setting.

DO'S AND DON'TS FOR GROUP COUNSELING

1. Often you should allow the group to select the subjects to be discussed. "Incident Reports" are excellent topics.

2. Encourage the group to set its own limitations.

3. Generally reflect most questions back to the group.

4. Encourage group members to say what they feel by reflecting feelings back, rather than by arguing against them or criticizing.

5. Maintain an accepting but neutral role, avoiding agreement or disagreement with strong feelings expressed by group members.

6. Staff should participate; but not too often.

7. Staff should express true feelings also.

8. With total group assistance, enforce all ground rules.

9. Don't be a lecturer, or deliver "sermonettes."
10. Don't be too defensive! Consider personal references as any other material—impersonally. Politely decline to discuss personal matters by pointing out that the purpose of the meeting is not to discuss the life of the staff.
11. Avoid asking individuals direct questions or making strong decisive statements.
12. Don't insist upon conclusions to subjects discussed . . . let it "soak."
13. Don't criticize group feelings, no matter how much yours differs.
14. Don't identify with antisocial or distorted feelings. Simply recognize feelings.
15. Don't allow one or two members to either disrupt or continuously dominate the group.

REFERENCES

Brookover, W. B., and A. Patterson. "Self-Concept of Ability and School Achievement: Final Report of Cooperative Research Project No. 845, *The Relationahip of Self-images to Achievement in Junior High School Subjects*." East Lansing: Office of Research Publications, Michigan State University, 1962.

Coleman, J. S., E. Q. Campbell, C. J. Hobson, J. McPartland, A. M. Mood, F. D. Weinfeld, and R. L. York. Equality of Educational Opportunity. Superintendent of Documents, Catalog No. FS5.238:38001. Washington, D.C.: Government Printing Office, 1966.

Deutsch, Martin. *Minority Group and Social Class as Related to Social and Personality Factors in Scholastic Achievement.* Society for Applied Anthropology Monograph No. 2., Ithaca, N.Y.: Cornell U. P., 1960.

Edwards, T. B., and S. W. Webster. "Correlates and Effects of Ethnic Group Identification," in *Research Relating to Children.* U. S. Department of Health, Education, and Welfare, Children's Bureau, Bull. No. 17. Washington, D.C.: Government Printing Office, 1963, p. 85.

Glasser, William. *Reality Therapy*. New York: Harper & Row, 1965.

Glasser, William, and Norman Iverson. *Group Counseling in Reality Therapy.* Los Angeles: Reality Press, 1966.

Gordon, Edmund W. "Characteristics of Disadvantaged Children," in "Education for Disadvantaged Children," *Rev. Educ. Res.*, Vol. 35, No. 5 (December 1965), pp. 377-389.

Harlow, Harry F. "The Nature of Love," *Amer. Psychol.*, Vol. 13 (1958), pp. 673-685.

Hunt, Joseph McV. *Intelligence and Experience*. New York: Ronald, 1961.

Liddell, Howard. "Psychoneuroses in Animals." unpublished ms., Cornell University, Ithaca, N.Y., 1958.

Mink, Oscar G. "Experience and Cognitive Structure," *J. Res. Sci. Teach.*, Vol. 2 (1964), pp. 196-203.

Rice, Robert. "A Reporter at Large—the Persian Queens," *New Yorker* (Oct. 19, 1963), pp. 153ff.

Schwebel, Milton. "Learning and the Socially Deprived," *Pers. and Guid. J.,* Vol. 43 (March 1965), pp. 646, 652.

Schreiber, Daniel. "The Higher Horizons Program," *New York State School Boards Association Res. Bull.* Vol. 4, No. 3 (September 1962).

Sears, Pauline Snedden. "Levels of Aspiration in Academically Successful Children," *J. Abnorm. Soc. Psychol.*, Vol. 35 (1940), pp. 498-536.

Whyte, William Foote. *Street-Corner Society*. Chicago: U. of Chicago Press, 1943.

Wylie, Ruth C. "Children's Estimates of Their Schoolwork Ability as a Function of Sex, Race, and Socioeconomic Level," *J. Personality*, Vol. 31 (June 1963), pp. 203-224.

10

Behavioral Counseling and the Total Educational Environment

Oscar G. Mink
Willard A. Mainord

PART 1. EDUCATION

Recent developments in the counseling movement italicize the shift in emphasis from the traditional position of insight to more objective behavioral changes. Traditionally, counselors relied upon the development of the client's understanding and insight into his condition. The newer position regards objective behavioral changes of the client as the goal of the remedial process. In part, the movement from the subjective to the objective focus was the result of the uneconomical as well as unsuccessful nature of the former. The traditional technique succeeded in teaching the client how to speak at great length about himself, while he unfortunately retained most of his problem behavior. The present behavioral technique, by contrast, regards problem behavior as a function of past experience and, therefore, a function of learning. Going ahead one more step in logic, then; Since troublesome behavior has been learned, improved behavior can be achieved through a similar learning process.

But what is this learning process? Learning appears to be evident through changes in an individual's behavior which have been effected by positive reinforcement or behavioral consequences, i.e., individual will repeat behavior which has brought him successfully to his goal. By the same token, if his behavior does not lead to the desired goal, the individual is less likely to repeat it. It has been noted that learning is best described as a gradual accumulation of minute behavioral changes which eventually become evident in a changed behavior pattern rather than a dramatic reversal or abrupt modification in behavior. Change, and therefore learning, is gradual, despite the impression that under certain conditions it appears to take place suddenly. In such cases, usually a more thorough understanding of the individual's learning history reveals that he has merely shifted from one behavior to another, both of which had been previously learned. The foregoing rule has one known exception—avoidance behavior as a function of intense noxious stimulation.

In keeping with the shift in emphasis to behavior as the basis for teaching and learning, all methods of inducing behavioral changes will be considered as counseling or teaching and all results will be considered as learning.

While there has been a shift in the approach to counseling and teaching, there has also been another shift in the direction of counseling. The key word in this second development is "social." It has been found that it is possible to design a program which has integrated within it the principles of learning and has social goals. In the past, an individual's maladjustments were defined as essentially private disorders. Recently, however, evidence has accumulated that the maladjustment is actually between individuals who are either working together or in opposition to each other. It appears that maladjusted behavior arises and is modified in social situations only. If it is ignored, it is maintained by social situations. The task of the counselor, then, would be to employ learning principles as remedial rules when an individual's social defects have been exposed. In other words, what was previously called psychotherapy or counseling is now more appropriately labeled teaching. (Mink, 1970)

A common term and an essential element in the behavioral approach to learning is "reinforcement" (or sometimes "reinforcer"), which generally describes a potential instrument of behavioral modification. It is used when desirable goals of the individual are identified. An effective learning program uses reinforcements as systematically as possible. Controlled reinforcement provides consistent direction to what could be a bewildering diversity of behavior which would be nonproductive and aimless. There are only three sources for social reinforcement: the individual himself, the counselor, and the community.

Bandura (1961) has found that the learner's awareness of the teacher's control of the reinforcers increases the teacher's effectiveness as a behavior modifier. Equipped with various sanctions, the counselor can establish a program designed to help the student uncover important social defects and correct them through a systematic use of reinforcements. The counselor thus enables the student to learn new, more effective skills and helps the student attain his goal in a way that neither alienates the student nor harms others.

However, it is not enough for the student to learn skills with the help of the counselor. The student must eventually become self-directed. To prepare for this, the student must have had an opportunity to deal with problems which would become significant to him after the counseling program has ended. Because of this, an institution needs a teaching community which reflects the problems that must be solved in society. The primary difference between the school community and society would of necessity be that the school is controlled by professional people who regulate the teaching community so that it is ultimately benevolent[1] rather than impersonal. When the student acquires the skills that enable him to be self-directing and to cope with his immediate social

---

[1] Benevolence does not mean that unpleasant consequences can be removed from a socially based teaching community.

problems, he is then equipped with those skills that are necessary for him to function in most social environments.

Thus the task of a total educational community is to graduate students who have acquired those skills essential for him to extract reinforcements from the community in a personally satisfactory and socially acceptable way. But in order for the school to utilize many social situations as constructive learning experiences, it must carefully delineate the methods in a unique framework.

For example, initially the counselor must rely upon his own ability to control the appropriate application of reinforcements. To do this, the counselor must control the individual's environment so that the reinforcements teach neither irrelevant nor destructive skills. However, learning can occur vicariously, so the school could be a place where the student could observe effective problem solving. In either case, whether the student solves the problems directly or observes their solution, his behavioral change will be determined by the consequences of his problem solving. Obviously, then, the school and its counselors must properly manage the consequences if they hope to reach their objectives. Walls and Smith (1969) using videotape sequences for modeling of voluntary delayed reinforcement found that counselor modeling has a significant impact upon subsequent client behavior. Data suggest that older adolescent and young adult clients of both sexes model more closely the counselor standards then peer standards in the same problem situation.

Scientifically, learning theory offers schools and counselors the most comprehensible framework from which they may develop a functional program designed to produce desirable behavioral modification in their students. Experimental efforts have provided several postulates about which there is general agreement. They include the following ten points.

1. Any persistent behavior is maintained by reinforcement, even if the observer is unable to identify the reinforcer and even if the behavior appears to be self-destructive.
2. Any persistent behavior will eventually disappear if reinforcements are not forthcoming but such a process is often distressingly protracted.
3. Any behavior that avoids unpleasant consequences will not only be persistent but it will also deprive both the client and the observer of an important source of information. For instance, the person who fears public scrutiny will seek isolation, thus effectively depriving himself of the discovery that social interaction can be rewarding and perhaps misleading the observer into a false hypothesis that privacy is a positive reinforcer.
4. Occasional reinforcement enables an individual to maintain well-learned behavior. Thus the teaching system must be tight enough to prevent, as much as possible, occasional reinforcements for self-defeating or ineffective behavior.
5. It is better to teach an individual a new behavior then to eliminate

existing behavior, since such a strategy leaves the direction of change uncontrolled. The most efficient strategy, then, is to provide new behavioral routes to existing goals, and then to control the reinforcements in such a way that success (payoff) is possible only through the new behavior.

6. Even if a behavior is elicited from an individual by vicarious means, it still must be reinforced if it is to become habitual.

7. In order for learning to occur, behavior must not only occur but it must also be reinforced. An individual's stated intentions to behave more efficiently cannot be taken as evidence of adequate learning although such statements may indeed be carried out.

8. Social reactions can be reinforcing, punishing, or irrelevant. In each case the social environment will provide most of the teaching.

9. Learning is an involuntary process, leading to changes in behavior that would be described as appropriate or inappropriate by an observer.

10. Effective teaching is accomplished only when student and teacher deal with observables. Again, effective teaching can be measured only by concentrating on observables. Inferences of needs, feelings, or repressions weaken and frequently undermine the teaching process. It also often introduces both error and irrelevancies into the process.

In addition to these ten postulates, there is an important working principle concerning the attitude of the student toward himself. In order to cope with a student's lack of self-esteem it is essential that the teacher maintain a workable definition of honesty and responsibility. Individuals develop self-esteem; it is neither suddenly acquired by introspection nor can it be bestowed. Self-esteem is a function of self-evaluation plus social validation, but it is not a product of either of these alone. People who honor their own ethical codes favorably evaluate themselves according to those codes whenever their behavior warrants it, When the individual realizes that he is violating his own ethical code, he weakens his self-esteem. But if he does not receive social validation, he will be forced to question his own worth.

A permissive social atmosphere is potentially damaging to a student's self-esteem, since permissiveness is not considered approval, specific, or definite enough to lead to confident social intercourse; if however, an individual knows that his portion of society disapproves of him, he will be less able to maintain self-esteem, despite his assertion that he is privately adhering to his ethical code. The presumption here—a relatively safe one—is that an individual's own reference group shares his particular code.

Since social feedback is needed both to build an individual's self-esteem and to effect behavioral change, the teaching community must have a framework that provides social evaluation and reinforcement. The concepts of honesty and responsibility may be defined and utilized as the basis for a social learning process. Since efficient learning is assisted by accurate knowledge of the facts, rigid honesty would provide all the vital social data. So, too, responsibility as a social concept provides a guideline for the systematic application of reinforcement. If both responsibility and honesty are to be basic to a social learning program, they must be operationally defined, clearly communicated, and consistently observed as the criterion for satisfactory performance.

What, then, is honesty? A person is honest if he consistently provides pertinent information *accurately* to another for whom that information has significance. This definition eliminates the traditional notions of confidentiality and the undesirability of tattling. It also excludes the withholding of information. The definition of honesty could be applied to the educational setting. If the educational institution operationally defines honesty and demands it of the student and staff alike, the result will be clear and accurate communication. After the utility of having both the facts and useful feedback demonstrated, resistance to the rule may diminish.

Responsibility may be defined as the obligation to contract and to sustain social agreements.[2] It is every individual's responsibility to have social agreements with the staff and students as well as others. The individual's compliance with the stricture of responsibility is measured not only by his willingness to enter into such agreements (for problem-solving purposes) but also by his consistent fulfillment of such agreements. Behavioral adherence to operationally defined demands for honesty and responsibility enable learning to occur. Responsible behavior leads to self- and social reinforcement; conversely, irresponsibility leads to social reinforcement withheld or withdrawn or to negative group judgment. Under optimal circumstances, individuals learn to be responsible in increasingly difficult situations and each success leads to a more generalized sense of responsibility which can be maintained in a larger society even if it is not as consistently rewarded as it can be in an educational setting.

While learning theory suggests the tools to achieve behavioral change, it does not provide the content which would most usefully be taught. However, the content must be derived from the specific objective—which is the acquisition of skills appropriate to help the individual cope with a social world.

For learning theory to provide the appropriate material, an institution must have a teaching community which offers the usual problems of social living but which differs from society by the help it provides for the individual to acquire essential personal skills. Unlike an impersonal society, an educational program may have as one of its objectives a remedial response whenever an individual displays a lack of skills. Then the teaching community must have methods of inducing its members to reveal their social defects if appropriate social teaching is to occur. Although the exposure of anyone's defects is painful, the pain is momentary and the individual's eventual triumph and the concomi-

---

[2] In the larger society, such agreements are often implicit. One advantage of this definition is that *sub rosa* agreements are forced out into the open and can then be modified or enforced, or both.

tant sense of pride and pleasure more than compensate for it. In fact, the very nature of the learning task demands that the student experience discomfort if that discomfort leads to the desired knowledge.

However, one should be able to distinguish between painful exposures that can be desirable and painful consequences that interrupt, stop or eliminate behaviors. Since the goal of an educational program is to achieve positive behaviors which are designed to reach a student's goals, painful consequences should be utilized only to eliminate behaviors that actually interfere with the learning process. An individual learns through a four-step process—desire, notice, action, and payoff (reinforcement). A counselor has no control over the individual's desires; therefore, he must try to control what the individual notices, how he acts, and what he receives as a payoff.

There is still one more important area to be considered if there is hope for successful learning, and that is in the large area of communication involving emotional contacts with others. It is generally acknowledged that most people need the affection, warmth, and proximity of others. Barriers are built when one feels oneself to be socially deficient, fears that he may seem deficient to others, that he may not inspire their affection. Unless these barriers to warmth and affection are removed, the individual has no freedom to seek and find them. Affection or love should not be misconstrued to be an indiscriminate expression of sympathy and understanding or nurturing emotionality. Love, behaviorally expressed, means that an individual extends himself to be of benefit to another, although sometimes such behavior will not be immediately welcomed by the recipient.

PART 2. COUNSELING

As we have noted, recently there has been more concern expressed with a kind of learning that is seldom part of an educational curriculum. Historically, society left the training of an individual's character and demeanor to the chance instruction of the environment. For the majority in society such haphazard instruction has worked reasonably well. But as we have become more concerned with the victims of poverty and inadequate cultural background, we have emphasized and modified the role of the teacher or counselor.

The more traditional counseling relationship which emphasized the student's insight considered a modeling relationship as theoretically irrelevant or even damaging—à la Freud. Therefore, the counselor did not consciously create in the individual a desire to imitate or model his behavior after the counselor's. One of the difficulties of therapies that deemphasized the counselor-counselee identity relationship was that the counselor tended to communicate or be perceived by the client as having an indifferent attitude. In this more recent therapy, however, the counselor, having the reinforcers, can more effectively serve as an identification model.

If it is accepted that there is a high correlation between a lack of educational background and a lack of social skills, there is then a logical justification for including counseling as an integral part of a total educational environment. Counseling is the process of transmitting social skills to students. However, because of the nature of some students who are in penal institutions or mental health facilities, the counseling process may be compromised because the students may not wish to learn.

In relating the behavioral approach to education, we noted that learning is continual and automatic, that reinforcement determines the direction of a student's change, and that during the learning process the counselor must control most of the consequences of behavior if he is to be an effective teacher. The counselor cannot, of course, be omnipresent and manipulate all reinforcements daily. Instead, he must have a program that will result in rules of reinforcement, which will in turn be observed by the student in the absence of the counselor. In other words, the school culture must reinforce behavior following the same contingencies as would the counselor. The counselor, then, should find ways of implementing the basic rules of the academic subculture.

If the counselor implements the proper set of rules, he will help turn the institution into a total teaching community which reflects society both in the nature of its problems and their solutions. Having the counselor in control of instructional consequences adds also to his effectiveness as a model (Bandura and Walters, 1963) If modeling by a superordinate is the same process as that of identification (which seems likely), then the counselor will be advantageously situated so that his expressions of approval and disapproval will be meaningful to the student. (Walls and Smith, 1969)

A word of caution should be added concerning the effects of unpleasant consequences, their use, and their control by the counselor. Many therapists are fearful of the deleterious effects of unpleasant consequences in remedial programs. If punishment is used indiscriminately, the results will probably be unsatisfactory. However, as we have noted for the educational environment, unpleasant effects can interrupt, suppress, or even eliminate behavior. If punishment, then, is the only available teaching device, it should be employed only to eliminate behaviors that are actually interfering with the learning program. If, in addition to the punishment, alternative routes are available to the same reinforcers which appear to be the goal of the undesirable behavior, and if the reinforcer is indeed acquired by a new and acceptable behavior, the result will be maximum learning efficiency. Punishment, after all, is one form of information and learning is always enhanced by the acquisition of pertinent information in a problem-solving task.

Others object to the use of punishment as a teaching device because they feel that it negates the acquisition of self-esteem. Such an attitude, however, seems to reveal a misunderstanding of the social nature of self-esteem. A counselor who expresses only approval without considering the student's behavior is reinforcing the student's substandard behavior. The student remains oblivious to his substandard behavior. He must then account for his persistent failures in other terms. His conclusion often is that he does not measure up to others or to his own potential or that he has been victimized. Under such circumstances, the student can only conclude that he is so inferior that he needs to be excused from the demands of first-class citizenship, or that his counselor is unaware of the nature of society, or that there is no hope. None of these conclusions helps to build self-esteem. An individual's self-esteem is increased either by his acquisition of social approval or by meeting his own standards—both highly correlated processes. It *cannot* be the "gift" of well-meaning counselors.

Along these same general lines is the concept of love or affection and its role in the counseling situation. As noted, the student may possess barriers that deprive him of the warmth and affection of others. Unless these barriers are removed, the student will be unable to seek or find such a relationship. But more vital at this point is the counselor's role and his expression of affection. Love will be expressed if the counselor attempts to help the student eliminate his defects. In this sense, love becomes another word for concern—that is, it becomes the extent to which a person will concern himself in an effort to be of benefit to someone else. What is essential here is that frequently such love or concern is rejected by the recipient. Counselors sometimes feel they have demonstrated their love when the students have reciprocated through verbal expressions of affection. Such an attitude could be destructive. The therapist who is always "a nice guy" may be willing to sacrifice a student's welfare for his own personal gratification and self-esteem.

Clearly the use of reward and punishment by the counselor requires that he possess and display a judgmental attitude. In the past, therapists believed that such an attitude would irreparably damage the counseling relationship and inevitably silence the client's free discussions, particularly those relating to his feelings. Yet empirical evidence refutes the old attitude. Waskow (1963) discovered, somewhat to her own bewilderment, that a counselor's display of his judgmental attitude in a group therapy situation was the ingredient which was most likely to produce discussions about personal feelings. But should this be so surprising? Discussions which are the results of moral judgments will reasonably be concerned not with the metaphysical question of "Who am I?" but rather with the more vital search, "What am I worth?" The latter question appears prepotent in the thinking of America's problem youth.

REFERENCES

Bandura, A. "Psychotherapy As a Learning Process," *Psychol. Bull.* Vol. 58 (1961), pp. 143-159.
Bandura, A., and H. Walters. *Social Learning and Personality Development.* New York: Holt, 1963.

Mink, O. G. *The Behavior Change Process*. New York: Harper & Row, 1970,
Soloman, R. L. "Punishment," *Amer. Psychologist*, Vol. 19, No. 4 (1964), pp. 239-253.
Walls, R. T., and T. S. Smith. "Counselor and Client Modeling Influence upon Voluntary Delay of Reinforcement," unpublished ms., Social and Rehabilitation Research and Training Center, Division of Clinical Studies, West Virginia University (May 1969), 12 pp.
Waskow, I. E. "Counselor Attitudes and Client Behavior," *J. Consult. Psychol.*, Vol. 27, No. 5 (1963), pp. 405-412.

11

Counseling in a Women's Job Corps Center—A Case in Social Crisis

Susan Zaslow Jackson
Tennie Smith

INTRODUCTION

Title I of Public Law 88-452 provided for the establishment of Job Corps Centers for Women. These Centers were to be operated by private industry under contract with The Office of Economic Opportunity (OEO) utilizing government funds and under direct government control.

Proposals to establish centers were submitted to the Office of Economic Opportunity (OEO) and contracts were given to a variety of companies whose products ranged in nature from electronics to copying machines. One proposal, written and submitted by Basic Systems, Inc., of New York City reflected four years of experience with innovative educational concepts and materials. The Company had a full-time staff of over twelve Ph.D.'s and some 250 doctoral-level scientists as affiliates in the field of education and related areas. These scientists were in the main behavioral scientists who had specialized in learning methodologies, systems analysis, social psychology, reading, management, systems programming, and programmed learning. The proposal which they developed reflected a vast pool of knowledge and creativity.

However, by the time OEO granted this company a contract to establish the Center they had proposed, Basic Systems was no longer an independent company; it had been purchased by the Xerox Corporation and became a Xerox educational subsidiary. Nevertheless, it was largely members of the original Basic Systems staff that recruited and trained personnel to staff the Center. The Center's location was to be in Huntington, West Virginia. Recruiting Job Corps staff was done on a national basis. Full-page ads appeared in major newspapers in New York, Los Angeles, San Diego, and other cities.

At interviews prospective teachers were briefed on new educational devices and systems. At the time of the interview most applicants seemed eager to learn and to work with the proposed system. Prospective counselors were told about the latest developments in group counseling and felt themselves to be on the threshhold of important and new discoveries. All were warned that the experimental nature of the program required great flexibility, and all were reminded that this represented a unique opportunity to contribute to their country—to join John F. Kennedy's New Frontier—by providing opportunity to America's disadvantaged young people. Without doubt each staff member's notification of his acceptance to the position was characterized by feelings of great excitement, due to the personal challenge and opportunity to contribute to humanity.

These feelings were heightened by eight weeks of intensive staff training conducted at the Center in Huntington. The arrival of the first group of Job Corps enrollees was anticipated to occur on or about January 11, 1966. Beginning November 1, 1965, the staff gathered to engage in a variety of activities and training. Experiences included: (1) sensitivity to human relationships; (2) dynamics of cultural and economic deprivation;[1] (3) total Center program; (4) the innovations in their areas of speciality, as they applied to the development of the curricula. By the time of the opening of the Center on January 11, 1966, each staff member had a dedication to the Center of the type found usually only in moments of national crisis. Perhaps engendered by their new understanding of the critical nature of the problem as a partial solution to America's future the staff was poised to function. But over and above their dedication to the job was a dedication to the yet unseen Job Corps enrollees—to each one as an important human being—arising from their new knowledge that for most of these girls this Job Corps Center might well be their last chance to pull out of the poverty cycle and enter the mainstream of American life.

THE CHOICE OF REALITY THERAPY

The responsibility for the choice of counseling approach to be used at the Center rested with the staff of Senior Scientists at BSI who had designed the Center, among them was the future Director of Counseling and Residential Affairs at the Center[2]

William Glasser, M.D., was hired as a consultant and spent a day in New York City with the Basic Systems central office staff, discussing and demonstrating "reality therapy" before the Huntington staff recruiting began. BSI Senior Scientists concurred that the social learning model on which reality therapy operated would work most suitably with Job Corps enrollees. It had the primary advantages of total staff involvement and of putting the counselor out of his office and placing him into the midst of center programming.

---

[1] From such written sources as Claude Brown *Manchild in the Promised Land*; James Conant, *Slums and Suburbs*; Harry M. Caudill, *Night Comes to the Cumberlands*; Michael Harrington, *The Other America*; and James Weller, *Yesterday's People*. Also many lecturers and consultants from Basic Systems, Inc., various agencies and educational institutional were utilized.

[2] See the immediately preceding Chapters 9 and 10 on counseling. These chapters reflect many of the basic theoretical and practical tenets of reality therapy as practiced in the Center under the direction of Oscar G. Mink.

Thus when Huntington staff recruiting began, the Center's design was clearly defined. At this point the first basic mistake occurred: staff members were not hired on the basis of their concurrence with program objectives. From the onset, conflict existed. It was during Staff Training that BSI personnel attempted to create a cohesive staff, committed to the use of reality therapy as well as individualized instruction as a total staff approach and knowledgeable in their uses and rationale.

To this end the counselors conducted some staff training sessions at which they shared their backgrounds with the rest of the staff. Guest speakers were brought in to talk about various counseling approaches. All this information was designed to communicate with the staff with respect to the applicability of reality therapy at the center. However, staff training was misinterpreted, perhaps deliberately, by some, who believed that the decision of the counseling and educational approaches to be used at the Center should be determined by the entire staff.

These staff members were threatened by new methodology and predicted failure. With the implementation of reality therapy as the predetermined choice of a counseling approach, many attempts to disrupt the process occurred. Even though the majority of the staff were supportive of this choice, some were decidedly opposed. The schism thus created was further heightened by the fact that some of those resistant staff members were people in key positions of power and authority.

REALITY THERAPY THEORY IN BRIEF[3]

The beginning assumption of reality therapy is that behavior difficulties (social problems) arise because of learning, and that behavioral improvements are possible only by the same process. The first principle of learning is that behavioral change is the result of the consequences of previous behavior. It is generally agreed that people tend to repeat procedures that work for them and abandon those that do not. These "consequences" which encourage behavior to recur are said to be "reinforcing." The manipulation of reinforcements is the counselor's primary tool. But ultimately the community will be the most important source of reinforcement. Since reinforcements determine the direction of behavioral change (i.e., learning), the counselor must have control of most of the consequences of behavior if he is to teach new behaviors effectively. The counselor, of course, is not always present to determine these consequences. So he must have a program which will result in consistent application of the same rules of reinforcement that he is applying whether or not he is present. This means the total environment must reinforce the same behavior the counselor would reinforce.

---

[3] See Chapter 10 for details. In addition, see W. Glasser, *Reality Therapy* (New York: Harper & Row, 1965), and W. Glasser, *Schools Without Failure* (New York: Harper & Row, 1968).

Otherwise, a serious problem could result. For example, a girl who was feeling the frustration of modifying her behavior could manipulate others involved with her in order to gain reinforcement without changing her own behavior.

What behavior should the counselor reinforce? In order to correct social problems, the counselor, and therefore the total environment, must extinguish socially unacceptable or irresponsible behavior. They must realize that frustration will occur if a more socially acceptable behavior is not substituted for the old behavior in order to gain the verbalized goal of the girl. Therefore the reinforcement of responsible behavior must occur. The criterion, then, is: "Will this behavior be acceptable and hence facilitate success in the outside world to which the individual is returning when she leaves this environment?"

The question arose concerning whether or not the girl in this structured environment would develop a dependency upon that environment. Certainly the counselor had to admit that a certain amount of dependency would occur since he was the prime controller of reinforcers. However, as the girl progressed through the program, she gained a feeling of success. She realized that her own behavior was determining her success in the program, and with this new method of behavior she could determine her life's expectancy in the outside world. In a very basic sense, girls on the move tended to shift their feeling of locus of control from the external world to their internal world.

Basically this is the reality therapy approach to effective therapy; ergo, as one behaves, he gets environmental feedback. If his behavior is consistent with his value system, he feels good. If not, he feels bad. Reality therapy is the development of counseling techniques and principles to facilitate this process. One of the most atypical features of the techniques of reality therapy is the demand it makes on the counselor to become involved. This involvement is of a specific nature. Interest, of course, and sensitivity are called for; likewise a willingness to reveal oneself and admit one's faults. The only limit to involvement is that it must always be for the counselee's good. If it helps the counselee toward accepting responsibility, the counselor must be willing to watch the counselee suffer in anxiety and must not intercede. Reality therapy has built sets of suggestions to help the counselor attain the proper relationship with his counselee. It has also built procedures, such as community problem solving groups, for the manipulation of reinforcements and the applications of principles of learning. Reality therapy, thus described, can be seen to have the following advantages for use at a Job Corps Center.

The total environment, which was a similar yet more restricted example of the community at large, consisted primarily of: (1) Job Corps personnel, (2) Center staff, and (3) students. In staff training and regular staff meetings the counseling staff can communicate its program of rules of reinforcement to the total staff. The students, because of past learning experiences, will not submit to consistent applications of the rules, but a great deal can be done in this direction through community groups (to be discussed below). Thus the Job Corps is particularly suitable for the use of reality therapy because the total environment can be manipulated to the advantage of the enrollee.

Another advantage can be more easily described in terms of the disadvantages of conventional counseling in the Job Corps situation. Conventional therapy can give appearance of functioning in an institute for delinquents or a mental institution, because the "inmates" must comply in order to get out. At the same time conventional therapeutic approaches tend to encourage "acting out" behavior which must be avoided in the majority of Job Corps communities because of public relations problems. In addition, at the Job Corps, girls are there by choice and can leave upon desire, so a less overtly disciplinary method of coping with problems is desirable. The community problem-solving group is such a method, where self-discipline is more or less transferred from the staff to the student body.

An examination of how reality therapy operated at the Huntington Women's Job Corps Center may suggest even more ways in which reality therapy is particularly suitable for the Job Corps.

THE OPERATION OF REALITY THERAPY AT HUNTINGTON

Staff Training

Some of the characteristics of staff training have already been indicated. In addition, the total staff had to be prepared for its role in reality therapy.

Let us examine first the specific role of the noncounseling staff in reality therapy. It was their job, as already mentioned, to reinforce responsible behavior when it occurred in their presence, and negatively reinforce, or better yet *not* reinforce, irresponsible behavior. To be able to carry out this task effectively the staff had to be aware of possible manipulative behavior of the enrollees who were placed under stress as their behavior was being modified. The staff, then, would have to be familiar with the particular problems of the girls, and be sensitive to the many subtle ways these problems are manifested in behavior. For example, while it may be perfectly responsible behavior for one girl to volunteer to help the teacher, for another this may be a way in which she avoids relating to her peers. Thus the entire staff attended the community meetings at which problems were discussed and solutions "worked on." Literally nothing was "confidential." In addition, the staff had to be sensitive to their students, in order not only to detect their irresponsible behavior but also to know how to reinforce each girl. One must recognize the needs and goals of each girl in order to reward her responsible behavior in such a way as to make it more likely to occur again.

To this end the counseling staff undertook sensitivity training for the total staff. It is most difficult to evaluate the success of these "T-Groups." Their purpose was not well understood by all group members. Many felt personally threatened by them. Some thought the counselors were using them as guinea pigs on which to practice. Others thought the intention was to give them therapy and resented the implication that they were in need of it. Thus for some staff members another factor was present in the developing schism between teachers and counselors that was later to plague the success of the reality therapy program and the entire Job Corps Center. In some cases it developed into a predisposition against counseling which resulted in some staff members refusing to attend community group meetings (and discouraging or disallowing the staff under their direction to attend). This same attitude spilled over to the girls. However, without the T-groups communication problems may have been even more difficult. Perhaps the greatest single caution might be that for in-service work on communications use of "in-house" staff for trainers should be avoided. Also, the design of the lab should be in the direction of criterion performance of each participant and not set to time limits.

The Community Group

The basic tool of reality therapy was the community groups. The groups met three times a week, one and a half hours a meeting. In the beginning the entire community formed one group. (OEO gave the Huntington Center special permission to open with only forty girls to make such a group feasible.) As the size of the Job Corps grew to full capacity (approximately 300), groupings of approximately 40 girls each were maintained. Because behavior problems would be dealt with in these groups, it was felt that the natural living unit, where much of the interaction occurred, would be the most useful organizational unit for grouping. Thus all the girls who lived together on a floor met together as a "Group," and were assigned to the counselor of that floor. This seemed to be the best procedure for arbitrarily assigning incoming enrollees to Groups. In this manner the problems brought up in group were handled as a community living condition. Anything could be brought up, and the basic rule was that nothing would be repeated outside of Group and no retribution would be taken after Group. This does not carry the same meaning of confidentiality as in the traditional sense. A girl's behavior was openly discussed in order to aid her in change of behavior. (This applied to staff-student affairs as well as student-student.) Although anything could be brought up, problems were to be discussed in terms of behavior. Both enrollee and staff must give facts concerning a girl's behavior such as the "who," "where," and "what" of an act. For this reason an important distinction was made between punitively telling just to get even or get someone into trouble (finking) and giving pertinent information to help in the solution of a problem. Also, in order to facilitate solution of problems each girl in the group agreed to be honest and responsible. Honesty was defined as having to say anything relevant that one knows about a situation under discussion. Responsibility was defined as a willingness to enter into plans decided upon by the group to solve problems by making and keeping simple commitments with each other. Enrollees tested and learned that others could and did care for them, because enrollees and involved staff entered in as part of the plan to help a given girl keep her commitment to herself and to the group.

When counselors as well as girls were very inexperienced with groups and unsure of how they should operate, it was found that written "Ground Rules for Groups," distributed to staff and students, helped keep the first groups on the right track. The rules and their purpose were discussed when they were originally distributed. Anyone was free to call a girl or staff member for violation of the ground rules and it was recognized that this was done for the benefit of all. Following are some typical ground rules.

1. Meeting will start and finish on time.
2. Anything may be brought before the group for discussion.
3. No one is excused from Group unless for medical reason.
4. No one is permitted to leave the meeting.
5. All guests are to be introduced at the beginning of the meeting and asked to participate.
6. *One topic* will be discussed at a time.
7. Language should not be offensive.
8. There will be no physical acting out behavior.
9. One person at a time will speak.
10. Side conversations are not permitted. Information is for the entire group.

These were a few of the ground rules utilized by the counselors to facilitate a smoother functioning group. The wording of the rules varied from group to group but essentially were of the same basic idea. These rules were adapted from previously established groups in other settings. Additional ones were suggested by consultants knowledgeable in the field, other Center staff members, and perhaps more important by the girls themselves. (For broader Center regulations, see Appendix, "Rules and Regulations for Huntington Women's Job Corps.") As the groups gained in experience and the rules were internalized the list faded in importance.

As behaviors were isolated and defined, recurring patterns would appear. The group began to recognize problems whose solutions depended upon one or more of their members changing some of their irresponsible behavior. Each enrollee began to recognize the fact how her behavior affected others, especially those with whom she lived and to whom she felt close. When this occurred, the group would formulate plans to help the girls involved change their behavior. One test of an appropriate plan was whether or not it *helped* the girls involved. In this way plans that were purely punitive, perhaps generated by the emotions of the moment, were detected and corrected by the group. It should be pointed out that sometimes plans were formulated that, for various reasons, did not work. The same problem often happens in the outside world. This gave the group opportunity to experience good, hard, critical thinking. The "whys" and "wherefores" of the plan's failure were openly discussed, and from that discussion grew a "well-thought-out" approach to the difficulties. Thus the girls, possibly for the first time in their lives, make wise decisions—the product of sound critical thinking and problem solving.

It was the counselor's role to see that the group process was orderly, that it kept moving positively, and that appropriate plans were formulated by the group. While allowing tension to build, if necessary to pressure the group toward solution, the counselor must never allow the group to dissolve while tension is high enough to cause new problems to occur before the next group meetings. The staff other than counselors contributed to the group in much the same way as the girls. By contributing observations of behavior they helped define the problems. They also contributed their ideas on possible plans for solutions, though generally only if the girls were at an impasse. No plan was put into action that the group did not accept, although the girls were aware of the fact that the final decision was the counselor's. But by the same token the group had the responsibility to work until appropriate solutions were found. At the end of the group the staff met for about five minutes for an open critique of the group (the girls had the option to stay, and sometimes decided to do so). This critique revolved around what group processes occurred. Later in a *staff* critique, leader strengths and weaknesses as well as good and bad procedures were discussed.

A discussion of some of the ramifications of the Group follows. The Group had several overt benefits to enrollees. Besides the solution of problems so necessary in a dormitory living situation and with a population characterized by social problems, the actual process of problem solution was learned. The Group also provided a consistent source of reinforcement for positive behavior and negative reinforcement for irresponsible behavior.

The Student Incentive System

OEO provided a $30 monthly income for each girl. In addition it provided a series of four $5 increments, but only a certain percentage of the girls could attain each income level. The OEO increment system lent itself to a competitive situation, in which the top few percent earned $50 monthly, the next few $45 monthly, etc. But the Huntington Job Corps Center, with OEO permission, developed a system in which student attainment determined the level of income with no competitive consideration. This was accomplished in the following manner:

Every course offered by the Job Corps—cooking, IBM keypunch, reading—was described in behavioral terms. Then an estimate of the average time needed to perform each task was make. Every course was then broken down on paper into nine-hour sections. (The choice of nine hours was relatively arbitrary.) Thus a nine-hour section of cooking was equal to a nine-hour section of reading, or any other course, in that both would take the average girl nine hours to complete. The completion of a nine-hour section earned a girl one point. This gave every girl an equal opportunity to earn points. Although girls were enrolled in different courses, they all attended school for the same amount of time each day.

Attainment of a raise was based on the number of points accumulated. When a girl reached x number of points she received her first $5 increment, earning now \$35 a month; when she earned $(x + y)$ number of points, she received her next increment, etc. The quantities x and y, etc., were arrived at mathematically, by considering the total number of girl/hours worked each week, and attempting to set the points at such a level that each increment would be attained by approximately the same percentage of the girls as in the OEO system.

So while it might be true that only a certain percentage of the girls would be earning at each level, and while the quicker girl would earn a raise sooner, this in no way affected any other girl in reaching points needed to get a raise.

This system was particularly relevant to reality therapy. It provided individualized reinforcement for each girl's responsible behavior of progressing in class. It also provided concrete behavioral information on each girl's classroom performance. If the system were competitive and a girl failed to earn a raise all that could be said of her was that her work was not as good as certain others' work. This does not indicate if her work in class has been responsible or not. But if a girl has been in classes for six weeks (180 hours) and has earned only five points (where average progress would be one point for each nine hours, or twenty points), then this says that the girl's performance in class has been irresponsible.

Other Reward Systems

"Hospital terminology" was a system both for reward and as a means of control. It was an integral part of community groups. There were three lists maintained in public view: "Serious List," "Critical List," and "Terminal List." A girl was placed on a list by her Group. This was seldom done upon the first occurrence of some irresponsible behavior unless the particular behavior was of such an extreme nature that the Group felt the girl involved needed a great deal of help from others and needed immediately the restrictions that accompanied being placed on the list in order to stay out of further trouble. More commonly a girl was placed on the "serious list" when she manifested a recurring pattern of irresponsible behavior over a period of time. Any refusal of a girl to work on her problem would also result in her being placed on the serious list. In accordance with each girl's commitment to responsibility (willingness to enter into agreements) it was expected that girls on the "serious list" would start working their way off the list. As hospital terminology indicates, a girl on the "serious list" needs special attention and therefore the Group concentrated extra effort to help her to get off the list. As a means of helping they observed those on the list in order to report improvements in behavior to the rest of the Group. When a girl's reported behavior showed steady improvement the Group would remove her from the list. If this did not occur then the Group would move a girl from the "serious" to "critical list." Here even more restrictions were applied to the girl but concurrently more of her friends became involved in helping her make and follow-through with commitments to the Group. When a girl on the "critical list" showed signs of steady improvement she was moved to the "serious list" and with further improvement was removed from the "lists" altogether. Any girl on the "critical list" who continued to show no signs of improvement was placed on the "terminal list" and was terminated from the Center. This was an extreme and rare thing. By publically posting the lists, peer-group pressure was brought to bear upon the listed girls to improve. One could see in one's friends the disappointment that appearance on the list evoked in those who felt responsible to help each other solve problems. Likewise, removal from the list was a source of common celebration. In addition a great deal of personal pride and self-worth was felt by a person who was able to work her way up and off the lists by her own behavior. The girls soon learned that one earns self-esteem and cannot receive it as a gift.

Life at the Center involved many potential rewards weekend passes away from the Center, late passes on Friday and Saturday nights, trips, and parties. All of these payoffs were made contingent upon responsible behavior and utilized by the counseling staff. (See Appendix A for specifics). But it was not left to the counselor to arbitrarily decide whether the girl had been behaving responsibly. There was a list of criteria for each reward—for example, no negative incident reports and acceptable room checks over a specified period of time. In the case of a weekend pass the period was a month. But for a smaller reward such as late passes, a week was deemed more appropriate. A girl with a negative record at the Center who started to improve could be reinforced immediately for her improvement without being repeatedly penalized for something that had occurred two or three weeks past. In the context of community groups, the Group could deny a girl any of these rewards if they felt it was a necessary part of a plan to change her behavior.

Community Groups were able to reward by mention of positive accomplishments of girls. These mentions were brought up by other girls and by staff as well. They were entered into a girl's permanent files by means of incident reports, which could deal with desirable as well as undesirable behavior. Thus within the Groups girls were mentioned by others if they had noticeably improved their physical appearance, kept exceptionally clean rooms, did careful work in class or more than called for, improved radically academically (going from fourth-grade reading level to ninth-grade level in a couple of weeks), scored well on the High School Equivalency Examination. The Huntington Center was the recipient of three of six scholarships offered by Litton Industries to Job Corps girls for furtherance of their education. One of the three winners also received first place in a Job Corps writing contest as well as a place in its art touring exhibit. These accomplishments brought their own rewards and were further reinforced by the peer group approval of the Community Groups.

It was planned that, in time, the entire Job Corps environment would be systematically designed in terms of work units and payoffs. The total would thus

be integrated into the system of reality therapy social learning to serve as reinforcers, producing behaviors that would prepare girls to succeed when they left
the Center.

SUCCESSES AND FAILURES

During the time that reality therapy was a functioning system, the Huntington
Women's Job Corps Center was notable in several ways when compared to other
Centers.

First, it had the lowest dropout rate of any Center. The fact of low
dropout rate was related to the mutual responsibility that was fostered by reality
therapy. The dropout of a girl was a failure for all; so all worked hard to prevent
it. Another explanation for the low dropout rate can be found in the cohesive-
ness that groups create. Assuming that a dropout indicates a problem unsolved,
group problem solving must also have contributed to a reduction in the number
of dropouts.

Second, the Center was characterized by no major incidents of vandalism,
such as other Centers experienced. The group as a tension-releasing mechanism
was partly responsible for this. The concept of mutual responsibility made it
unlikely also since such incidents are usually the product of a negative group;
but few negative ideas survived when shared with others because there were
always some in the group who perceived such ideas as ultimately harmful to
those who conceived them. And in accordance with the concept of mutual
responsibility, it became their responsibility to dissuade others from self-destructive activity.

Third, it is significant that there was not a single pregnancy[4] at this Center
of 300 women during the ten months reality therapy was being used. After its
discontinuation the first pregnancy occurred.

Successes with individual girls could be described at great length, as could
notable failures. But failures of reality therapy in a more general sense would
probably be more enlightening.

It has already been mentioned that certain schisms developed among the
staff, starting with the failure to hire staff committed to the BSI Center design
and objectives, and perhaps increasing during staff sensitivity training. These
schisms certainly worked against the success of reality therapy with its total
environmental approach. In particular, some staff members used the students
against other factions of the staff. This even included staff members organizing
students to picket the Center.

In some cases staff never did fully comprehend the theory and practice of
reality therapy. One staff member saw it as a "communistic" system. This can

---

[4] Although some girls arrived at the Center in this condition they were properly cared
for and returned to the appropriate environments. According to OEO regulations, the girl
was permitted to return to the Center after the birth of the child.

only be attributed to some failure of the counseling staff in training the rest of the Center staff.

Another factor in the failure of reality therapy was the interference of OEO, Washington, D.C. While certain OEO personnel may have understood what the Center was doing, as an organization it remained suspicious of reality therapy and was quick to blame any of the Center's problems—problems that were occurring at all centers—on reality therapy. In addition, OEO encouraged students at the Center to go straight to OEO with problems. This behavior was not unsupported but encouraged by certain members of the staff. Where a student's problem was the consequence of her own irresponsible behavior, this gave her a source of reinforcement for such behavior and sabotaged Center attempts to extinguish the behavior and reinforce more responsible behavior.

Still another factor in the failure of reality therapy, ultimately providing the final blow to the system, was the changing administration. The first change, of course, was the purchase of Basic Systems by Xerox. Thus the very top administrators had no particular knowledge of or sense of commitment to reality therapy. In addition to this, in a six-month period the Center had six directors. Each one had different feelings about reality therapy and its role at the Center. Some were interim directors who promoted a state of laissez faire that allowed reality therapy to exist but through a refusal to make decisions prevented it from ironing out its problems. One of the final directors and his assistant director knew nothing of reality therapy. First they changed its substance, turning Community Group into a time for reading announcements. Then they cut the groups back to once a week. At this point fewer than half the original counseling staff remained. The newer counselors were for the most part informally trained in reality therapy. The remaining trained counselors were discouraged to continue defending it. In a move typical of industry the new administrators further destroyed it by giving charge of the counseling staff to a man who was not a counselor, who had no experience in behavior modification, and who had little experience in counseling. In addition they hired unqualified people as counselors to replace the departing professionally trained counselors.

Suggestions for Utilizing Reality Therapy Successfully in a Similar Setting

1. A commitment must be made by all administrators to use reality therapy. In this case, Xerox administrators should have made this commitment so that even if administrators at the Center changed, new ones would have to be committed to reality therapy.

2. Likewise, all staff must understand and agree to implement reality therapy as a total educational environment approach. This may require more extensive staff training, with more attention paid to the manner in which reality therapy is presented to the staff. It would also be a factor in hiring staff. Commitment to the process and to its tenets like honesty and responsibility ought to be a condition of employment.

3. Related to (2) above is the fact that at the Job Corps Center most of the staff are professional people. They may view reality therapy as an affront to their professional competence or an infringement on their professional domain. An orientation to and appreciation for the work of the counselor might help the professional staff to accept the counselor's expertise in an area in which most professions function, albeit unsystematically. One common fallacy in the thinking of educators who emphasize the "art" of teaching is a tendency to confuse "belief" with scientific fact. In addition, the relationship of staff and staff functions should be worked through as part of staff training. A more formal system of communication and information flow would facilitate solution of some of these problems. At the Huntington Women's Job Corps Center these systems were developed by a team of systems analysts but not utilized by management. Gradually and informally sub rosa systems developed thereby contributing to many problems.

4. There was a basic weakness in our approach, partly dictated by OEO policy. From the time the girls arrived at the Center everything was provided for them. They received their allowance, money for clothes, and of course comfortable living quarters. There was no OEO policy regarding attending classes, or any policy with respect to discipline with the exception of the most serious problems. A girl could skip every class for two weeks and at the end of that time receive her $15 allowance. Not only was this policy unrealistic in terms of the way in which our society functions, but it deprived the counselors of some major reinforcers. Worst of all it gave the student no way of establishing personal dignity and self-esteem in their own eyes—it was a fatal OEO policy error to assume that any agency can give another person self-esteem. It simply must be earned. It would certainly be advisable to restructure the institutional setting so that all but the basic necessities can be manipulated by the staff to reinforce responsible behavior.

SUMMARY

Dr. Bennetta Washington, head of the Women's Job Corps, Office of Economic Opportunity, has outlined[5] some of her thoughts about counseling and counselors based on her Job Corps experience. Dr. Washington summarized some of the major problems of the counseling function today. An examination of the way reality therapy handles some of these problems will reveal many of its advantages over traditional counseling techniques.

1. Dr. Washington mentions the interrelated problems of discipline and authority. On the subject of discipline she laments the fact that counselors have not "actively involved themselves in the teaching of worthy values." Dr. Washington cites the counselors' refusal to directly attempt to correct misbehavior on

[5]*National Vocational Guidance Association Newsletter* Vol. 5, No. 2 (January 1966).

the "dubious assertion that counseling and discipline don't mix." Nonetheless, she points out, the counselor is still seen, in the student's eyes, as an authority figure, and therefore suspect.

Reality therapy overtly deals with the changing of misbehaviors. Yet it does so in a way that minimizes the authoritarian role of the counselor. It is the group, the students themselves, who discipline. With the skilled leadership of the counselor, the group evolves its own values, and through a system of reinforcements (discipline) it changes the misbehavior of the group members to responsible behavior.

2. Another problem for the counselor who refuses to engage in discipline and insists on being neutral in terms of value judgment is that the students interpret this acceptance as indifference. Thus when a girl tested those involved with her, she might well discover that they (the involved) did not really care for her.

Reality therapy does not presume to function in a value vacuum. The whole process of group is one of evaluating behavior in terms of the students' and society's values. In addition, the counselor is encouraged to become involved with the student. He is free of constraints that force him to accept all behavior. Although he is as loving and accepting of a fellow human being as in any other type of traditional therapy, he is free to be himself as a genuine human having feelings, faults, and values. Therefore, he is encouraged to react honestly to the student and accept only responsible behavior. In such a relationship the *last* thing a student can feel about a counselor is that he is indifferent.

3. Finally, Dr. Washington reprimands the counselor who believes he has an exclusive function. "Our experiences with Job Corps girls show clearly that they respond to, and seek help from, the person with a sincere interest in them as individuals. This may be the cook, the switchboard operator, or the snack-bar manager."

It is here that reality therapy has its greatest advantage over traditional counseling approaches. In its total environmental approach it trains all staff members to deal with students in a way that supports the students' positive progress as the counselor works with each student and the "group." It is well adapted to work with the girl who doesn't respond to the counselor but does to the cook. The cook or others, just as well as the counselor, can use reinforcement to shape the girl's behavior. They need only understand the girl's problems, and the basic rules of reinforcement, and genuinely desire to help the girl.

CONCLUSION

For all of these reasons reality therapy is thought to be a remarkably advantageous counseling approach for a Job Corps Center or similar institutional setting where a total social learning environment can be designed and implemented.

APPENDIX

Rules and Regulations for the Huntington Job Corps Center

I. General Expectations
   A. Students will *respectfully* refer to staff members by the name with which both are most comfortable.
   B. Students will not resort to *offensive* physical force.
   C. Students will not curse at each other or staff members.
   D. Students are all responsible for keeping their commitments.
   E. Students will treat each other courteously and respectfully at all times.
   F. Students will not make direct phone calls to the homes of staff members. On-duty personnel will decide if a call is warranted.
   G. Students will not shout, throw anything, or lean out of the windows.
   H. Students should not make use of staff equipment, i.e., typewriters.
   I. Students and our guests are all responsible for taking care of furniture (e.g., keeping feet off furniture, putting cigarettes in ashtrays, etc.) and for respecting personal and private property (e.g., stealing and defacing).
   J. Students are not permitted to drive private cars (OEO).
   K. Possession of fireworks is not permitted in the Center.

II. Acceptable Behavior within the Residence Lobby where all students are "On Display"
   A. Students will meet their dates in the lobby, not on the street or in neighboring business places.
   B. Girls will act as hostesses and be responsible for the behavior of their guests.
   C. Students will pick up after themselves and guests and will leave the lobby clean.
   D. Students will be responsible for reminding themselves and others to use proper containers (e.g., pop-bottle racks, trashcans, and ashtrays) when disposing of trash.
   E. Students will refrain from necking in or around the lobby.
   F. Students will not go into the lobby improperly dressed.
   G. Visiting hours will be from noon until midnight on Friday and Saturday and from 9:00 a.m. until 10:00 p.m. on Sunday, except for special pre-arranged official programs.

III. Within the Residence Halls
   A. Quiet hours (no excessive noise from record players, etc.) from 11:00 p.m. Sunday through Thursday and 1:00 a.m. Friday and Saturday will be enforced.
   B. Bed check will be at 11:00 p.m. on Sunday through Thursday, and at 1:00 a.m. on Friday and Saturday.
   C. Lights out at bed check.
   D. Students will sleep in their own rooms.

E. Periodic checks will be made of the residence floors to assure that no students will be "sleeping in."

F. Girls will be dressed in halls. Bathrobes are considered acceptable dress.

G. Students will move in the halls quietly and orderly.

H. Drinking will not be tolerated as an excuse for loud, boisterous, or aggressive behavior. We will not tolerate drinking under age 18 for beer, 21 for liquor.

I. Students will be courteous and quiet around the phone when it is in use, and will stay within the 10-minute time limit. Students will not give out information such as names of other students to callers they do not know. The telephone will not be used after quiet hours. A girl will have her callers call her on her own residence floor and own side of floor so others will not have to search on other floors for her. Students will not write names or other information on the wall by the phone.

J. Students will not go upon the roof.

K. No appliances, such as irons, will be used in student bedrooms.

L. No nails or plastic tape may be used for decorating purposes in student rooms.

M. No washers or dryers may be used during quiet hours.

IV. Within the Dining Hall

A. Students will be *on time* for meals.

B. Good table manners will be observed by all at meals.

C. Students will not cut into lines nor cross to get food.

D. Students may not go into kitchen.

E. Students will be appropriately dressed for meals.

   1. Slacks, and shorts in the vicinity of the knee, will be allowed at all breakfast and evening meals (except on one "dress up" night during the week to be announced).

   2. Hair rollers will be allowed at breakfast and at evening meals on Friday and Saturday.

      (a) Please note that slacks, sport clothes, and rollers are not permitted at any noon meal (except Saturday), since this is the time most visitors eat in our cafeteria.

      (b) The Sunday noon meal will be a "dress up" meal.

   3. No nightwear, including bedroom slippers, pajamas, nightgowns, robes, etc., will be allowed at any meal.

V. Health Regulations

A. No unauthorized medicine will be kept by students.

B. Students will keep appointments that are made for them by the Health Service Department.

C. Students will not violate the services of the infirmary by going for the purpose of missing a class or meeting. (Notice is given at what time students are to be excused from class for doctor or dental appointments.)

D. Medical excuses for class absence or lateness are available *only* through Health Services and will not be given to anyone arriving after 7:30 a.m. and 12:30 p.m.

E. Medication will be dispensed during the following hours only:

6:30 a.m.– 7:30 a.m.
11:30 a.m.–12:30 p.m.
5:00 p.m.– 6:00 p.m.
9:00 p.m.–10:00 p.m.

F. No live animals of any kind, nature, size, or description are permitted in the Center.

VI. Acceptable Behavior Within the Classrooms
  A. Students will be present and on time to classes.
  B. Students are expected to behave responsibly within the classes.
  C. Students may smoke in the classroom if the instructor permits it.
  D. Dresses must be worn to classes.

VII. Recreation Regulations
  A. The Recreation Hall will close at 10:00 p.m. Sunday through Thursday and Midnight on Friday and Saturday nights.
  B. There will be no smoking while dancing.
  C. Records once started playing on the turntable will not be rejected.
  D. On equipment on which a deposit is required—i.e., record players, and bicycles—such deposit will be applied toward any repair necessary due to irresponsible treatment.
  E. Good sportsmanship on the part of both spectators and participants is expected of our girls.
  F. Specific requirements for sports participation will be presented in each activity.

VIII. Acceptable Behavior on Elevators
  A. Students are not to lean on the elevator buzzer.
  B. Students are not to operate or ask to operate the elevator without authorization.
  C. No smoking will be allowed on elevators.

In the event of circumstances not covered by the above rules and regulations, the Staff Leadership Team and the Center Director reserve the right to make all final decisions.

IX. Signing Out and Curfew
  A. Any student leaving Cabell Hall after 7:00 p.m. or expecting to return after 7:00 p.m. must sign the register at the Reception Desk in the lobby. A second sign-in book will be used after curfew. (Time will be called so the changeover is not open to dispute.)
  B. Curfew hours will be at 10:00 p.m. Sunday through Thursday, and at 12:00 midnight Friday and Saturday.

C. Students will not sign in for other students.

D. All dates must register at the Reception Desk.

E. Because of city ordinance, 16-year-old girls must have special passes to be out after 11:00 p.m. on Friday and Saturday.

F. Late Passes

All applicants should be free from any violations of the following criteria for at least one week (Thursday to Thursday) prior to making application for a late pass which is 1:30 a.m. on Friday and Saturday evenings. Student shall have been at the Center for one (1) month prior to applying for a late pass.

1. Applicant shall not have more than one *unexcused* absence from any class.

2. Applicant shall have *no* negative incident reports.

3. Applicant shall have had *no* curfew violations.

4. Room check report shall be "good" or "excellent."

5. Applicant must not be on either *serious*, *critical*, or *terminal* list.

No request will be considered later than Noon on Fridays. If an individual is granted late passes for both Friday and Saturday nights, and she violates the former, the latter will be rescinded.

G. Weekend and Overnight Passes

A "pass" serves as a privilege and reward for exceptional behavior. To be eligible, a student must have been at the Center for two (2) months. All applicants should be free from any violations of the following criteria for at least one (1) month prior to making application for this pass.

1. Applicant shall not have more than *one unexcused absence* per week (or a total of four (4)).

2. Applicant shall have had *no* curfew violations.

3. Applicant shall have had *no* negative incident reports.

4. Room check report shall be "good" or "excellent" on each report.

5. Applicant must not be on either *serious*, *critical*, or *terminal* list of her Community Problem Solving Groups.

No requests will be considered later than Community Problem Solving Group, Wednesday, as it is necessary for all of the students' teachers to approve the granting of a weekend pass. Students must complete the weekend pass form not later than noon on Thursday. A weekend pass will generally extend from after Community Problem Solving Group on Friday until curfew on Sunday night.

Extended weekend passes (up to 72 hours) may be given on some occasions.

When a girl stays away from the Center more than 72 consecutive hours, the entire amount of time she was absent will be deducted from accumulated leave time.

X. Community Relations
    General Expectations
    A. Students will not wear hair rollers below the second floor or outside the Center except at designated meals (breakfast daily and evening meals on Friday and Saturday).
    B. Students will not use profane language on the street.
    C. Students will practice good manners at all times.
    D. Students will show respect for other people and for themselves at all times.
    E. Students will not hang around on the streets and corners in and around the Center.
    F. Students should not leave the Center walking in sports clothes, slacks, or shorts.

    In the event of circumstances not covered by the above Rules and Regulations the Staff Leadership Team and the Center Director reserve the right to make all final decisions.

part V

Action Projects

12

Mobility Upward—STEP*

Charles Savitzky

A CAPSULE DESCRIPTION OF STEP

STEP (School To Employment Program) is a work-experience program directed toward those students who have potential to achieve at higher levels by combining education and work; it motivates potential early school leavers to remain in school, as well as preparing those who leave before graduation for a smooth entrance into full employment. It is not an appendage to the school program but organic to it; it is part of the school day, creditable for school record on satisfactory performance, and supervised by a teacher-coordinator who extends as much supportive action as possible.

It is not a program for students who have left school but it is rather an in-school program. It accepts the proposition that training in responsibility, attitude, and performance is an important task for education and it is possible to bring feedback from the job to instruction and vice versa to benefit both employer and student. Unlike other work experience programs, it does not ask employers to hire students as a charitable gesture. STEP's approach is realistic and positive, upgrading the students and program without requesting special consideration for them or giving guarantees as to their performance. It is not an alternate-week program but a daily work program.

The basic program design of STEP in New York City is not completely supportive; it keeps the group intact for two periods of the day under STEP orientation, but also assigns them to two other subject classes. In this manner, the students are not separated from the mainstream of the school. The students meet daily with a teacher-coordinator in a double class period with a great deal of instructional emphasis on job guidance and related subjects. Feedback from visits and jobs is used in group and individual instruction. Provision is made for individual conferences and visits by the coordinator to places of employment, homes, social agencies, and other groups interested in the growth of students in this program.

The work experience is as major as the school phase; in most cases, it is the

* School To Employment Program (Ed.). See Savitzky (1963).

121

catalyst helping to build a better image of the school's function. It is part of the school day, fully supervised and rated for school credit. It cannot be treated as another part-time job after school hours. The employer understands it as part of a regular school program accompanied by additional supervision. Emphasis is on adjustment to the world of work and attitudes rather than on training in occupations related to school studies. Jobs in private industry are predominantly in small commercial, distributive, and service establishments.

Begun in New York City as a pilot Work-Experience Program in two high schools in 1955, it has expanded in 1958, 1961, 1962, 1963, 1964, and 1965. It is now known as STEP. The expansion of the program in 1961 and to date has been supported jointly by the New York City Board of Education and the State Education Department which sponsors similar programs in other school districts. The program in New York City now (1970) includes nineteen high schools and one "600" school. (These schools are known principally for their difficult to manage problem students.)

A heartening development is the decision of some employers to set aside, as a matter of policy, a number of positions in their companies for STEP students.

From the "Poor Scholar's Soliloquy":[1]

> No, I'm not very good in school. . . . I don't know why the teachers don't like me. . . . Seems like they don't think you know anything unless you can name the book it comes out of. . . . I just can't memorize the stuff. Last year I stayed after school every night for two weeks trying to learn the names of the Presidents. I never did get them straight. . . . I'm not too sorry, though, because the kids who learned the Presidents had to turn right around and learn all the Vice-Presidents.
>
> I don't do very well in school in arithmetic, either. Seems I just can't keep my mind on the problems. We had one the other day like this: If a fifty-seven-foot telephone pole falls across a cement highway so that seventeen and one-sixth feet extend from one side and fourteen and nine-seventeenths feet from the other, how wide is the highway?
>
> That seemed to me like an awfully silly way to get the width of a highway. I didn't even try to answer it because it didn't say whether the pole had fallen straight across or not. . . . Civics is hard for me, too. I've been staying in school trying to learn the "Articles of Confederation" for almost a week because the teacher said we couldn't be good citizens unless we did.

Following are a selection of unsolicited letters from former STEP pupils.[2]

---

[1] Stephen M. Corey, "The Poor Scholar's Soliloquy," *Childhood Education*, 20, 5 (January 1944). Copyright © 1944 by the Association for Childhood Education International, 3615 Wisconsin Avenue, N. W., Washington, D.C.

[2] A sampling of unsolicited letters from former STEP students to their coordinators. *Thank You*, New York City Board of Education, April 1965.

Washington Irving High School   June 5, 1964
Dear Miss Tierney:

   Thank you for everything that you have done for me. I shall never forget you. I wish that there was more I could say in appreciation to you. You have been the most wonderful and thoughtful teacher I have ever had. I hope that some day I may get a new job. I shall come to you and talk about how it comes along. I miss our class and the girls too. I wish we could all stay together. I have to go now. And thank you for everything. I want to wish you the best in everything.

                                          Your former student,

                                          Christine Kowalczyk

Sheepshead Bay High School   March 1, 1965
Dear Mrs. Turner:

   I attended Jasper County Junior College in Joplin, Missouri, in which I received a C+ average. This was all possible due to you, Mrs. Turner, and the WX (STEP Program). Mrs. Turner, you helped me understand my immaturity in my early school years and helped me understand the importance of furthering my education. When I entered the WX Program, I didn't even expect to continue high school, but now, thanks to you, Mrs. Turner, I am able to further my education. I plan to attend Long Island University summer session of 1965. I am proud of my achievement thus far and hope I can help other students as well as Mrs. Turner did.

                                          Yours truly,

                                          Steve Schraeder

P.S.   I am majoring in physical education and would like to become a
       teacher so that I can and will help boys and girls like myself who
       are too immature to make something of themselves.

John Jay High School   November 1, 1964
Mrs. Ann Bender
Dear "Mom":

   I wouldn't mind if you read this letter to your class; as a matter of fact, I wish you would. You always try to talk your boys into straightening out and flying right, so they're hearing it from one of the boys who straightened out and flew right. Say hello to everyone for me. I'll expect an answering letter soon.

                     With respect,

                     Mike Cuomo (QMSN, USS Bordelon)

Port Richmond High School   January 4, 1965
Dear Mr. Hochron:

   I've been kept busy with my schooling. I wish I could tell you about my training but all of it is classified.

   How's the program coming along? I've done a lot of talking about it to the guys up here and they're all pretty envious about it. If you ever need a promoter for the program, let me know. I know, it helped me a heck of a lot and I'm still proud to have been in it. It really helped me to wake up and realize what life's all about. I don't think anyone will ever really know how happy and proud I was when Mr. Tague handed me that diploma. I know that was the biggest day of my life so far. I don't know what the future will be like for me but I do know that I'll never be able to forget the Work Experience Program or you or Mrs. Van Horn for the help you gave to me. I know it's not enough to just say "thank you" but it's all I can really do right now.

                                   Mac

                              Private Marvin H. McAdams

   A wide, harsh gap separates the balanced lament in the "Poor Scholar's Soliloquy," (Corey, 1944) a symbolic of traditionalism and rigidity in education, and the optimism and appreciation of former STEP students expressed in unsolicited letters to their teacher-coordinators. Their mass soliloquy compressed from individual school records previous to entering STEP would, by comparison, place our "poor scholar" in a position of eloquence and achievement.

   How was this gap bridged? What are the characteristics in this work experience program that account for its viability and potential for success?

THE BROADER CONCEPT OF TEACHING

The catalyst for motivating students to learn is the teacher, but within a framework of a humanistic relationship and personal involvement. The primary concern is not subject matter in isolation, circumscribed and per se; it is rather the process of reaching students in a form and climate that will nourish more permanent and continued learnings. The explanation or understanding of a process, a computation, a movement in history, may be polished and correct, but to what avail if it is embedded in a zestless, dragging lesson with little interaction, challenge, and discovery? The learning, at best, may be for the moment or of short duration.

   As we consider, in retrospect, the qualities of teachers who have influenced us positively, the guidance aspect—direction and attitudes—was the extra plus that raised the teaching to a distinguished level:

   "It was how he presented the material. He didn't talk down . . . he had a sense of humor. You felt he enjoyed teaching, and I in turn enjoyed it."

"She showed devotion to the individual student and made you realize that almost everything was within your grasp of understanding. She encouraged me and went out of her way to build my confidence."

"He had a personal commitment to us. There was electricity in the lesson because there was something personal in it—his interest followed you after you left the class."

Effectiveness in teaching, especially for potential dropouts, is predicated on the more vital and functional approaches to facilitate the outcomes above. In STEP, it is built into the design of the program: the teacher of the STEP group (in a core of two periods) is also its counselor, coordinator, and employment supervisor. He extends supportive action, as from a centralized point, in an integrated manner at school and on the job and, at times, with personal problems. He also exercises initiative and imagination in arranging and modifying materials and approaches to assure success, disdaining the practice of reducing teaching into a boundless telling process or workbook assignments exclusively. The teacher-coordinator has an opportunity to gain an in-depth understanding of his students because he is not burdened in responsibilities beyond his STEP group. Job orientation, upgrading in basic skills, and subjects on developmental levels are the salient areas covered.

STEP students exhibit no hesitancy or reservation in sharing their insights on teaching that "takes." The following interview illustrates their openness.

Interviewer: How do you look upon Mrs._____as a teacher?

Student: She's more like a . . . like a friend or something. You know? She's not like a teacher that will just tell you to do this or that. She tries to help you. She really cares about you. The other teachers, they just do a job. They put it on the board and either you learn it or you don't.

Interviewer: Before you joined the STEP Program, you did have some trouble in other subjects. Do you find the same difficulty now?

Student: No, I don't find it so hard because she gives us more work. And—I can really work there. And if I don't understand something, I can ask her about it: "Could you help me out?" Like English last year. I really studied it.

Interviewer: Didn't you learn part of that arithmetic way back? In junior high school?

Student: Naw. I didn't really learn it. . . . I was supposed to learn. You can't learn if somebody just tells you to do it. But now I've changed my whole life. I used to walk out of the room; used to run out of the room; throw chairs. But now the whole thing's changed. I had some views that this class was a dumb program, you know, and everybody was just telling me it was for dummies and it was no good, you know. I was willing to try anything now . . . so I went into the class and it seems different than anybody said—the guys were smart and just needed a change.

Interviewer: Would you then advise someone else to come into the program?

Student: Oh yes, if they needed help, I'd highly recommend it. I'd just tell them as I said, how it saved my life, you know. If I had a problem, I'd talk to her [the STEP Coordinator]. She knows; she'd straighten me out. If I had problems with my employer . . . she'd talk to me. Yes, she actually helps me . . . let's say a second mother, almost. I never had anything like this in my whole life. The teachers and everybody seem to go in your favor now. Before everybody seemed to be against you. You've got to get a teacher who's experienced, somebody who takes up individual problems, like one boy might have a conduct problem and another might have a subject problem, and our teacher knows these things. She looks at our records, she looks at us individually, not as a class. . . . No one stays home because of a cold. I mean if you're not going to care too much about school then you're not going to care much about your job either. You learn all these kinds of things in the class.

The importance of guidance aspects in teaching has been pointed out in a number of studies. In one study, 600 students enrolled in college classes gave five principal reasons (listed below) for selecting certain teachers as most helpful. It is interesting to observe that the two most frequently mentioned reasons were not directly related to teaching. Similarly, in "California School Dropouts and Graduates' (McCreary and Kitch, 1953) students indicated that what they wanted most was personal contact with the teacher.

1. Encouraged student, gave self-confidence.
2. Helped with personal (not school) problems.
3. Taught students how to study.
4. Made work clear, interesting, worthwhile.
5. Was understanding, patient, friendly.

STUDENTS ARE ACCEPTED AT THEIR LEVEL

Although their financial assistance may not be needed at home, STEP students generally are job-oriented and eager to move into the world of work and gain more independence. For a good number this may be a rationalization to disguise their dislike for school, but at the point of enrollment it is real and operative for them; it has powerful attraction and promise—a release from cumulative failure and truancy.

STEP does not place students in a bind, cajoling them to continue with a regular, full-time program, or hurrying their exit. It accepts their reality or vision, but insists that the school phase extend to the job with supervision and guidance, and that they agree to accept responsibilities as well as privileges.

The work part of the school day now becomes a learning situation which feeds back materials and approaches into the classroom.

The effort is to avoid collision; the program is neither punitive nor down-grading. The upgrading in basic skills, an area of serious retardation for them, is incorporated into the regular stream of the STEP schedule of school studies and tied in to job opportunities and present employment.

THERE ARE STANDARDS TO MEET

Permissiveness and leniency in attendance or application to work (school and job) is destructive to character and achievement. STEP students are advised, in advance, of the rules and "hardness" in the program, specifically their account-ability. The complement of realistic work assignments are excellent laboratories, proving grounds for instilling wholesome character traits. Under proper opera-tion of STEP, there can be little compromise with ineptitude, surliness, or indif-ference. Realities may demand exacting patience as a copartner with firmness. "The educational system provides the young person with a sense of what society expects of him in the way of performance. If it is lax in its demands, then he will believe that such are the expectations of his society. If much is expected of him, the chances are that he will expect much of himself."

To change hardened attitudes, to exert influences on students to break with routines of smug self-assertiveness and disorganized behavior and thinking, including questioning of or disrespect for authority, is a formidable task that does not yield to fast and simple solutions. It is not made easier by spreading social theories and plans highlighting opportunity structures as true determinants of behavior without equal emphasis on individual responsibilities. But the effort must be made with complete determination if the program is to succeed.

This, too, is the function of education and it is stated in unmistakable terms by Thomas Henry Huxley:

> Perhaps the most valuable result of all education is the ability to make yourself do the thing you have to do, when it ought to be done, whether you like it or not; it is the first lesson that ought to be learned; and however early a man's training begins, it is probably the last lesson that he learns thoroughly.

STEP IS AN IN-SCHOOL PROGRAM

As an in-school program, STEP is in an advantageous position because the cord, however tenuous, has not been severed; the door has not been closed; there is chance and hope in a bridge of help—embracing both employment and school-ing, now offered to students. The atmosphere is more positive, not terminal;

someone still cares. To attempt to regain students after dropping out is treatment in reverse, not preventive, more expensive and fraught with additional complicating factors. Would it not be more practical to transfer considerable attention and monies from postdropout programs now developing to predropout programs along lines similar to STEP?

JOB PLACEMENT IS REALISTIC

It is an illusion to hold that students in STEP or similar programs (at time of enrollment) are prepared to make decisions on specific vocational goals or specific skill training. The prime value of the jobs they hold is to help change attitudes and build responsibilities on all levels, while at the same time exposing them to different categories of job opportunities and requirements. To agree with students that the more difficult or menial tasks are to be avoided in part-time work is a foolhardy policy, especially when the job market is narrow. It is not unusual to have students move from messenger work to responsible desk jobs with future training assured and assumed by companies, from checkers in supermarkets to assistant managerial positions. In all cases, whatever the nature of the job, the recommendation for future employment is most important.

A majority of the jobs in STEP are in small retail and service industries where personal relationships, "getting along," are often critical; the support to students here should not be underestimated. This has meaning for vocational goals, too, because our economy is shifting to a service-oriented society—retailing, wholesaling, civil service, insurance, real estate, banking, and finance. Firms are usually small and owner-managed.

Employment in a work-experience program before graduation is an insurance factor for better chances in placement upon graduation, to better meet competition for jobs in a restrictive market and a growing labor force. Experience and recommendation do count.

Placement in private industry is not sought as an act of charity or good will. Stipend positions for more sheltered jobs in public agencies and for temporary periods are preferable for selected cases where students are not ready for employment in private industry or when jobs are not available.

REFERENCES

Corey, Stephen M. "The Poor Scholar's Soliloquy," *Childhood Education*, Vol. 20, No. 5 (January 1944).

McCreary, William H., and Donald E. Kitch. "Now Hear Youth: A Report on the California Cooperative Study of School Dropouts and Graduates," *Bulletin of California State Department of Education*, Vol. 26, No. 9 (October 1953).

Savitzky, Charles. "S.T.E.P. Program for Potential Dropouts," *Bulletin of the National Association of Secondary School Principals*, Vol. 47 (December 1963), pp. 51–58.

13

The Madison Area Project

Joseph Congemi

The Syracuse, N.Y., Madison Area Project, which was directed toward the junior high school student of age 14-16, included 75 percent who were 15 years old. The project was called the World of Work. The program was designed to minimize the students' feelings that they were different; it was also designed to instill pride in the students by infusing the project with status so that the rest of the students in the school would respect it and its participants.

The basic belief behind the program is that every student regardless of his cultural heritage is inherently good. No one is born bad and no one is inherently bad. The patterns of behavior a student displays in class and the lack of tolerance of certain behavior patterns are believed to be manifestations of underlying causes. A child is to be considered as the product of his environment; his state of being is the result of external forces, not of his own efforts alone.

The project has underscored the realization that dropouts and potential dropouts have overwhelming feelings of inferiority and inadequacy. What then should be the approach to youngsters who feel inadequate, incompetent and hopeless? Can anything be effective in bringing a sense of worth, hope and equality to such a person?

In one approach to this problem, the project established a relationship with the Rotary Club in Syracuse and obtained the use of its camp for two weekends. Approximately twenty-five students participated. After they were brought to the camp and introduced to the program, they were permitted to do as they wished during the day; during the evening they participated in vocational orientation sessions. The prevailing atmosphere in the camp was intended to encourage trust, self-satisfaction and responsibility. The students were given the usual camp responsibilities; for example, a couple of students were assigned to wash the dishes, but no two persons repeated the chore.

During each day of the camp the students were able to participate in at least fifty different activities. No one was directed to join any specific activity at any time. An effort was made to promote freedom of choice so that the students could exercise their ability to choose wholesome activities. Over a period of two weekends, none of the young people, some of whom possessed lengthy histories

129

of antisocial activities, was involved in a single case of discipline. One reason for this remarkable performance could be the young people's response to the respect and faith with which they were regarded by the staff members. The participants were told that they were young adults and that they could follow simple directions. For example, directions were clear: "Clean up after yourself." Remonstances were brief: "You realize that you should not become involved in fighting," or "We don't have to explain this sort of thing to you—you know what's right and what's wrong." The youngsters proved that they were able to live by middle-class standards if they were given an opportunity to do so under the right conditions.

This portion of the project and its beliefs were tested on one occasion. The first night that the boys came to camp they were playing in the pool hall, which was some distance from the sleeping quarters. It was late and dark. There were few lights at the camp at night and it was difficult to see even a short distance. Three boys wandered into the hall to play pool, and they were gone for one-half hour. A staff member looked for them but they were not in the hall. There were loud calls for them; they were sought in the swimming pool and across the playing fields. Everyone thought that they might have gone swimming or perhaps had had an accident. No one knew.

Then the staff members remembered that there was a bar about two-hundred yards down the road. The youngsters had been warned on the first day that it would be a serious offense if anyone were to leave the camp; they were warned that any offenders would be immediately returned to Syracuse. The policy had been stated only once. And now the feeling among the staff was that these students had gone to the bar. Since one of the students had a history of emotional illness, the staff members tended to feel that he had coerced the others to leave with him.

After searching the grounds for ten or fifteen minutes and calling to the boys, the staff members heard the voices of the returning boys. As they returned, the leader of the project stepped forward and, by way of welcome, said, "Now I realize that you were swimming or that you were in the forest somewhere, but for some reason or another I know you weren't in the bar across the street, because if you were I would have no choice but to take you back to Syracuse." He told them that he had faith in them and that he knew they would not violate his trust. The ringleader later went to the office and told the staff that since he was not punished, he would not drink the beer that he had purchased. Instead he threw it away. The boy did not create another problem during the project, although he has since dropped out of school and run away to California.

The portion of the program at the camp emphasized the students' freedom of decisions and choice of activities and thus bolstered their dignity as individuals. To do so, the staff provided them with individual counseling. During the evenings there were unplanned discussions and the students were encouraged to talk about anything concerning their futures, particularly as employees. They discussed methods to obtain application papers for work and Social Security coverage. Most of the youngsters were not experienced in these areas; so, they held mock interviews with an employer and even learned to shake hands; they particularly enjoyed the interview activities since they were able to practice with other students and evaluate each other. The rudimentary act of shaking hands brought everyone into an activity and, as a result, each became a bit more important. It was symbolically their initiation into the world of employment.

During the discussion sessions the students were given the opportunity to say whatever they desired about school and their teachers. The conversations were taped for later referral. Many of the teachers considered good and effective by the staff were inadequate in the eye of the students. The students also revealed that while some of the teachers were considered excellent in their field, the teachers' real concern was with the subject matter and not with the student.

During these evening discussion sessions, the students revealed their confusion concerning the academic aspects of school. They knew that a certain amount of material had to be covered during the year, but they confessed that they were lost. They were unable to keep pace with their classes; once behind they were unable to catch up. As early as the second week of class the boys declared that they knew that they were going to fail and that they had stopped trying. The pessimism and hopelessness of the students enlightened the staff members and realistically introduced them to the World of Work program.

There had been some change among the boys in their self-concept over the two days. It was not much and no one knew how long it would last. When the students came to the camp, many of them needed haircuts and shaves. They did not seem to know about grooming. By Sunday afternoon when they were to depart, they had combed their hair and shined their shoes.

During the second weekend of the project, the staff decided to emphasize the roles of the sexes in social situations. The girls and boys dined together, the girls acting as hostesses to the boys, which enabled the camp to have a combined social activity. Opportunely, various dignitaries visited the camp at this point. Each guest was greeted by a boy and a girl who then escorted the visitor through the facilities of the camp. The students were self-assured enough to guide such people as the mayor. The experience evidently delighted the students who expressed enthusiasm when they later discussed it at school.

After the initial phase at the camp, the project resumed in the school. The daily program began at 8 o'clock in the morning in a group-counseling session. The students usually selected the topic for discussion, but sometimes topics were given to them. The purpose of the discussion was to enhance personality development rather than vocational development. The belief held by the staff members was that as long as growth is continuous and the approach to growth and discussion is uninhibited, vocational development should follow. In the past year the students who were involved resolved many of their personal problems. They had no trouble in their work stations. However, for these students who had severe personal problems, the problems were reflected at work.

Some of the topics discussed in the morning class were:

What's a Mother? What's a Father?
What makes a good teacher? How should principals act?
What should an employer expect from an employee?
If I were an employer, how could I be a good one?
What are some of the mistakes I should expect to make?
How should I be treated, or how should I treat someone else, for making errors while at work or at school?
What's a good husband like?
What's the role of a mother? How should a child respond to his parents?

While the topics may appear simple, the students had rarely, if ever, dealt with them. It may surprise some to learn that the values of the students were quite middle class when they were given the opportunity to reflect and express themselves, but they had never been given such an opportunity before.

The project matched the regular school program except during the 8 o'clock period, which was devoted to the discussions. Experience had indicated that the period was necessary. It presented a positive, nonassertive atmosphere to the students who were neither threatened nor restricted through fear of punishment. They were able to say whatever they wished. Unfortunately, none of the discussions could be taped. Included in the discussions were confessions of incidents in the home, profanity, and revelations of unwholesome activities that took place in the neighborhood. The tone of the hour enabled the student to unburden himself securely and comfortably. Gradually the student identified with the program, one which he in turn considered a good program. It had achieved status and was the object of envy on the part of the rest of the school.

After the hour of discussion in the morning, the students dispersed and met their regular classes in the core courses—English, social studies, mathematics, or science. For some, classes generally ended about 11:30. Others, who needed more credits, finished later. The program was flexible and individualized. If a student had an employer who wanted him at 2:30, his program was altered so that after 11:30 he would have less intellectually demanding subjects. The students could choose subjects for personal enjoyment—for example, music, physical education, and art.

When the student left school daily for work, he was independent. No one checked up on him. He went to work and the employer was responsible for his supervision. The school and the staff members relinquished control over the student after he arrived at his job.

However, the staff members were selective about placement. They tried to find a job suitable for each student. For example, one boy had a measured IQ of 58. However, he was not retarded; he was slow, but he was not a moron.

Whatever his ability, his reading was so poor that he could not score high on tests. In addition, he was an isolate; he seldom spoke and he did not enjoy being near people. The project tried to place him where he could be alone. Such a situation prevailed in a photographic shop where he was able to develop prints and learn a skill. Despite everyone's efforts and expectations, he was, unfortunately, unhappy there. He was then placed in the Onondaga Workshop for the Handicapped where both retarded and physically handicapped individuals are housed and work. The atmosphere is accepting and in it the boy blossomed. He even says a few words now. He is beginning to communicate. He has received good reports from his employer.

Obviously, the positions must be flexible. They must meet the needs of the students rather than the needs of the project. The staff members frequently check on the students so that if there are problems with a placement, they can try to remedy it. If they cannot, they change placements.

As a result of the project, excellent relations have been established between the business community and the school. Unlike most similar programs, the employers paid the fee; the school system financed only five of the 26 jobs assigned, and then only because the jobs were on the school system's property. The remaining 21 were financed by the individual employers at the base rate of 75 cents an hour. Some students earned as much as $1.25 and $1.50 an hour simply because the employers preferred this. Obviously, the project has been of little cost to the school system. A testimonial to the efficacy of the program is the repeated request from last year's employers; every job is available again this year.

In addition, each job available through the program has achieved status in the eyes of the students. One reason for this may be that the project has tried to avoid menial jobs such as sweeping; only one such job is included in the program. Other jobs included secretarial work for the Department of Urban Renewal and secretarial work for a lawyer who assumed payment of the student's salary. Another girl became, at fifteen, an assistant recreational leader at one of the recreational centers. One boy was assistant mechanic at a garage, while another worked in food services at Syracuse University. A girl assisted at the School of Social Work at the University. A boy operated the mimeograph machines and learned various skills at the Youth Development Center at the University. There was even one case of a boy with an IQ of 91 who attained quality points through the experience attained in his job. An explanation may be that he improved because of his job in the bookstore at the University, which gave him responsibility. He began by earning 75 cents an hour, and he now earns $1.20, having achieved the raises himself. Each of the jobs is respected by the students because of the status each possesses in the eyes of the students. The reasons for this vary; for example, one girl returned from her first days as an assistant recreational leader elated because, as she said, "I've got my own desk!"

As important in some ways as the jobs themselves was the counseling portion of the project which included meetings with the parents. The workers tried to work out a program with the parents whereby the students would be able to study at home. The intention was to teach the parents the importance of their childrens' study habits, the need for punctuality, and the need for regular attendance at school. The parents learned that their children were aware that they needed their parents' cooperation.

There are also individual counseling sessions with the students at least once each week. The session is unstructured; the student is permitted to discuss whatever he wishes. Intensive counseling is possible during this time, which is considered particularly important because often the sessions are devoted to personal problems.

Every program dealing with dropouts seems to point to a lack of an important element, the social development of the youngsters. They seem to be socially retarded. They do not seem to know much about their community. Their feelings of inadequacy prevent them from becoming involved in the various parts of the community. So this particular project introduced a social phase—that is, it involved various activities in other parts of the city away from their school. The staff arranged bowling matches at some of the finer bowling establishments in Syracuse. The students were taken as a group. One bowling proprietor was good enough to charge lower rates. The students who went there for a half-day on several occasions enjoyed themselves, probably because they felt comfortable. They were happy that they were there. They were also taken to basketball games. They saw the Harlem Globetrotters. The purpose of the excursions was to show them that these facilities in the community belonged to them as well as to others. They learned that they should use these facilities, that they could use them, and that they, as students, were acceptable there.

The year ended with a Junior High School Prom which was sponsored by the work-study program. It was called the "World of Work Spring Prom." The staff hired a band and the students were formals. It was the most successful event of the year.

Besides all this, the staff arranged some jointly sponsored activities. The students ran a successful car-wash project. Every person in the program volunteered two hours of one particular Saturday to the activity. They earned a reasonable amount of money which made them feel that they were middle-class. As they divided their earnings, the students felt rewarded for having participated in the car-wash activity. Other activities included several parties held throughout the year at homes of various teachers from the school and at various places in the community.

The program emphasized important facets of student life other than academic achievement. Social, personal, and emotional development are of more initial importance than high test grades. The staff members recognized that the students felt unwanted and rejected, that they did not believe they had many opportunities before them. The students knew that they appeared to be without abilities; yet the program revealed that many of the participants possessed abilities that became evident through their activities, but escaped detection on paper. For example, one group of students played five or six games which were donated to the project by the Parker Brothers Game Company. They enjoyed the games which they played at a party. Yet, these same students had measured IQs which were below normal; they would have been considered retarded if they had been measured by student IQ tests. But under favorable circumstances, such as the party in this case, these students not only played the games successfully but also enjoyed themselves. They were even reading directions; yet, they were students who typically were not reading in school.

Still another part of this many-faceted program was the tutorial effort. Students from Syracuse University, retired executives and retired high school teachers were kind enough to volunteer their services. One tutor served three students, which proved unwieldy. In the future there will be one tutor to one student. The students were tutored in whatever subjects they were deficient. In addition, the tutoring program took on aspects of a big brother or big sister relationship. Tutors could take the students outside the community. For example, a few of the students from the Community College who were interested in the program took several of the boys from the program on a camping trip. Two young women took some of the girls to concerts. This portion of the program, then, was more than just tutoring. It became a relationship that was being established with an adult, one who could be trusted, respected and probably admired. Because of the respect that the youngsters experienced, the expectations developed, and the status of the program, the students' feelings of inadequacy were greatly reduced.

Out of 28 students who participated last year, five failed and only four dropped out. Those who failed are still in school. They are all beyond the 16-year mark and are all returning next year. It is not a realistic hope that all of these youngsters will graduate from high school. The problems they have with reading and mathematics are severe. One boy who is in the ninth grade is still reading at the third-grade level. He was given an intensive reading program for one year and achieved an 85 in reading, but he still is not past the fourth year in reading. He is getting older; soon he will be 18. The possibility of this boy's graduating from high school is not high.

Despite its many facets, the program will be expanded and will concentrate its major effort upon helping the students to be useful, productive members of society. It is a realistic goal. The concentration will shift from the junior to the senior high school. Four staff members will be added and the decisive factor in their selection will be their personality and not their academic preparation. The qualities that will be sought include flexibility, a capacity for sympathy, understanding and sensitivity, particularly in relation to students. It is essential that each staff member be able to establish rapport with the type of student participating in the program. For these students, this ability is more important than the staff member's technical proficiency. Yet an effort will be made to include the selection of people who have a background in counseling, since counseling skills are also vital in dealing with these students. Without such skills, conferences could be hazardous for all involved.

Another innovation will be the introduction of "good samaritan" practices for these students. Although they themselves are considered culturally deprived youngsters, they are going to gather clothing, toys, and other appropriate items for distribution to orphanages in Syracuse at Christmas time. Much can be gained from such an experience. At the very least, it is hoped that the students will receive some satisfaction from helping others.

The World of Work project, then, has attempted to demonstrate that the youngsters who become dropouts and social problems are ignored while they are in school. If they are treated with regard for their dignity, with respect for their individuality and ability and with concern for their future, they will respond with feelings and values that will be useful to society and ensure their success as independent, vital citizens. They need and deserve the opportunities that can be created for them when there is still a chance to erase some of their feelings of inadequacy and pessimism.

14

Talent Search*

Margaret Carson

When the Madison High School "Talent Search" project started, there were only 13 children in it. Madison High School is situated in a low socioeconomic area in Rochester, New York. When the Talent Search started, the high school had a population that was about 50 percent Black. It is a challenging and deeply rewarding school with all types of children. Every counselor would profit from being a Talent Search counselor at Madison High. With enough counselors, each having 16 or 17 children, problems for any school such as Madison would be solved. What these children need more than anything else is the personal involvement of the counselor—the feeling that somebody cares.

That is said so often that it has become a cliché, but it is, nevertheless, essential. The youngsters themselves say it; the parents also say it. The counselors in the project cared. That, to the youngsters and parents, is the crux of the problem—the part that has the meaning—to care.

For example, one boy said to a counselor not too long ago, "You know the only trouble with being in this project? It's made me sad—very sad—in one way." "In what way?" the counselor asked. He replied, "I know now, after these years, that you care a lot more about what happens to me than my mother and father do and ever did. It shouldn't be that way. They should be the ones that care. At least I'm glad somebody does." It's hard to try to supplant a set of parents, and if one had 50 students, he could not begin to have the warm, friendly relationship that is possible with 15 or 17.

At the beginning of the project a counselor was asked to try to identify 13 to 15 children who had average ability and a test estimated IQ of at least 90. Some who were identified by the counselor had far above that. One girl, Jane, with an estimated IQ of 107, had been receiving D's and E's on her report cards. Her mother, who was mentally ill, lived with Jane and a younger daughter. Both of the girls were in constant fear of their mother and father. The father spent long hours tending bar and did not go to the house because the mother had said she would kill him if he did. Meanwhile, this child, a bright girl, was so nervous and tense that she could not possibly do her school work well.

*This article has been developed from typescript of a taped presentation and loses some of the spirit and enthusiasm of its author. For this the editors apologize.

The counselors, with the help of the school psychologist, tried to alleviate Jane's situation at home. A year and a half ago they finally were able to have a doctor from the State Hospital demand entrance into the house. The mother has since been placed in the State Hospital and probably will not be released for a long time. Jane is now doing good work. Her summer school English teacher said, "If I could only have had Jane when she was a freshman. Oh, what sensitivity, what comprehension of literature." The point, again, is that the special attention directed to the needs of this child effected some profound changes.

For the first two years the counselors and children did not meet as a group. At that time it was felt that it would not be good for the children to know who the others were. At the beginning of the third year, when they were in the tenth grade, the children asked if they could meet as a group in order to organize and declare a purpose. They met and became a club. They had a president, vice-president, secretary, and treasurer. During the junior and senior years they had their picture in the senior annual. They were delighted to have it there. Their club name is Project Mercury, which they selected because Mercury is the god of swiftness and of motion.

During the project's first year, the reading coordinator for Rochester, learning that the children had chosen this name, gave them a painting by Ralph Abry, a Rochester painter, of a statue of Mercury which had, for many years, adorned the top of a factory in Rochester. They were thrilled with the gift of the painting.

The children were eighth-graders when they started in the project. Out of the 265 eighth-graders who were in the school that year, the counselors selected 15 who qualified for the project by virtue of their estimated IQ, low grades, poor home situation, and lack of motivation. Each could have been classified at that time as a potential dropout. Because the students in this school are subject to a high mobility rate, only five of the original group remain among the 17 now in the project. Eleven of these were admitted at the beginning of the ninth grade, and all eleven are still in the group. One student entered the project at the beginning of the tenth grade after having been a member of a school-work program.

One boy asked to be allowed to reenter the regular program. He is the outstanding male vocalist in the school, possesses an excellent vocabulary, and can relate easily with others. The boy stayed in school and last June he was graduated. He was a distinguished-looking graduate and had been a source of pleasure to the counselors in the project. His case was dramatic testimony to the effectiveness of the Talent Search project. He graduated because someone went to his home and talked with his mother; someone went again and again and helped when the father left home. His case took time—a great deal of time—but it was obviously worth it.

A serious limitation of the program is directly related to the effort that a counselor must expend in order to achieve some success and the burden of numbers of students assigned to each counselor. The counselor involved here not only worked with the 17 youngsters mentioned but also counseled 300 seventh graders and then traveled to seven elementary schools in order to counsel those sixth-graders who would be entering Madison High School the following year.

The purpose of the project was to motivate these children to attain better marks and to relate better at home. The counselors cannot change the home but they can help the students to accept the home they have. The counselors tried to provide all kinds of cultural enrichment, plays, concerts, ballets, and to offer vocational counseling as well for the boys.[1] They present the students with the opportunity to listen to representatives of different kinds of work, which involves not only the professions, but also factory workers, policemen, mailmen, and similar workers. The representatives of various jobs met with the youngsters at a local settlement house.

Other assistance for the project came from the government. NDEA funds provided tutoring for the students in any subject in which they were weak. Last year 13 pupils were tutored in six different subjects for a total of 163 hours. They were provided a corrective reading program. By their senior year only one person was not reading up to grade level and still needed the program. The corrective reading was taught by Junior League volunteers who donated their time. They were trained by the reading consultant regularly hired by the Board of Education. They were always cheerful and gay, and the youngsters frequently entered one counselor's office to ask, "Honest, don't they get paid?"

The fact that they were not paid and that the volunteers worked with the students because they enjoyed it and because they really cared about these boys and girls impressed the students. As the children in the project reached their grade reading level, they were replaced with other children who needed help in developing reading skills. The Junior League volunteers talked so much about the joys of coming to Madison High School that other Junior Leaguers wanted to come also. Now there are three Junior League projects at Madison.

Others also contributed to the project. Over 400 tickets were donated by the faculty and community groups to Eastman Theater concerts where the students heard the Philharmonic Orchestra and the Civic Orchestra. They were given tickets to the Community Playhouse, where they saw *The Taming of the Shrew*. None of these children had ever seen a play except on their school stage. When the play, *The Sound of Music*, came to Rochester with a professional cast, a group of churchwomen donated tickets so that the group could attend.

Others who have been interested in the project have donated money. The children have even had after-concert supper parties in a restaurant downtown. Every time one counselor took the children to a downtown restaurant after the theater, the hostess or the head waiter or somebody said, "What a wonderful

[1] The author of the present chapter was not questioned as to why the girls were omitted from the vocational counseling. I would advocate vocational counseling for all students regardless of sex, participation in special projects, etc.—Oscar Mink.

group of youngsters. That's the nicest group I think we've had in here. They're so well-behaved."[2] If these adults could visit the homes of these young people, they would most certainly marvel.

The project group also had an all-day visit with lunch at the University of Rochester; the students visited Robert Wesleyan College and the State University College at Brockport. They toured the Strong Memorial Medical Center and they had a guided tour of the Airport and the Bausch Museum. They went to the Lamberton Conservatory at Highland Park.

The students were also urged to participate in school activities. Five of them have performed well in football, basketball, wrestling, and track; three are in the Madison School Band, Orchestra, and Dance Band; three are in the Inter-High Choir—one is the President and one is a lyric soprano soloist. All three went to Atlantic City when the Inter-Choir went there to sing for the National Music Festival.

Six are active in settlement houses as counselors of younger children and sit on various committees and boards; two went to visit the UN as representatives of their settlement houses; six of them have had scholarship help—three because of good grades and the other three because of good citizenship.

After school and Saturday jobs were found for 12 of the students. Eight of them are now completely self-supporting. One girl's mother and father were both alcoholics. Her home duties would weaken the hardiest; she could not take a job, so she started a sewing service for the faculty. She and the girl whose mother needed psychiatric help gravitated toward each other. They teamed up on this sewing service. Without being told, they went down to the Courthouse in Rochester and registered the name; it was the "Little Shoppe." They achieved a reputation for good workmanship—they mended, and sewed buttons for the faculty in order to earn money. They worked at home. The counselors recognized that their scheme was quite ingenious.

Then the project started a service group. During the school day students were assigned for one period to be a host stationed in the entry hall which gave them a trememdous sense of importance. Each wore a badge that said "Host" or "Hostess." When a visitor entered the school the student approached the visitor and said, "How do you do? Can I help you?" The host's service was to escort the visitor to his destination and then to return to his post, sit down, and await the next visitor.

The project also sponsors an annual Book Fair, which began with the help of the Junior League. Numerous people donated books. No book cost more than a quarter. The counselors always urge the children to bring their parents. While the Book Fair included the whole school, the project students handled the selling.

[2]Whereas "good behavior" tends to have a "middle class" ring to it, one should remember that a concern of this program was to teach young people how to succeed in the "establishment."—Oscar Mink.

Each year the project has profited from help from new sources. Last year the Junior Chamber of Commerce helped the project. They set up evenings for studying various careers. The students met and questioned a lawyer, beautician, doctor, mail clerk, policeman, and salesman.

One activity which the youngsters particularly enjoyed was visiting the home of one of the counselors who lives in the country on 13 acres of land. While the land is not a farm, it does have a pond and the students loved it. The counselor regularly took three or four to her home at a time. They usually dined and then relaxed and talked and listened to music. Sometimes the youngsters did not talk, preferring to listen to records. They would lie on the floor and listen. For them it constituted a wonderful evening.

It cannot be emphasized enough that personal involvement is the all-important component. Personal involvement permits the youngsters to experience the new awareness that an adult really cares about them. It appears that the effectiveness of the program on the students in itcan be measured in direct proportion to the amount of attention and love given to them.

One of the youngsters did not graduate; the others did. However, the one who did not graduate has a scholarship for Rochester Business Institute, as do thirteen others. Dr. Ernest Biegel, President of RBI, is so interested in this project that he offered a scholarship to any project student who wanted it. One of the girls has been accepted at Monroe Community College. A boy is going to enter the St. Barnabas Brotherhood. One boy is going into the Army. Another, who is the sole support of his mother, has a fine job in a lumber company and he is attending Rochester Institute of Technology at night.

The success of the program, while not complete, revealed that the effort expended by the counselors could bring about changes which were dramatic and lasting. The project has emphasized, moreover, the need on the part of the school staff for genuine concern and personal involvement. It succeeded when warmth and attention were recognized by the students and when the counselors could devote enough time to a youngster and his situation so that he could help alleviate some of the conditions that created problems. The project, in short, renewed the faith on the part of all participants, adult and adolescent alike, in the idea that people do care and that their help within the framework of a school program can be remarkably effective and far-reaching.[3]

[3] Worthy of note in this article are two obvious considerations: (1) the impact of counselor involvement; (2) the "outside of office" programing of the counselors. The article on the Woman's Job Corps Center in the counseling unit emphasizes the same pair of factors.—Oscar Mink.

15

Overview of the Job Corps, 1964 to 1969

Ellen Britz Mink

INTRODUCTION

At age 17, John Doe had been arrested five times for theft. He was black, poor, and the product of a broken home. Beginning with three strikes against him, John Doe was out before he really started.

Today, John Doe is twenty and a successful apprentice machinist in Beverly Hills, California.

What happened?

The Job Corps turned a liability to society into an asset. The Job Corps has had its ups and downs since 1964 when it was first authorized by Congress, and not all of its nascent expectations were lived up to. But there are enough cases like John Doe's to indicate that the program has had a major impact.

Snapshots of this impact are numerous, but another synopsis will do for now.

From *The New York Times*, Sunday, December 18, 1966, under title "Job Corps Helps Slum Girls Shed 'Mud of Gutter'," by Majorie Hunter:

> HUNTINGTON, W. Va., Dec. 17—"You see your future etched in the scars of the dirty counter, in every smashed vodka bottle you've drained, every obscene sentence you've spieled off in retaliation . . ."
>
> The words were those of a pretty young drifter named_____.
>
> Tossed out of school at the age of 12 (They called it a nervous breakdown, she said), she wandered alone into the world of pick-up jobs in dirty cafes, of cheap rooms with the vodka bottle waiting to say, "Welcome home."
>
> Last January, she joined the Job Corps. She was just 17 years old.
>
> Today, she is working in a San Francisco office and attending night classes in high school through a Litton Industries scholarship.

In a recent letter to a friend here she wrote:

"I'm going to keep on going to night school because I believe if I let myself slip once I may never stop slipping. This I had proven to me once."

Only, if I start slipping now, no Job Corps is going to come and weep over my broken bones and fix my sore teeth and wipe the mud of the gutter off my face."

A talented writer and artist,_____is among the most brilliant of the hundreds of girls who have passed through the Huntington Job Corps Center for women since it opened nearly a year ago.

But others, too, have had the mud of the gutter wiped off their faces.

They come here from the tenant shack of the rural South, from the dirty back streets or the ghettos of the big cities.

Some are tough and boisterous. Some are pathetically shy. Most are school dropouts. All are poor.

BACKGROUND

The Job Corps is a voluntary national residential program for underprivileged young men and women. It was authorized in 1964, by Part A, Title I of the Economic Opportunity Act. In 1966 Congress passed amendments requiring that at least 23 percent of the total enrollment be women. Congress also restricted the operating costs and gave the Center director of Job Corps Centers authority to dismiss students for disciplinary reasons, without approval from officials in Washington.

The purpose of the Job Corps is to provide the trainees with adequate personal, social, vocational, and academic skills necessary for them to function effectively in the mainstream of American life. In February 1969 the Job Corps was placed under the Department of Labor, having previously been administered by OEO. (See the Epilogue to this book.)

SELECTION CRITERIA

Job Corps enrollees must be 16 to 21 years of age, a citizen or permanent resident of the United States, and out of school three months or more. They must be unemployed or underemployed and come from culturally or education- ally deprived backgrounds. The Job Corps especially wants to recruit those employed in low paying, dead-end jobs that are beneath the individual's potential abilities. They look for those youths who are most likely to continue in poverty if forced to remain in their present environment—those in need of a change of environment in order to become useful and productive citizens.

Men are usually screened and selected by the U.S. Employment Service, Youth Opportunity Centers, and more recently by the AFL-CIO. Women's civic organizations, particularly the Women in Community Service (WICS), select the women. Any state employment office will refer an interested youth to the nearest screening agency.

Some Job Corps personnel believed selection was used to remove from the community many of the chronic troublemakers who were often on probation or on parole. The Job Corps still accepts trainees previously convicted of a felony. Provision can be made with the state authorities for parole supervision while in the Job Corps.

Since the program began, screening has been tightened gradually. In addition, the applicant is given a better preinduction orientation about Job Corps now. During the first years of the program the applicants were not always given a true picture of what to expect in the Job Corps, and often promised things that couldn't be done.

CHARACTERISTICS OF ENROLLEES

Many trainees come from backgrounds in which they have been grossly abused by environmental circumstances. Some are angry and defiant; a few have acquired deviant behavior patterns. Most are starved for affection and attention, yet suspicious of others' motives, finding it hard to believe someone could care about them. Many have a defeatist attitude. They come from all over the U.S.—urban and rural—and a wide variety of ethnic and racial backgrounds, including Indian, Puerto Rican, Negro, Caucasian, Hawaiian, Mexican.

Their academic achievement level ranges from illiteracy to college readiness. Reading and arithmetic comprehension for half of the enrollees is about the fifth-grade level, even though most have completed nine years of school. [11]   Nearly one-third are unable to read a simple sentence or solve a second-grade arithmetic problem. About 60 percent come from broken homes, and 39 percent from families on relief. [4, p. 3]   In addition, "63 percent come from homes where the head of the household is unemployed; 60 percent live in substandard housing; 64 percent were asked to leave school; 80 percent have not seen a doctor or dentist in ten years. Only 60 percent ever held a job, full or part-time, and their average annual salary was $639." [11]   More than half of the male recruits of draft age are unfit for military service because of educational or health deficiencies. Most enrollees have never slept between sheets; some have never had electric lights. Almost all have developed an acute resistance to conventional schooling. [11]

PROGRAMS, SERVICES OFFERED

Vocational guidance is provided in depth to assess abilities and traits. The total offering of the Job Corps Center must be broad enough to serve all the needs of all the students, and flexible enough to allow each student a variety of options. Unlike our secondary schools, the Center must have many alternate programs to retain those who dropped out or were pushed out of traditional schools.

The programs and services attempt to provide growth for the *whole* person. There are three types of educational training: (1) *vocational* training that is job- and skill-oriented, (2) *basic education*, which aims at general knowledge with a practical application and is integrated with vocational skills, and (3) training in *home and family living*, "life-skills classes," personal hygiene, and how to "make it" in the establishment. The women are also given classes in child care, managing money, buying food and clothing, and caring for the home in order to help produce more stable, responsible families.

This calls for new teaching methods and new counseling methods. The 124 Job Corps Centers make the following available: individual tutoring and counseling, both formal and informal; trained staff to supervise and help enrollees 24 hours a day; special new self-instructional materials to help enrollees move along at their own speed; modern equipment, developed and donated by business firms, to teach current vocational and academic skills. [11] Contractors who operate the Centers are encouraged to develop new approaches, methods and materials to provide the necessary education and work skills.

The student, in all phases of the program vocational training, basic education, "life-skills" classes, and counseling and recreation, should be rewarded at frequent intervals—by certificates, announced change of status, weekend passes, extended late hours, or some such acknowledgment of progress in order to keep motivation high.

Most *vocational programs* last from nine to twelve months (although an enrollee may stay in a program for two years or more). Vocational training is in almost any field the enrollee wants and is capable of handling. Curricula are developed in areas including surveying, forestry, power-tool operation (men's Rural Centers); office-machine operators, data-processing machine operators, accounting clerks, automotive repair, cooking, hospital workers (men's Urban Centers); business and clerical occupations, household services, food preparation, tailoring, retail sales, nursing aide, keypunch operator (women's centers). Vocational supervisors try to expose enrollees to a wide variety of job opportunities and to develop interest and skills needed to pursue vocational inclinations. They also train students to form good work habits, and to instill pride in a job well done. In addition, the supervisor teaches students the techniques of filling out job applications. The program often includes on-the-job training with local businesses.

The basic skills required for all other learning, such as reading (remedial, intermediate, developmental), language and study skills, mathematics, social studies and elementary science are taught by qualified instructors in small classes. Field trips highlight classroom subjects and "life-skills" classes—such as a visit to a bank to help explain budgeting and savings.

Physical education and swimming instruction are required courses. Voluntary recreational activities include group sports, arts and crafts, drama, music, trips to the theater, concerts, and dances.

"Nurses are on duty 24 hours a day. Doctors and dentists are available for regular and emergency care." [7, p. 3]   There is health and first-aid instruction; special attention is given to overweight and underweight problems.

Resident advisers live with the enrollees and are constantly available for advice and guidance. Actually, "all staff members become involved in counseling activities, and it is likely that each will assist corpsmen with particular problems. Coordination is achieved through the professional counselor." [3, p. 4]

"Laundry facilities are provided. Student government is encouraged and enrollees participate in setting and enforcing rules and regulations. Especially encouraged are group acitivties, such as student newspapers, and participation in extracurricular activities, both on and off the center." [7, pp. 3, 4]

The men's Rural Centers have performed conservation work worth $38 million to the nation. Corpsmen have built and maintained 4,900 miles of roads, and thousands of picnic tables, fireplaces, and parking spaces. They have developed and improved fishing streams, and 16,500 acres of fish and wildlife habitat. They have planted 15,900 acres of trees and shrubs, and improved and reforested 12,800 acres of timber. [11]   They are called in to help build camp grounds and other recreational areas, and to help control forest fires.

Enrollees are encouraged to participate in community activities. They work with the handicapped, sponsor little league baseball teams, and donate evening time at homes for the aged. Some work with retarded youngsters or shop for elderly people in the area. Several women's Centers operate nursery schools for local children. [11] Although the "service of these young men and women to the communities is extracurricular, such service is an important part of the overall objective of making good citizens of these people." [12]

"What Job Corps has learned about educating the school dropout is being applied in public school systems across the nation with the aim of helping to keep potential dropouts in school as long as possible. The interchange of teaching methods and materials between Job Corps and the public schools began in the summer of 1966. . . ." [11] It has continued.

After graduation, corpsmen are assisted in finding jobs, returning to school, or entering the armed forces. While many large Job Corps Centers are staffed with placement officers, OEO has also set up regional placement centers to serve graduates who seek employment. Two voluntary agencies, Women in Community Service and Joint Action for Community Service, help graduates adjust to community life and stick with their jobs.

DISCIPLINE

While rules at Centers vary, all have regulations regarding class attendance, bed-time, curfew, etc. Discipline ranges from temporary loss of special privileges to fines, extra work, or dismissal from the program, depending on the severity of the offense.

MONEY

Free room and board, and medical and dental services are provided for enrollees. Five dollars for incidentals on arrival at the center; $30 monthly living allowance (later raised to $50), less deductions for Social Security and taxes, is given to each enrollee. The federal government also gives the enrollees $50 readjustment allowance for every month satisfactorily spent in Job Corps. (The enrollee can use up to half of this to help support his family if they have been partially dependent on him previously. If he does, the government matches his contribution and it is sent monthly to the dependents. Three of every four youths take advantage of this.) Recently this readjustment allowance has been denied those who dropped out during their first 90 days. [4, p. 26]

Initially, each man is given a full issue of clothing and every month there-after is provided a small sum to maintain his clothing. The women are given a clothing allowance.

The enrollees travel to and from the Center at government expense. After satisfactorily completing six months, they may make one round trip home a year at Government expense.

All these allowances are given at the time, rather than the delayed rewards of conventional programs.

CRITICISMS

1964. The House Committee on Education and Labor Report on the Economic Opportunity Act (Rept. No. 1458, 88th Cong., 2d Sess., June 3, 1964) contains criticisms of the Job Corps as proposed. (These are contained on pages 70-72 of that report.)

Their major points were (1) high cost for the first year of operation; estimated $4,700 per enrollee, in actuality it was $11,252—raising the question of whether the Job Corps was the best use of financial resources; (2) whether the Job Corps would effectively remove the causes of youth unemployment and poverty. (Dr. Bronfenbrenner said it would if the youth could use his new-found skills when he returned home and if "he has learned patterns of social and civic behavior which are appropriate to that community.") [13, p. 5]

1966. Hearings on the proposed 1966 amendments to the Economic Opportunity Act of 1966 were held before the House Committee on Education and

Labor (Subcommittee of the War on Poverty) during March 1966. Criticisms of the Job Corps received a great deal of attention: (1) high costs, (2) general inefficiency, (3) incidents of vandalism, rioting, and crime rate, (4) high initial dropout rate of 32 percent, (5) high salaries paid Job Corps employees, and (6) sending the half of the enrollees 1,300 miles from their home and often to isolated areas. (Examples of criticisms made of the Job Corps can be found in the Minority Report on the Proposed Economic Opportunity Amendments of 1966, House Report No. 1568, 89th Cong., 2d Sess., pp. 95-148.) [13, p. 9] The House Minority Report also said: "A potentially good program is faced with failure because of excessive cost, political profiteering, permissive disciplinary policy, and a distant unenlighted, centralized control . . ." (p. 95, House Minority Report). [13, p. 10]   (If an incident occurred, the Center Director had to make a report to Washington and wait to see if the enrollee should be dismissed from the center.)

Congress in 1966 added the amendments stated earlier in this report in the second section; and also put a ceiling on cost per enrollee at $7,500 for those centers open for more than 9 months, and sent enrollees closer to their home.

STATISTICS

By June 1967 there were 122 Centers (102 for men and 20 for women), with a total enrollment of 39,400 trainees. [4, p. 4] Costs were [14]:

Fiscal Year	Millions of Dollars
1965	$196
1966	308
1967	211 [4, p. 9]
1968	282
1969	201-(Funds as of December 31, 1968)

On January 23, 1969, there were 33,266 youths enrolled in 109 Centers— 23,332 men and 9,934 women. [14]

The average cost per student in the fiscal year 1966 was $11,252; the men's Urban Center having the highest, $12,510 (including starting costs). [13, p. 9]   But the men's Urban Centers' cost per student dropped in fiscal 1967 to $8,664, placing women's Centers' costs highest, with $9,735 per student. [4, p. 10]   (This mainly due to only a few hundred women living in one Center, and the high rentals of leased residential buildings and facilities.) The Rural (conservation) Centers' cost in fiscal 1967 was $7,315 per student. [4, p. 10]

Mr. Shriver, then Director of OEO, pointed out in 1966 that costs per enrolee were much higher where the enrollment was below 49 percent capacity, as in Breckenridge, Kentucky, Atterbury, Indiana, Tongue Point, Oregon, and Rodman, Massachusetts. This, he said, was partly due to bad management and to problems caused by contractors which had been replaced. (Pp. 570-577, House Hearings on proposed 1966 amendments, 89th Cong., 2d Sess.). [13, p. 9]

Only one in nine enrollees remained for a year in 1966, and half of the enrollees left within two months. The median length of stay doubled in 1967. (And the average length of stay increased with the age of the Centers.) It was found that the older the youth, the longer he stayed. (Six months represents the crucial cut-off period needed to make the Job Corps experiences a success.) [6], [4, pp. 16-20]

Studies show that a longer stay in Job Corps means educational gains, higher wages, and more stable employment. A sophisticated cost-benefit analysis by Dr. Glen Cain found that those who spent 9 months in a Center equaled 1.6 years of schooling. [2, pp. 13, 14], [4, p. 21]   Louis Harris, the pollster, found (1967): Prior to enrollment, the median hourly rate to be the same ($1.19) fro two groups of corpsmen; the group which stayed more than six months raised their median hourly wage by 32 cents compared with those who stayed less than three months who increased their (median) wages by only 15 cents. And of those who had stayed in the Job Corps more than six months and were employed, 90 percent had full-time jobs with the balance working in part-time or seasonal industries. The comparable rates for former corpsmen who stayed less than three months were 79 percent and 21 percent. [6], [4, p. 21]

Of the 1,167 Job Corps graduates who were placed by March 13, 1966: 571 were employed, 380 were in the armed forces, and 216 were back in school. An additional 1,500 corpsmen had gone on to advanced training in Urban Centers, after training at rural conservation centers (p. 595, House Hearings on proposed 1966 amendments, 89th Cong., 2d Sess.). [13, p. 8]   As of May 1, 1967, 75,410 youths had gone through some phase of Job Corps training: 52,985 (70 percent) got jobs, joined the armed forces, returned to school or entered college. Of the 52,985 youths, 40,269 (76 percent) got jobs (average wage was $1.71 per hour); 7,418 (14 percent) went to school; and 5,298 (10 percent) joined the armed forces. [15, pp. 366-367]

OPERATION

The men's Rural Centers (93 in 1968) were operated by public agencies, the Departments of Agriculture and Interior, and in four instances by the states. These Centers were small and housed only about one-third of the youths enrolled in the Job Corps. They were located in national and state parks and forests. (There was a problem of isolation and distance to travel for recreation, shopping, and the like). The emphasis in the Rural Centers was mainly on conservation and basic education, and less on job training as in the urban centers.

The bulk of the Job Corps training effort was in the 28 (in 1968) Urban Centers and three Special Centers. The Urban Centers for both men and women were operated on a contract basis from OEO. The men's Urban Centers were advanced Centers for further training and were usually located on surplus military bases and installations. The women's centers were all in urban settings, usually in leased facilities. (Often there were problems of community resistance. The

Women's Job Corps Centers involved use of the community's facilities, and the renovation of residence buildings, at vast expense. The basic issue for local criticism was a fear that wild youths would cause havoc in the community. And, there was often antagonism to any federally administered operation. [15, p. 367])

In 1968, eighteen of these Urban Centers were operated by private industry (such as Federal Electric, Science Research Associates, Xerox Corporation, and Litton Industries). The remaining Urban Centers were contracted to non-profit institutions, including two universities, two YMCA's two educational foundations, and one national women's sorority (women's center in Cleveland). These organizations recruit and employ all Center staff.

OEO welcomed corporate involvement because it gave an image of respectability and acceptance by the business community. "Though profits were small, contractors had no financial risk since they operated on a cost-plus-fixed-fee basis." [4, p. 4]   (No fee exceeded 4.7 percent of the contract cost). Corporations were interested because of increased pressure for involvement in aiding the poor, social responsibility, and profit. Corporations could also use the centers as laboratories for developing and testing new teaching methods and materials. [4, p. 4]

Education-run Centers had the highest rate of failure, mainly because big corporations had the ability to tackle large organizational problems and could make decisions quickly. Yet some corporations had difficulty in developing new educational techniques for training the disadvantaged. (Money was cut for educational research, and this hurt attempts to attract top-level educators and administrators.)

FUTURE OF THE JOB CORPS

Considerable progress had been made during the Job Corps' first five years of operation. Discipline in the Centers has been improved as a result of more effective screening and decentralizing control from Washington to the Center Directors; the experience gained by center staffs; more has been learned about educating the disadvantaged; course curricula have been further developed; the average length of stay of enrollees has been longer; and relations between Centers and surrounding communities have improved. However, much remains to be done before the future of the Job Corps is insured. [4, p. 23]

One of the biggest problems relates to the fact that recently more and more sixteen- and seventeen-year-olds have joined the Job Corps (at the end of 1966 they constituted 55 percent of total enrollment). The problem is twofold: (1) younger enrollees tend to drop out early (only 10 percent of the sixteen- and seventeen-year-olds stayed six months or longer in 1966, compared to 32 percent of the eighteen- and nineteen-year-olds and 46 percent of the twenty- and twenty-one-year-olds); (2) often arbitrary age requirements prevent them from immediately using the training they did receive. [4, pp. 16, 17 and 25]

Several proposals to remedy the situation are being considered. Some are already in practice—sending the enrollee closer to his home environment to help remedy homesickness, increasing the monthly allowance to $50, denying readjustment allowance to those who drop out during their first 90 days, and specifically educating young enrollees to qualify them for a high school equivalency certificate. One proposal not yet a reality is to concentrate the sixteen- and seventeen-year-olds in special Centers, using the older corpsmen in leadership roles and in performing chores the younger ones can't do by law, such as driving vehicles and handling certain equipment. An alternative would be to secure a commitment from enrollees that they would stay in the center for at least a year and then design special curricula suitable for a longer time period. Another alternative, and perhaps the more promising, would be to convert some conservation Centers to experimental institutions stressing education to prepare sixteen- and seventeen-year-olds for passing high school equivalency examinations and receiving high school diplomas, in order to pursue further education and training. [4, p. 25] Yet, to date, not much has actually been done to alter the Centers and their programs to make them more attractive to this age group. The younger enrollees still have the highest dropout rate. "Designing ways to keep, as well as educate and train, the younger enrollees remains a crucial problem." [4, p. 25]

A second major and continuing problem of the Job Corps has been the continued increase in the proportion of Negro and other nonwhite enrollees, a factor which has contributed to the tensions experienced in centers and to the early departure of some enrollees, particularly those from the South. To help alleviate this, a drive was began in the spring of 1967 to enroll youths from Appalachia, a region of predominantly white population. [4, p. 24]

A third problem is that from the outset Job Corps decided not to involve the local vocational educational establishment and state vocational education institutions, even though a number of states had previously operated vocational residential Centers. "Closer cooperation with state vocational authorities could have broadened support for the program and added to its available professional capability." [4, p. 23] Involvement of state institutions might have relieved some of the tensions between centers and their neighboring communities. State-operated Centers might also provide opportunities for experimenting with new and different program approaches. As early as 1966 the Advisory Commission on Intergovernmental Relations recommended that OEO "take positive steps to interest states in acting as prime or supporting contractors for Job Corps facilities. . . ." [1, p. 187], [4, p. 24] The Commission's recommendations were ignored by OEO. (Only 2 percent of Job Corps enrollment were in state-related conservation Centers in May 1967.) It might be necessary then for Congress to take steps to assure that the recommendation is carried out. [4, p. 24] (Before the 1966 Amendments, the law provided that local educational agencies be utilized, *if* training was equivalent, "with reduced federal expenditures." The words "at comparable costs" are substituted by the 1966 Amendment). [13, p. 10]

For youths who stayed long enough to complete a course of study, the experience has been meaningful, and has helped them to gain employment at a higher wage level than they might have otherwise anticipated. Extensive studies by Dr. David Gottlieb (1966) have indicated that the aspirations of youths from impoverished homes are not very different from those of middle-class youth. But lower-income youth find their goals more illusive. [5, p. 20]   "The Job Corps is one institution with the potential of helping poor youth to bridge the gap between aspirations and reality." [4, p. 26]

The harsh fact is that it has helped only a minority, despite the relatively ample resources allocated to it. The future of the Job Corps as a viable institution remains in doubt. It will depend upon its ability to operate efficiently in residential Centers where youths will stay long enough to gain experiences meaningful to their future, and on its ability to persuade the public that the effort is worth the investment. [4, pp. 26-27]

At this writing, President Richard M. Nixon and the new Republican administration, coupled with reactionary Congressional and public support have all but written finis to the Job Corps. (See the Epilogue to this text.) But *finis coronat opus* (the end crowns the work). Will this mean that once again the portion of America's problem youth served by Job Corps will be free to wander the streets of our troubled nation?

REFERENCES

1. Advisory Commission on Intergovernmental Relations. *Intergovernmental Relations in the Poverty Program.* Washington, D.C.: Government Printing Office, 1966.
2. Cain, Glen G. "Benefit-Cost Estimate of Job Corps." Mimeo. Office of Economic Opportunity, May 22, 1967.
3. *Education in the Job Corps Conservation Center.* Washington, D.C.: Job Corps, Office of Economic Opportunity, n.d.
4. *Examination of the War on Poverty: Staff and Consultants Reports.* Vol 1. Printed for the use of the Committee on Labor and Public Welfare. Washington, D.C.: Government Printing Office, 1967.
5. Gottlieb, David. "Poor Youth Do Want to Be Middle Class But It's Not Easy," paper delivered at the 61st Annual Meeting of the American Sociological Association, Miami Beach, August 30, 1966. Mimeo.
6. Harris, Louis, and Associates. "A Study of August 1966 Terminations from the Job Corps." Mimeo. March 1967.
7. *Facts of Women's Centers of the Job Corps.* Government brochure J-23c. Washington, D.C.: Office of Economic Opportunity, March, 1967.
8. *Is There a Job in Your Future?* Washington, D.C.: Government Printing Office, 1966.
9. *Job Corps Facts.* Government brochure J-1c. Washington, D.C.: Office of Economic Opportunity, 1968.

10. *Job Corps Facts*. Washington, D.C.: Government Printing Office, 1965.
11. *Job Corps, the First Three Years*. Washington, D.C.: Office of Economic Opportuntiy, n.d.
12. *Job Corps Youth, Neighboring Communities Help Each Other*. Government brochure J-46. Washington, D.C.: Office of Economic Opportunity, January 1967.
13. Lister, Sara. *A Brief History of the Job Corps*. Library of Congress Legislative Reference Service, Washington, D. C.: Education and Public Welfare Division, 1966.
14. OEO programs, weekly national summary, Feb. 10, 1969.
15. Parker, Franklin. "Whom the Public Schools Failed: the Job Corps in Perspective," *Phi Delta Kappan*, Vol. 49, No. 7 (March 1968), pp. 362-369.
16. *Quick Facts on the Programs of the Office of Economic Opportunity*. Government brochure E-1c. Washington, D.C.: Job Corps, Office of Economic Opportunity, May 1967.
17. "Some Questions and Answers about the Job Corps Center for Women in Huntington, West Virginia." Unpublished report, Job Corps Center for Women, Huntington, W. Va., 1965.
18. *Step Up to Job Corps*. Government brochure J-7c. Washington, D. C.: Office of Economic Opportunity, n.d.

SUPPLEMENTARY NOTES

The following are reports written by one of the editors and his associates at Basic Systems, Inc., as a result of visits to various women's Job Corps Centers prior to the opening of the Job Corps Center for Women in Huntington, W. Va. The material is included as a supplement to the foregoing chapter on Job Corps.

Notes on a Job Corps Center No. 1

Selection of Enrollees

Some personnel at the Center are not very satisfied. A few people think that selection may be used to clean out the community's chronic troublemakers who are often on probation or parole; the center thus becomes a repository for community rejects.

One of the counseling staff seemed to think that changes in the method of selection might be forthcoming; mentioned was the inclusion of professional people in the nominating process. Exactly what is intended by his statement is not clear, but it probably means that social caseworkers will play some role in suggesting candidates for the program.

Some personnel thought that a Center should be able to return a girl; it was noted that it is practically impossible to send an enrollee home once she has arrived at the center unless she is pregnant. The number of girls arriving who were pregnant could not be exactly determined, but the approximate figure was

10 percent. One of the girls in the first group was in her eighth month of pregnancy, and this raises some questions about the purpose and efficacy of the health screening.

OEO seems to be very sensitive about the subject of returns. In one case, a Center had felt that they had convinced OEO that a particular girl just could not make it through the Center program. Several days later OEO directed that before she would be sent home, her case would have to be reviewed in Washington by psychiatrists or counselors for possible alternatives to dismissal.

A member of the counseling staff was asked if they had some opinions that might be used to formulate improved selection criteria for the Centers which would maximize the gains for the enrollees and lessen some of the staff's problems. The staff members did not seem willing to make an intellectual commitment, but finally indicated that they would contribute something to the selection process.

A number of girls leave the Center voluntarily. Some want to return after stepping off the plane, some after their first weekend in a new city. The counseling staff agreed that if a girls wants to go and her parents support her decision (but most parents are apathetic), she will go.

Two observations were made at this point. The first is that a girl who has lived with, been abused by, and has actively hated females all her life will (not surprisingly) have and provoke huge problems in a women's residential center. The second observation was that nothing is easy; even the distribution of bus fare presents a problem.

Beginning the Program

The hiring and the establishment of the physical plant at one Center were done very quickly. There were many complaints about the administration of the program. Some people had been hired for the summer only, and some others have quit because their position was so insecure and too ill-defined.

When the Center took over the hotel, there was a lot of renovation and cleaning to be done. The building even now has a kind of mismatched, donations-from-the-relatives appearance. The furnishings, even those in the offices, lend an aura of impoverishment.

It was strongly suggested that if the hiring of staff and the organization of facilities had been accomplished before the enrollees began to arrive, the number of problems and crises would have been fewer and the orientation would have gone more smoothly. The staff at one Center evidently voiced objection to the lack of orientation given the girls upon arrival. They suggested that the enrollees be involved in a large-scale orientation program when they arrive, including such activities as a tour of the city and recreation activities. Evidently the spirits of the girls were high when they arrived, and these activities would have been a means for expending their excitement, occupying their time, and lightening the load of some of the persons involved in the intake process.

Community Relations

Since the enrollees come from all over the country (purportedly to remove them from the tensions and strains of their home environments), they are consequently disinterested in community activities and lack an identification or loyalty to their temporary home. Moreover, the community tends to associate the Job Corps Center with a reformatory inmate of some type. For instance, the staff cited examples of requests made to the schools in their city (for the girls to attend community colleges) and to a hospital (for the Licensed Vocational Nurse program) where the appeals were answered by affirmative replies; later on these requests were denied. In each case the staff felt that unsatisfactory reasons were given for the refusal. These refusals have hindered the training program severely.

Favorable and unfavorable stories about the Centers appear in all papers. Sometimes an effort is made in one town or another to have the press agree to bury extremely unfavorable stories in their Saturday editions.

In a couple of Centers the "creeps" who hang around the center doors waiting for the girls to come out are noxiously visible to passers-by. They present problems: to the public acceptance of the Center on one hand, and to staff and security on the other.

Security

Staff, visitors, and enrollees sign in and out; everyone except the enrollees has a nametag or badge. The enrollees are given passes by the assistant or counselors on their residence floor. The following information is recorded on the pass: name of the girl, destination or purpose (a walk, to church, to the post office), name of the girl accompanying her (for they cannot go out alone), time leaving, and time of expected return. The pass is left at the desk where the enrollees sign out of the building.

Enrollees have a certain amount of free time each day, which may be the hours 3:00 to 5:00 p.m. or perhaps 7:00 to 9:00 p.m., during which time they may do errands or other outside chores.

By requesting at least two days in advance, they can stay out until midnight or 1:00 a.m., provided they are in the company of an adult. This regulation satisfies the local ordinance regarding curfew, which is different for persons over eighteen. Girls are allowed a certain number of late nights per month, a greater number if they are over eighteen.

There were two security men near the front desk and door at all times. The security staff runs the Center at night; the counseling staff run it during the days on weekends.

Vocational Training

At this Center, a few girls (eight or ten out of about 230) will attend a local college to major in such fields as music, recreation, or journalism. A number are going to a technical school for courses in bookbinding and food catering. Some attend a secretarial school to learn shorthand, typing, switchboard operation, and other office procedures. Another eight or ten will be trained as dental assistants.

Two fairly large groups are being trained at the Center. One group will train to be LVN's (Licensed Vocational Nurse); the other group will learn simple clerical procedures that do not require or justify outside training. A smaller third group will remain at the Center to receive "prevocational training" where it has been decided that these enrollees are too young, too dull, or otherwise unsuited or unready for vocational training.

Supplementary Education

In conjunction with the vocational training, the enrollees are attending classes in public affairs and family life as required by OEO. They also attend classes in music, art, reading, and mathematics. The greatest difficulty is encountered in public affairs and family life classes; it seems to stem from the fact that the content of these courses is irrelevant to the enrollees, particularly when approached in the conventional manner. Some difficulty may arise from the teachers hired to instruct in these fields.

The art class was also said to be one of the best. The girls showed talent and enthusiasm and the teacher was one who "came across."

The classrooms used as reading labs evidenced hardware and reading kits (SRA and EDL) with an emphasis on self-pacing.

They are acquiring a library and encouraging the girls to read and use the study materials on their own, and with some success. One teacher said that the materials used were designed for boys and were insulting to girls who could not read but had been to school.

Sex Education

Most of the girls are sexually experienced. A number have been prostitutes, and it seems that quite a few have made some money this way since their arrival at the Center.

The Center is legally responsible for the girls; if one becomes pregnant or is picked up on charges of prostitution the center is held accountable. They are about to begin a program of sex instruction. There is hope that items from the classroom, movies, and discussions of the topic will be fed back into the group counseling sessions called here Psychology I.

No one would say anything about or even acknowledge the existence of contraceptives. They are probably doing the best they can in the situation they are caught in, but it is my feeling that the only realistic aspect is the girls' behavior. If a girl becomes pregnant, she will be sent home (this has not occurred in the time this Center has been in operation). If a girl becomes infected, she will be treated (they evidently keep a close check on this). But they will not or cannot hand a pill to her on twenty days of the month, or at least they will not discuss it.

Staff Morale

In the main the morale is good, the staff is enthusiastic and willing. They are pleased by what they are accomplishing and feel that this center is probably more successful than others they have heard about. Some staff members are more effective than others; the successful ones are those who like the girls, can give them affection, can tolerate but not be frightened by or dislike them for behavior that deviates from the staff's mores. It seemed to make no difference whether the basis for this behavior was intellectual, pragmatic, or emotional. Incidentally, many of the staff have worked in a reformatory or probation and parole. One of their prides is that two Job Corps girls were at the New York World's Fair for seven weeks representing Job Corps to the public.

The staff has some complaints: the administration is not organized. Some very effective teachers have left or been let go while ineffective ones were retained. Vocational training is beginning before sufficient remediation. The accounting department has no flexibility, no realization of needs other than those dictated by their responsibilities. The demands for time (which may originate from administration, other staff members, or an unexpected need on one of the residence floors) can be debilitating, requiring 12-18 hours a day at times. Several thought that the Center had too many enrollees to accomplish its goals.

The Girls

The observer sat on the floor where the Resident Assistant's office is located as the girls wandered in and out, and wondered whether and how many of the BSI staff comprehended what they are going to work with.

There are thirty-five or forty girls living on the topmost floor. They are geographically and ethnically various. These kids are not from the middle class; they are raw—and this creates a tremendous barrier. But there is one thing I heard over and over and saw demonstrated in a most appealing way which tends to cross this barrier; they are starved for affection. Caring for them—really caring for them no matter what they do or say—works. For many of the girls, it is the first time in their lives that they have felt cared for.

A counselor has been able to say "Don't give me that shit, Audrey," mean it, and be comfortable saying it. There is a lingo and a set of attitudes and preferences which must be recognized. Some people are able to speak and understand the lingo; some lose the girls when the girls or the counselors become angry.

A number of the girls staged a protest demonstration about the food. No more roast beef and apple pie—they want soul food, necks and greens, and they will get it.

Head Counselor wants a male and a female counselor on each floor; staff discussed this, and noted that, predictably, a passive male with a dominant female is a fatal combination; the girls resent the woman and trample on the man.

According to OEO policy, the Job Corps' task is to educate or train. They really do not want it to become a mental health project. Most counselors also have found that it is absolutely impossible to limit their efforts to vocational guidance. With what they are regarding as a weak administration, they feel that their service has become one of primary importance in the functioning of the Centers. There are difficulties in this; one girl is such a problem that maintaining her in the center absorbs a great deal of the counseling services' time.

The girls sometimes complain about being in prison. This is understandable. They cannot come and go as they please and there are no 3 o'clock bedtimes. Their whereabouts are supposed to be known at all times. The answer to their complaints, "We are legally responsible for you," does not always satisfy.

The main disciplinary problem is coming in late; there are also AWOL cases—about one each weekend. If a girl is late, her counselor speaks to her, and she is usually punished either by being restricted (i.e., no passes for a certain amount of time) or assigned to work (but she can choose what she wants to do).

Lists are printed daily of those girls who are confined by illness, AWOL, or restricted.

If a girl is aggressive (fights with another), she will be restricted or given work. There are two legitimate means for dissipating aggression—recreation or work; the work is in the canteen or help to the Resident Assistant. There is a swimming pool available, and the girls and staff have gone on a number of excursions.

Notes on a Job Corps Center No. 2

Characteristics of Students

Students are approximately 60 percent Caucasian and 40 percent Negro. Average reading level is six years and nine months. Student dropouts have resulted from the following factors:

Interpersonal problems, primarily resulting from racial prejudice.
Return to public schools.
Difficulty with the basic education and home-and-family programs (sometimes seen as like the traditional school courses).
Difficulty with rules and regulations.
Lack of appropriate vocational options.
Severe psychological problems.

Characteristics of Staff Members

There are about 135 staff members including maintenance personnel and food service personnel. Staff members are 85 percent Caucasian and 15 percent Negro. Staff resignations have occurred for the following reasons:

Lack of long-term job security.

Interpersonal problems (prejudice of a racial basis).

Lack of appropriate work experience.

Vocational Options and Distribution of Students

Business occupations	100
Sales and marketing training	12
Health occupations	60
Practical nursing program	3
Child care program	2
Cosmetology (subcontracted)	30
Recreation aide program	12
Arts and crafts specialist	1
Photography specialist	1
Commercial art specialist	2
Waitress training program	1
Basic education aide program	1

Guidance and Counseling

Counselors have a minimum of an M.A. degree and a supervised practicum and are considered professionals.

Counseling is by appointment, walk-in, or on-call, as necessary. There is no evening counseling, and only one scheduled individual interview each month. The girls are not referred to counselors for disciplinary problems. Severe psychological conditions are referred to psychiatric services in the community.

The counseling program uses the Job Corps test battery for evaluative purposes with the Job Corps Test A, Part 1, excluded because it has been found to be too probing. The guidance tests alone require 15-20 hours during the initial processing period which lasts 15 days.

There is a continuing in-service training program for the counseling staff. It was emphasized that the success of the counseling program and the ultimate success of the overall program requires education on an integrated basis for the total staff of the Center.

Residence Program

All residence affairs are handled by live-in residence advisors, aged 21-50. It has been observed that the younger advisors are more successful because of their flexibility and greater permissiveness. All advisors have the B.A., with some background in education and/or social service. Work schedule is 48 hours on duty followed by 48 hours off duty. The ratio of advisors on duty to enrollees is approximately 1 to 45.

Advisors perform the following functions:

A. Supervision of students on the floor.
B. Maintenance of discipline on the floor.
C. Room inspection.
D. Mail distribution.
E. Lights-out and bed check.
F. Provision of some tutorial functions for individual girls.
G. Distribution of information to students by public announcement.
H. Observation of personal problem areas and provision of information to the counseling staff.
I. Room changes as required.
J. Volunteer activities in any recreation area of personal competence (teaching piano, dance skills, etc.).

Residence advisors have no assignments for supervision of public areas, counseling, instruction, or regular recreation activities.

Recreation Program

The recreation program is very strong. It is probably the single most important factor in the overall program.

All recreation is handled by a recreation staff of professional personnel. No resident leaders are involved in the program.

The program offers a multiple choice of the following activities each night and on weekends:

A. Library.
B. Music library (earphones).
C. Choral group and voice teaching: one night a week, using a consultant.
D. Charm school: one night a week.
E. Gymnasium: two nights a week (all activities including trampoline and parallel bars).
F. Swimming pool: available four nights a week.
G. Movies: two nights a week (run in the canteen with informal attendance).
H. Entertainment: rock-and-roll band one night a week.
I. Coed dances: Saturday nights with regular attendance with boys.
J. Canteen: available daily, 4 p.m. until lights out.
K. Arts and crafts: five nights a week.
L. Coed bowling league: Sunday afternoon.
M. Summer camp: 50 girls each weekend.
N. Softball: intramural competition one night a week.
O. Rollerskating rink: one night a week on a scheduled basis.

P. Millinery shop: on a continuing basis.

Q. Piano lessons: intermittently (taught by Center staff members).

R. Courses in photography and commercial art: one night a week.

S. Oil painting.

T. Dramatic Club.

U. Cooking course: available each night for six girls on a sign-up basis.

V. Serving course: available each night for six girls on a sign-up basis.

In addition to the comprehensive full-time recreation program, vocational training is given in recreation as a profession. The recreation/vocational program provides 14 through 16 months of training in physical education, aquatics, arts and crafts, and leisure-time activities. Literacy requirements for enrollees are set at the tenth grade. Employment opportunities for graduates are very great, with a starting salary of approximately $4,000.

Home and Family Living Program

There are seven subject areas in the home and family living program:

A. Food and nutrition.

B. Child care and development.

C. Home furnishings.

D. Home nursing (a three-week program supported by the Red Cross and various other paramedical and medical groups).

E. Consumer education.

F. Human relations.

G. Clothing and textiles.

The following program items are of interest:

A. Most of the girls have never seen sewing machines. The sewing-course should have a variety of old machines, some with treadles.

B. There is a diet club in which the girls monitor each other.

C. In the food and nutrition course, one day a week is devoted to consideration of regional food interests.

Logistics

The following logistics information is of interest:

A. The educational facilities are in a number of separate buildings. This separation of facilities has been the most serious problem faced by the Center because of difficulties in transportation of girls and problems caused by girls in the streets.

B. The schedule for processing of new girls arriving at the Center is as follows:

1. The center is informed of arrivals two weeks in advance.

2. The schedule for processing is set up.

3. The girls are picked up at the point of arrival by drivers, resident advisors, and student hostesses who have been selected by the resident advisors. There is no formal greeting procedure.
4. The girls are taken to the Center where they are greeted by an administrative coordinator.
5. Each girl is given a $5 advance and introduced to the residence staff. She is given a room assignment, draws her linen, and is shown how to make her bed.
6. She is given a meal, if required.
7. Each girl is then escorted through and shown the facility.
8. An orientation to the Job Corps and to residence regulations is held on the residence floor.
9. The actual processing schedule is initiated on the following day.
10. The first item of processing is a cursory health examination.
11. Processing activities are scheduled over approximately 15 days during which no vocational training takes place.

C. The girls get an annual leave between December 17 and January 4. During that time the Center is basically shut down. OEO regulations provide that leave is accumulated at the rate of two days per month and transportation is paid for one annual leave after six months of enrollment.

Staff vacations are scheduled by supervisors.

Discipline

There are three levels of discipline at the Center:
A. Moderate discipline by the elected student government.
B. Discipline by the resident advisors.
C. In severe cases, discipline by the Director of Administrative Coordination.

Discipline may consist of reprimand, restriction of privileges, fine, or, in the worst case, recommendation for separation.

Visitors and Curfew Policies

Curfew policies are as follows:
A. Weekday curfew is set at 10 p.m. with lights out at 11 p.m.
B. Friday and Saturday curfew is set at 11 p.m. with lights out at 12:30 a.m.

Some girls have expressed dissatisfaction with the lights out requirement and it will probably be revised, providing a public area on each floor where girls can read or smoke after lights-out time.

There are regular visitors (boys) at the Center each night and especially on weekends. All such visitors must fill out a registration form on their first visit and provide at least five references. Visitors can only be on public areas of the building and must leave by 10 p.m. However, despite these restrictions, the social life at the Center is apparently active and happy.

Community Relations

There have, in the past, been difficulties with respect to community relations. However, the situation is now alright and there has been no bad publicity for quite a long time. The Center has developed a community group of approximately 150 women, called "Friends of the Job Corps," who provide regular social activities and social outlets for the girls.

Health and Medical

A part-time dentist and a doctor on regular consultation are used for cursory medical and dental examinations prior to the actual medical processing program. Medical processing is accomplished through use of community facilities.

Notes on a Job Corps Center No. 3

The recent visit was extremely fruitful in that it allowed us to check our assumptions against a certain amount of experience in many program areas. The following are my more or less randomly organized recollections of interviews with personnel.

Vocational Education

In an initial orientation session, the Director of Vocational Education tells the girls that they may choose any vocation at all and he will try to help them attain it. His plan is to offer clerical skills, beauty culture, practical nursing, and child care in the training Center, and to provide on-the-job-training in whatever other vocations the girls choose. For example, a girl who wants to become a telephone operator will have an initial *n* weeks of practice in clerical skills and office procedures at the Center, and then will go to an OJT program in the local Bell System facilities. There she will receive no pay for her work, but will be apprenticed to a telephone operator and will spend a regular schedule of hours working under that person. The system is very flexible. One girl elected upholstery as her vocational choice, and an upholstery shop was located that would accept her for an OJT program. Apparently these local merchants and business men were willing to accept enrollees without any financial remuneration.

I saw a list of the frequency of vocational choice of the 281 girls at the Center. One hundred and thirty or so of them had chosen clerical skills, approximately 35 had chosen nursing, about 50 had chosen beauty culture, and the rest of the choices were twos and threes for upholstery and telephone operator, etc. The Director of Vocational Education was enthusiastic about the possibility of tailoring vocational objectives to the students' real desires, rather than trying to help the student adjust to an inflexible, locked goal, educational system. I think it is not only feasible, but to be highly recommended that we emulate his approach to vocational training.

Licensing a school of practical nursing involves hiring nurses with particular profiles and equipping a facility according to government standards. A book describing such specifications is available from the Board of Health. The name of the nurse in charge of practical nursing education is available.

It seems impractical to operate our own beauty culture facility—there are stringent government standards. We would have to install one work station per trainee. (We have the name of the only beauty school in Huntington which is licensed, and should decide on the appropriate course of action very soon since it involves facilities alterations.)

Basic Education

Basic education is given in literacy, math, and science. The enrollee's reading skills range from total illiteracy to high school graduation. We could not ascertain what basic reading materials were used, but we did see SRA Graded Readings and other free reading materials on the shelves in the Remedial Reading room. We were not able to talk to anybody who was familiar with the science program, but it seems that the Job Corps programmed instruction series is being used for mathematics. On the upper end of the mathematic skill continuum, algebra classes are being given.

Medical

They had twelve pregnancies upon admission. One of these was in the fifth month, and two were complicated by syphilis. Because it has been functioning only a short time, it is impossible to predict the pregnancy rate for the training period. A physician has been hired to give sex education, but according to the Acting Director OEO has been opposed to referrals for contraceptive devices, although they have allowed some discussion of contraception in terms of future family planning after marriage.

Pregnancy cases are "processed out" by referral to hometown welfare departments, and are given leave from the Job Corps. They may return within six months of the baby's birth provided that Welfare people are satisfied by arrangements for its care.

The Head Nurse reported that the most serious medical problem is gynecological. There was a high incidence of vaginal infection, so high that it was deemed necessary to take smears from each girl as part of the initial medical examination. In a group of girls who had been in the Center approximately one week, and who had not been off limits as far as the staff knew, live sperm were found in many cases. Physical evidence of virginity was noted in "a few cases."

The seemingly high sexual activity of enrollees, coupled with the restriction of birth-control information (if that is indeed the current OEO policy) points to a potentially explosive problem for our own Center.

The second major area of medical concern has been dental problems. The Head Nurse reported that the mean cost for estimated dental work for six girls (chosen as a stratified sample of which two seemed to have very severe dental problems, two to have moderate dental problems, and two to have very good teeth) was $275. This figure agrees quite well with our estimates. Many of the girls required extraction of teeth which held bridgework in place, and therefore also required new prosthetic devices.

Thirdly, there were problems of mental disorder or behavioral disturbance which took a great deal of time and usurped a great portion of the medical facilities in the infirmary. Homosexuality had been noted in several cases, one of which was so severe that the girl had to be isolated in the infirmary. She had chosen a family from among her peers, a mother, father, sister, and infant. She was having active sexual relations with seven girls on her dormitory floor before she was isolated for "medical" reasons which were carefully trumped up by the nursing staff. Severe psychotic episodes have been noted in about 5 percent of the entering enrollees. The policy of the Center has been to return these girls to the community or make referrals to other agencies. However, OEO procedures require that such cases be processed through the Washington office, and this processing takes approximately one week. The Center has no isolation facilities for behavioral disorders, no staff, except the medical staff of nurses, to care for them, and it must use the infirmary beds to house them. In some cases of what appeared to be simple schizophrenia, the patients were left for a full week in their dormitory room in which four other enrollees lived. A local mental hospital accepted one severely disturbed enrollee, but refused to keep her more than a few days. In each case requiring an enrollee to be "processed out," the enrollee's hometown welfare department must be located and contacted, and acceptable provisions for the care of the enrollee, an itinerary for travel, pocket money, etc., must be worked out (this is true in the case of pregnancies also).

Another problem is obesity. Many of the enrollees are on special diets which require the cooperation of the kitchen staff.

Recreation

A student lounge is attractively decorated with a dance floor, juke box, and adjoining snack bar. Students are allowed to invite dates to this lounge for informal evening activities.

Here enrollees will be exposed to many arts and crafts opportunities, such as ceramics or leatherwork. They will also be provided with facilities for table tennis and other indoor games.

Enrollees have physical education classes two days a week. An area of the recreation building will be used for physical education one day a week—"small area indoor sports" such as tumbling and calisthenics. On one day a week the facilities of the local "Y" are made available to the enrollees. Dances are planned with a Men's Job Corps.

Residence Affairs

They have a staff of resident advisors which is organized much like our own proposed staff. The pattern of work they have adopted is three days on, three days off. They reported having tried two on, two off, but found that this system did not allow for enough continuity. There is some complaint about the three-on, three-off pattern because it means that the resident advisors must miss several weekends in a row. They plan to try a three-two-two-three pattern next.

The ratio of resident advisors to enrollees is approximately 1 to 30, like ours. The resident advisors were young college graduates who had received virtually no training. They reported that their major duty was to be available in their rooms on the residence floors from 5:00 p.m. until midnight. At this time, they interacted informally with the enrollees, and maintained discipline when necessary. They reported that enrollees went to bed very late—three o'clock in the morning on a typical day. They also reported that while they very often heard out an enrollee's problems, they did not try to give advice because that was the guidance counselor's role, a role which two people could not share. They recommended that we should plan to have a "cooling off" room in the dorm, where girls who got into trouble at night could be isolated for the remainder of the night under the close surveillance of a resident advisor.

We had originally thought of using married couples as resident advisors, but were convinced after talking that men could be of little use on the residence floors.

Rules of conduct were evolved as the need for them arose, we found, and everyone stressed the necessity of formulating a set of rules prior to the start-up of Center operations. Each enrollee must show an ID card with her name and photograph on it upon leaving the Center. Centering—restriction to the building for disciplinary purposes—is simply a matter of taking away an enrollee's ID card.

During the day, resident advisors scheduled appointments for enrollees with counselors, met new enrollees at the airport, took enrollees out on emergency shopping trips, arranged for distribution of money to enrollees who had special need for it, and so forth.

Public Relations

The Director of Public Relations at the Center conducts tours around the Center and operates a speakers' bureau. She mentioned at least one problem of interest to us. Security was a function subcontracted out—five inside building guards were retained for this purpose, which is just what we estimated. However, crowds of objectionable sorts of men began to loiter around the outside of the building, and two off-duty policemen had to be hired by the Center itself to patrol the outside areas. Small towns are really sensitive to such appearances, and the girls themselves must be discouraged from congregating outside the building.

Notes on a Job Corps Center No. 4

Attached [to the original report] you will find a copy of a fact sheet about women in the Job Corps. In light of some of our discussions, it could be useful. The data from the fact sheets should prove to be interesting. In addition my personal observations follow:

The enrollees receive one hour of reading instruction per day.

Before entering the regular vocational courses which take them away from the center for long periods of time, the enrollees are assigned to the prevocational program. This program is essentially an exploration into various vocational areas. The enrollees participate in work-study activities which provide them with direct experience in some of the alternative vocations available to them.

Other areas of vocational programming:

A. Cosmetology is contracted out. A group of about thirty girls out of 242 in the Center are enrolled.
B. Business is the preferred vocation. Center-operated. A group of about forty or fifty girls are enrolled.
C. Nursing practical license is operated by the center itself. A group of forty girls are enrolled.
D. Dental Assistants. Contracted out. There are three girls enrolled.
E. Power sewing. Contracted out. Two girls are enrolled.
F. Food service. Contracted out. Three girls are enrolled.

Security

The security staff numbers ten. Two are part-time and contracted for. Eight are full-time and work directly through a retired sergeant from the local police force.

Medical

Because of the legal problems involved when nurses administer various kinds of medications, they found it necessary to hire as a staff member an M.D. from the community. The M.D. works two hours a day on a five-day-week basis. In addition to the M.D., they have also hired from the local community a psychiatrist who works two hours per day on the staff. The psychiatrist works primarily with the staff. Any type of extended psychiatric care is taken care of on a contractional basis outside of the center. There are between 92 and 96 medical contacts daily with the dispensary. Dental education is seen as being a necessary prerequisite for any kind of dental-care treatment. The equivalent of the deputy director for resident affairs informed me that they literally had to hunt the girls down under their beds to get them to attend their dental appointments. Dental care was quite extensive, ranging in many cases anywhere between $750 and $1,000 per enrollee.

Recreation

The recreation staff consisted of 9 full-time persons and a few part-time persons. Recreation is not called recreation as such within the Center, but *program services*. Recreation includes canteen, tours in the community dealing with cultural activities, art museum, concerts, and similar events as well as trips to other communities, training sights, industrial settings, and to special programs. It also includes team sports such as volleyball and basketball. Every girl is required to take swimming and participate in some type of physical activity on a daily basis.

Education

All labs (cooking, art, sewing) dealing with the education program are kept open during the waking hours of the girls' weekends and evenings, with somebody available to assist the girls with activities in the labs during those periods.

Counseling

For the counseling program they have hired all individuals with master's degrees in social work. And the approach to the girls is what they call the team approach and group orientation. They have one resident advisor, one counselor, and one recreational person to work with a group of 37 girls. They are called floor teams. Every floor and every floor team has the use of an office, a day room, and counseling facilities.

Notes on a Job Corps Center No. 5*

JOBS CORPS GIRLS' SCHOOL HERE ALIVE WITH HOPE
AND A RAH-RAH SPIRIT
Paul Weeks, Los Angeles Times
(Section F—Metropolitan News)

The walls aren't covered with clinging ivy. They are dirty brick.
The campus has no rambling walks where one can scuff through fallen autumn leaves or linger at the wishing well.
But the old 13-story Case Hotel, where downtown traffic rumbles by and

the tang in the fall air is eye-watering smog, is alive these days with a rah-rah spirit that you would expect at Vassar or Smith.

Most of the 234 young women in residence probably have never heard of exclusive girls' schools—much less dared to dream of ever attending one.

But they are—a school exclusively for 16- through 21-year-olds whose families are mired in poverty. And this is a $1.9 million gamble by the taxpayers to see if the young can pull themselves out of it.

The name is terribly prosaic: The Los Angeles Job Corps Training Center for Women, at 1106 S. Broadway—an equally prosaic neighborhood.

The contractor with the government to operate it: The Young Women's Christian Association.

Shriver Swamped

"Our first job," antipoverty director R. Sargent Shriver said in his Washington office one day last summer, "was to find out if the young people were interested in a program like the Job Corps. We were swamped.

"If we arouse hope in teenagers and prove that they want a chance, it's up to Congress after that."

The center here was the third of the first five organized. The first, at St. Petersburg, Florida, situated in a residential hotel in a neighborhood of retired, has survived a storm of criticism that it was sort of a playpen for boisterous delinquents.

In Los Angeles, the YWCA snagged the Case for a $38,400 first-year's rental, raced through a renovation and staff-procuring period, then opened its doors with much trepidation and little fanfare on June 11.

Olive King Bray, the first director, followed a Washington directive in pleading in a memorandum to news media:

". . . [that] on opening day your reporters refrain from interviewing the arriving enrollees and that your photographers do not take closeup shots."

"Most of these women have never been more than 30 miles from home," she wrote. "When they arrive, most will have just taken their first plane or train ride and will be stepping into a new and temporarily overwhelming world."

How is it four months later?

Forty-four girls—and Olive King Bray—were dropouts, a casualty rate that "compares very favorably" with other centers, says Miss Barrying H. Morrison, YWCA executive director who has taken over the center directorship temporarily.

"In our planning stage, we figured if we were 60-to-70 percent successful, we would be doing all right. In retrospect, we now figure it will be 85 percent."

By that, she said she means that percentage of girls will stay, will be more physically able, will have developed challenging attitudes for the future and will have acquired a job skill.

The girls may enroll for two years. If they stay here, it will require an extension of the YWCA's contract which expires next July.

Their living quarters, with two or three to a room, are on the top six floors. Classes run from 8:30 a.m. to 4:20 p.m. Courses range from basic reading, writing, and arithmetic to typing, practical nursing, homemaking—and swimming.

Weekdays, about 50% leave the center for other campuses where their tuition is paid for specialized courses at seven academic or vocational colleges. Other students don't know they are from the Job Corps, unless the girls tell them.

A staff of 174 is employed to operate the center for a capacity of 252 enrollees. The $50,000 a month budgeted for staff was an underestimate, Miss Morrison said. It is costing more.

Tests administered the young women after their arrival will serve as measuring sticks of the center's success. They show the median arithmetic level was fifth grade; reading, sixth grade; number of years of school attendance, 10.4.

29 Finished High School

Twenty-nine have finished high school; five have no more than three years of schooling.

One of Shriver's announced purposes for the Job Corps was to pull young people out of hopeless, stultifying environments and transplant them miles from home into new, more hopeful surroundings.

In the Los Angeles center, 35% are from the South (including Appalachia); 32% from North Central states; 3% Middle Atlantic; 30% the West.

Fifty per cent are Anglo; 37%, Negro; the remainder, other ethnic groups.

Everything, including living arrangements, is racially integrated.

"We don't give lectures about it," says Miss Morrison. "We assign them to their rooms and let them work it out themselves."

Only one incident resulted, she said, in conflict between a Southern white and a Negro. The Negro girl was transferred to another center.

Could See Fires

"During the time of the August riot," Miss Morrison said, "the girls could see the fires from the top floor. They were frightened, but nothing happened. If anything, it brought the girls closer together."

Shortly afterward, a picket line of "18 or 20" girls marched through the building. They were complaining about the food.

A frantic call was placed from one staff member to another, reporting the demonstration.

"Is it integrated?" the second staffer asked. She was assured it was.

"Then don't worry about it," the second one said, and hung up.

A committee was formed to discuss the food problem. It turned out, the girls were homesick for their own regional dishes.

"Somebody mentioned particularly they'd like neck bones and greens," a staffer said.

It was worked out so the girls occasionally could cook their own specialties.

Passes Once a Week

Curfew is at 10:30 p.m., with special late passes once a week for girls on the honor list. Curfew violation poses the biggest discipline problem.

"The majority of these girls had no real kind of discipline at home," says Miss Morrison. Twelve girls in all have been disciplined for being away without leave overnight.

Despite high crime rates spawned in poverty over the nation, Miss Morrison said only one of her enrollees has been arrested here.

"Some time after the riot, she was in that area when a disturbance occurred," the director said. "She said she wasn't involved and was indignant at a policeman's questioning her. She kicked him."

Subsequently, the young woman was convicted of disturbing the peace and was placed on probation as the center's responsibility.

"She's still with us," Miss Morrison said.

Getting the young women to discuss their gripes with a stranger is difficult. Three of them agreed to sit down for a give-and-take session.

One thought for a minute, shrugged her shoulders. "You really can't knock a good thing," she said.

What they like best: The girls make their own rules, set their own penalties, are "recognized as individuals."

"They [the staff] don't force anything on you," one said. "They say you're on your own. Some of the girls got homesick or couldn't accept responsibility. They're the dropouts."

Schoolgirl-like, one decided the worst feature was the lack of opportunity "to meet boys." She thought it might be due to the downtown location.

A staff member almost choked. "Boys seem to find their way here all right," she laughed. Dances and outings are on the schedule, and some of the girls, she said, are actually reticent to go.

One of the unexpectedly high costs of the program, said Miss Morrison, has been medical and dental treatment.

Needs Underestimated

"We underestimated these needs," she said. "We didn't realize a large percentage of them had never been to a doctor or a dentist."

The young women get $30 a month each for spending money and $50 a month is put aside to be given them when they leave the Job Corps.

Their "free" time, a weekly calendar shows, is loaded with in-center recreation: Art, crafts, homemaking, volleyball, chorus, swimming, canteen dates, movies, guitar classes, jukebox dances—plus such outside activities as camping, passes to Hollywood TV shows and dances at the men's Job Corps camp.

The emerging college-type loyalty to their "campus" is exhibited by such things as sewing Job Corps emblems on their sweaters.

And like numberless regular schools, they have set their own words to "Hail to Thee, Cornell"—their L.A. Job Corps hymn, plus a "fight song" written to the tune of "Hey, Look Us Over."

epilogue

Job Corps Thoughts Before It Passes On

Colman McCarthy

When he was still running OEO, Sargent Shriver, a user of metaphors, often referred to the Job Corps as "the Nation's dumping ground." Occasionally, the term would throw off or offend someone. "Go To a Job Corps Center," Shriver would say, "and see for yourself. It'll be filled with kids this country has literally dumped."

Most were content to take Shriver's word for it. Besides, statistics soon began coming back on the dumpees, grim enough to convince anyone. Fifty percent of the kids had never seen a dentist or doctor, 24 percent had eye trouble, they averaged 9 years of schooling but only read at fifth-grade level, 33 percent had behavioral problems, 29 percent of the Negro enrollees left school because they were bored, as did 56 percent of the white enrollees.

In addition, there were curious little stories the statistics didn't tell. For example, a girl from Appalachia was being shown her room in the dormitory of an urban women's center. When showing her the bathroom, her guide flushed the toilet to be sure it worked. The Appalachian girl jumped back in horror. It was the first one she had ever seen and her comment was, "But I could fall into it."

Early reports also came back from many Centers that homosexuality was going to be a problem. The judgment was based on the habits of enrollees who, during the middle of the night, would slip out of bed and into that of a companion. Psychiatrists discovered later that it was not homosexuality at all, but loneliness. The youths in question had never slept alone in a bed by themselves before, being forced by poverty to share a bed with one or more brothers or sisters.

Occasionally outside observers complained that Job Corps officials often did not give out permanent clothing when new recruits arrived. What appeared as cruelty was really practicality; most of the enrollees had lived on such poor diets that it was better to hold off fitting them for clothes until they gained 10 or 20 pounds, usually a matter of weeks.

It was little wonder the country had no use for kids like this. They didn't

173

even qualify for the dirty-work jobs that every well-run society, if it's going to be neat and clean, needs done.

Early in 1965, when Job Corps began, two things became immediately clear about the program. First, it was not going to be just another job-training program. Many of the youths were so physically, socially, and psychologically shattered that training them for jobs right off was impossible. It accomplished little to take a young man into a mechanic shop and say, "Here, I'm going to make a mechanic out of you," when everything about the youth shouted back, "Please, make a human being out of me first."

Thus Job Corps was basically a human reclamation program, reclaiming exactly the youths society made worthless and then damned because they *were* worthless. The situation was similar to Shaw's comment in the preface to *Man and Superman*: "The haughty American nation . . . makes the Negro clean its boots and then proves the moral and physical inferiority of the Negro by the fact that he is a bootblack."

The second fact immediately clear about Job Corps in its early days was that of all the poverty programs, it was destined to become the most picked on. Spending tax money on dropouts, punks, welfare cases, and the hopeless was probably the subconscious reason why so many righteous Americans were revulsed by the idea of Job Corps. Essentially, the same thing was being done in a program like Head Start, but here the kids were small and cute and cuddly and who but maybe Strom Thurmond would dare speak out against children?

A further reason to wax vehement against Job Corps was "the Harvard argument." Critics pulled out figures saying it cost $10,000 a year to train a Job Corps enrollee—or about three times the cost of a year at Harvard. Few bothered to get the accurate cost of Job Corps—$6,725 in 1968—or to consider that the program did a lot more than educate, or that Harvard, through alumni, gifts, endowments and other contributions, subsidizes each student for $7,570, which means a year at Harvard comes out to more than $10,000. Ironically, the Harvard argument boomerangs in another, more topical way—no Job Corps enrollees, no matter how "disadvantaged," have yet rioted and shut down their center.

When Richard Nixon resurfaced on the national scene, he also picked on Job Corps. The night before he was elected president, he said on national television that the program was a failure, that it costs $12,000 a year to train an enrollee (Mr. Nixon had been using the figure $10,000, but on election eve it escalated to $12,000) and that he planned to eliminate it.

Evidently candidate Nixon didn't know that many large corporations were running Job Corps centers: IBM, Litton, Westinghouse, Philco-Ford, Packard-Bell, Burroughs, IT&T. Nor did he know that about 123,000 of the 177,000 youth who enrolled since 1965 are either working, back in school, or in military service. As president, Nixon has apparently heard from his businessmen friends that Job Corps isn't all bad: slander Job Corps and you slander us, their reasoning went. So instead of trying to eliminate Job Corps, the President is now merely going to emasculate it.

What it means is that for many of the dumped, they will get dumped again: into programs too narrow for them, or back into a society too uncaring. Either way, the dumped feeling is nothing new.

Selected Bibliography

MONOGRAPHS AND COLLECTED WRITINGS

Bard, Bunard. "Why Dropout Campaigns Fail," in Don E. Hamachek (ed.), *Human Dynamics in Psychology and Education*. Boston: Allyn and Bacon, Inc., 1969, pp. 525 532.

Beilin, Harry. "Teachers' and Clinicians' Attitudes Toward the Behavior Problems of Children: A Reappraisal," in Don E. Hamachek (ed.), *Human Dynamics in Psychology and Education*. Boston: Allyn and Bacon, Inc., 1969, pp. 477-490.

"The Disadvantaged Student. Specific Collegiate Programs: Admissions, Financial Aid, Instruction." Middle States Association of Colleges and Secondary Schools, New York, New York, November 1968.

Dooley, B. J. "A Comparison of Inductive and Deductive Materials for Teaching Economic Concepts to Culturally Disadvantaged Children." Paper presented at Georgia University, Athens, February 1968.

Entivisle, Doris R. "Semantics Systems of Minority Groups." Baltimore, Md.: Johns Hopkins University Center for the Study of Social Organization of Schools, June 1969.

Haimowitz, Morris L. "Criminals Are Made Not Born," in Don E. Hamachek (ed.), *Human Dynamics in Psychology and Education*. Boston: Allyn and Bacon, Inc., 1969, pp. 459-476.

Lloyd, Helen M. "Is the Reading Instruction That We Are Providing the Disadvantaged Adequate?" Paper presented in Boston, Massachusetts, April 1968.

McCreary, William H., and Donald E. Kitch. "Now Hear Youth: A Report on the California Cooperative Study of School Dropouts and Graduates," *Bulletin of California State Department of Education*, Vol. 26, No. 9 (October 1953).

"Project PEP: An Evaluation of the Summer Program for Disadvantaged Students Held at Skidmore College." New York State Education Department, Albany, March 1968.

Redl, Fritz. "Our Troubles with Defiant Youth," in Don E. Hamachek (ed.),

Human Dynamics in Psychology and Education. Boston: Allyn and Bacon, Inc., 1969, pp. 451-458.

Shery, Roger W. "Teacher Training and Urban Language Problems. Prepublication Version." (To be published in "Teaching Standard English to Inner City Children," Center for Applied Linguistics, Washington, D.C., Fall, 1969) June 1969.

Silverman, Ronald H., and Ralph Hoepfner. "Developing and Evaluating Art Curricula Specifically Designed for Disadvantaged Youth. Final Report." California State College, Los Angeles, March 1969.

"Summary of the Instructional Conference on the Dropout." Conference held at Roanoke, Virginia, by Virginia Education Association, Richmond, December 1968. 49 pp.

PAMPHLETS

Fantini, Mario, and Gerald Weinstein. "Toward a Contact Curriculum." B'Nai B'rith New York Anti Defamation League. Pamphlet to be published by Harper and Row, New York, 1969.

BIBLIOGRAPHIES AND BOOKS

Amos, William E., and Jean Dresden Grambs (eds.). *Counseling the Disadvantaged Youth*. Englewood Cliffs, N.J.: Prentice-Hall, 1968.

Booth, Robert E., and others. *Culturally Disadvantaged: A Bibliography and Keyword-Out-Of Context (KWOC) Index*. Detroit: Wayne State University Press, 1967.

Cheyney, Arnold B. *Teaching Culturally Disadvantaged in the Elementary School*. Columbus, Ohio: Merrill, 1967.

Cipolla, Carlo M. *Literacy and Development in the West*. Baltimore, Md.: Penguin Books, Inc., 1969.

Cockburn, Alexander, and Robin Blackburn (eds.). *Student Power: Problems, Diagnosis, Action*. Baltimore, Md.: Penguin Books, Inc., 1969.

Cowles, Milly (ed.). *Perspectives in the Education of Disadvantaged Children: A Multi-Disciplinary Approach*. New York: World Publishing Co. © 1967.

Cronbach, Lee J., and Patrick Suppes (eds.). *Research for Tomorrow's Schools: Disciplined Inquiry for Education*. New York: Macmillan Company, 1969.

Dawson, Helaine. *On the Outskirts of Hope: Educating Youth from Poverty Areas*. New York: McGraw-Hill, 1967. © 1968.

Deutsch, Martin. *The Disadvantaged Child: Selected Papers of Martin Deutsch and Associates*. New York: Basic Books, 1967.

Deutscher, Irwin, and Elizabeth J. Thompson (eds.). *Among the People: Encounters with the Poor*. New York: Basic Books, Inc., 1969.

Doll, Russel C. *Variations Among Inner City Elementary Schools: An Investigation into the Nature and Causes of Their Differences*. Kansas City: Center for the Study of Metropolitan Problems in Education, 1969.

Educational Research Information Center. *Selected Documents on the Disadvantaged.* (ERIC has many indexes and publications. If your library carries ERIC publications (on microfiche), this should be a pretty good source.)

"Education for Socially Disadvantaged Children: Reviews the Recent Literature for a Special Noncycle Topic," *Review of Educational Research*, 35 (December 1965), 373-442.

Edwards, Harry. *The Revolt of the Black Athlete.* New York: Free Press, 1969.

Ehrensaft, Philip, and Amitai Etzioni (eds.). *Anatomies of America: Sociological Perspectives.* New York: Macmillan Company, 1969.

Fantini, Mario D., and Gerald Weinstein. *The Disadvantaged: Challenge to Education.* New York: Harper and Row, 1968.

Gilman, Merritt, and Elizabeth Gorlich. *Group Counseling with Delinquent Youth.* Washington, D.C.: U. S. Department of Health, Education and Welfare, Social and Rehabilitation Service, Children's Bureau, 1968. 38 pp.

Glock, Charles Y., and Ellen Siegelman (eds.). *Prejudice U.S.A.* New York: Frederick A. Praeger, Publishers, 1969.

Goldstein, B. *Low Income Youth in Urban Areas.* New York: Holt, 1967.

————. *An Evaluation of Total Action Against Poverty in the Roanoke Valley.* New York: Greenleigh Associates, Inc., 1969.

Jackson, Bruce. *A Thief's Primer.* New York: Macmillan Company, 1969.

Hellmuth, Jerome (ed.). *Disadvantaged Child, Volume I.* New York: Brunner, Mazel, Inc., 1967.

————(ed.). *Disadvantaged Child, Volume II.* New York: Brunner, Mazel, Inc., 1968.

Kozol, Jonathan. *Death at an Early Age: The Destruction of the Hearts and Minds of Negro Children in the Boston Public Schools.* Boston: Houghton Mifflin, 1967.

Lago, Armando M. *Benefit-Cost Analysis of Manpower Training Programs: A Critical Review.* Silver Spring, Md., Los Angeles, Boston, Ottawa: Operations Research Incorporated, 1968.

Miller, Harry L. (comp.). *Education for the Disadvantaged: Current Issues and Research.* New York: Free Press, 1967.

Moynihan, Daniel P. (ed.). *On Understanding Poverty: Perspectives from the Social Sciences.* New York: Basic Books, Inc., 1969.

Noar, Gertrude. *Teaching the Disadvantaged.* Washington, D.C.: National Education Association, 1967.

Ornstein, A. C. (ed.). *Educating the Disadvantaged.* New York: AMS Press, Inc., 1970.

Passow, A. Harry (ed.). *Developing Programs for the Educationally Disadvantaged.* New York: Teachers College Press, 1968, pp. 343-52.

Paulston, Rolland G. *Educacion y El Cambio Dirigido De La Comunidad: Una Bibliografia Anotada Con Referencia Especial Al Peru.* Occasional Papers in Education and Development. Cambridge, Mass.: Graduate School of Education, Harvard University, 1969.

Potts, Alfred M. *Knowing and Educating the Disadvantaged: An Annotated*

Bibliography. Alamosa, Colorado: Center for Cultural Studies, Adams State College, 1965.

Rees, Helen Evangeline. *Deprivation and Compensatory Education: A Considera-tion*. Boston: Houghton Mifflin, 1968.

Schreiber, Daniel (ed.). *Profile of the School Dropout*. New York: Vintage Books, 1968. Minorities Collection.

Storen, Helen Frances. *The Disadvantaged Early Adolescent*. New York: McGraw Hill, 1968.

Stratton, John R., and Robert M. Terry (eds.). *Prevention of Delinquency: Problems and Programs*. New York: Free Press, 1968.

Sundquist, James L. (ed.). *On Fighting Poverty: Perspectives from Experience*. New York: Basic Books, Inc., 1969.

Tiedt, Sidney W. *Teaching the Disadvantaged Child*. New York: Oxford University Press, 1968.

Warden, Sandra. *Leftouts: Disadvantaged Children in Heterogeneous Schools*. New York: Holt, 1968, pp. 187-96.

Weisbrod, Burton A. "Preventing High School Dropouts" in Robert Dorfman (ed.), *Measuring Benefits of Government Investments*. Washington, D.C.: The Brookings Institution, 1965, pp. 117-171.

Wilson, Alan B. *The Consequences of Segregation: Academic Achievement in a Northern Community*. Berkeley, Calif.: Glendessary Press, 1969.

Witty, Paul A. (ed.). Educationally Retarded and Disadvantaged. Chicago: National Society for the Study of Education Yearbook 66th, part 1, 1967.

JOURNALS

Aikman, A. L. "Rural Poor," *Illinois Education,* 55 (April 1967), 349.

Allen, Q. "This Way Out; Slum Youngsters Choose College, but It Takes Courage to Stick," *American Education*, 3 (July 1967), 2-4.

Angel, F. "If's on the Way Back from Alienation," *Educational Leadership,* 24 (April 1967), 607-610.

"Annotated Bibliography," Contemporary Education, 39 (March 1968), 235-239.

"Antidotes to Poverty," *Times Educational Supplement,* 2737 (November 3, 1967), 993.

Axtelle, G. E. "Bright Promise: Review of Educating the Culturally Disad-vantaged Child," by L. D. Crow and others, and "Teaching the Disadvan-taged," by J. O. Loretan and S. Umans," *Educational Forum*, 31 (May 1967), 507-511.

Baker, E. H. "Motivation: For the Disadvantaged, Special Problems," *Grade Teacher*, 85 (March 1968), 104-107, 116.

Barbe, W. B. "Identification and Diagnosis of the Needs of the Educationally Retarded and Disadvantaged," *National Society for the Study of Educa-tion Yearbook*, 66, pt. 1 (1967), 97-120.

Biber, B. "Educational Needs of Young Deprived Children," *Childhood Educa-tion*, 44 (September 1967), 30-36.

Biber, B. "Impact of Deprivation on Young Children," *Childhood Education*, 44 (October 1967), 110-116.

Blatt, B. and F. Garfunkel. "Educating Intelligence: Determinants of School Behavior of Disadvantaged Children," *Exceptional Children*, 33 (May 1967), 601-608.

Boney, J. D. "Some Dynamics of Disadvantaged Students in Learning Situations," *Journal of Negro Education*, 36 (Summer 1967), 315-319.

Branson, H. "College Admissions: Helping the Disadvantaged Student Choose a College: Upward Bound Program," *NEA Journal*, 55 (October 1966), 43-44.

Bressler, M. "White Colleges and Negro Higher Education," *Journal of Negro Education*, 36 (Summer 1967), 258-265.

Brickman, W. W. "Educationally Disadvantaged," *School and Society*, 96 (March 30, 1968), 196.

Brittain, C. V. "Preschool Programs for Culturally Deprived Children," *Children*, 13 (July 1966), 130-134.

Brockman, J. T. "The Role We Play in Education," *School and Community*, 54 (March 1968), 16.

Brooke, E. W. "Crisis in the Cities," *Kentucky School Journal,* 46 (January 1968), 12-14. *Pennsylvania School Journal*, 116 (February 1968), 308-310.

Brown, C. W. "Upward Bound; Project Stimulates Capable, Impoverished Youths To Go to College," *Texas Outlook*, 51 (April 1967), 30-32.

Brownell, S. M. "Preparing Teachers of the Disadvantaged," *North Central Association Quarterly*, 41 (Winter 1967), 249-253.

Bryan, D. M. "Education for the Culturally Deprived: Building on Pupil Experience," *Social Education*, 31 (February 1967), 117-118.

Bumpass, D. E., and R. L. Gordon. "Bridging the Gulf for the Disadvantaged," *Audiovisual Instruction*, 12 (May 1967), 442-445.

Caliguri, J. "Self-Concept of the Poverty Child," *Journal of Negro Education*, 35 (Summer 1966), 280-282.

Calkins, P., and J. Gussow. "ERIC: Data on the Disadvantaged: Yeshiva University's Information retrieval center on the disadvantaged," *Phi Delta Kappan*, 48 (March 1967), 362-364.

Carton, A. S., R. Fulton, and R. M. Cordasco. "Education of the Underprivileged," *School and Society*, 95 (February 18, 1967), 108-110.

"Communication: The Key to Learning," *Ohio Schools*, 45 (September 1967), 23-25.

Cooper, David. "Relevancy and Involvement: Literature for the Disadvantaged," *The Eng. Record*, Vol. 19, No. 1 (October 1968), pp. 45-51.

Cordasco, F. M. "Challenge of the Non-English-Speaking Child in American Schools," *School and Society*, 96 (March 30, 1968), 198-201.

Cordasco, F. "Educational Pelagianism: The Schools and the Poor; Review of the Disadvantaged: Challenge to Education," by M. Fantini and G. Weinstein. *Record*, 69 (April 1968), 705-709.

Corey, Stephen M. "The Poor Scholar's Soliloquy," *Childhood Education*, 20, 5 (January 1944).

Crewson, W. "How New York Tests for Pupil Achievement," *Nations Schools*, 81 (May 1968), 81-82.

DiLorenzo, L. T. "Effects of Year-Long Prekindergarten Programs on Intelligence and Language of Educationally Disadvantaged Children," *Journal of Experimental Education*, 36 (Spring 1968), 36-42.

Dial, D. E. "Programs and Planning for the Disadvantaged," *School and Community*, 54 (May 1968), 81.

Douglass, H. R. "Salvaging the Underachiever," *Clearing House*, 41 (May 1967). 523-526.

"Down East with the Deprived," *Times Educational Supplement*, 2696 (January 20, 1967), 172.

Dranov, P. "Taste of College: Upward Bound Programs," *American Education*, 3 (April 1967), 25-27.

Duncan, J. A., and G. M. Gazda. "Significant Content of Group Counseling Sessions with Culturally Deprived Ninth Grade Students," *Personnel and Guidance Journal*, 46 (September 1967), 11-16.

Eames, E. "Culture of Poverty," *Pennsylvania School Journal*, 116 (February 1968), 329.

"Educating the Children of the Welfare Poor: A Record Symposium," *Record*, 69 (January 1968), 301-319.

Epstein, J., and others. "Teachers for the Disadvantaged: Project Mission," *National Elementary Principal*, 46 (January 1967), 13-16.

Fagan, E. R. "Disadvantaged as a Collective," *Phi Delta Kappan*, 49 (March 1968), 396-399.

Fantini, M. D., and G. Weinstein. "Reducing the Behavior Gap," *NEA Journal*, 57 (January 1968), 22-25.

Gallogly, F. D. "Working with the Disadvantaged," *Instructor*, 77 (August 1967), 44-45.

Gattmann, E., and others. "College? Man, You Must Be Kidding! College Readiness Programs for the Disadvantaged," *NEA Journal*, 56 (September 1967), 8-10.

"Getting Them to the Starting Line Together: Dade County, Fla.," *Times Educational Supplement*, 2671 (July 19, 1966), 248-249.

Gold, M. J. "Programs for the Disadvantaged at Hunter College," *Phi Delta Kappan*, 48 (March 1967), 365.

Grande, P. P. "Attitudes of Counselors and Disadvantaged Students Toward School Guidance," *Personnel and Guidance Journal*, 46 (May 1968), 889-892.

Grossman, B. D. "Early Childhood Education and the New Frontiers," *Elementary School Journal*, 68 (April 1968), 340-342.

Haberman, M. "Materials the Disadvantaged Need and Don't Need," *Educational Leadership*, 24 (April 1967), 611-615.

Harris, A. J., and R. J. Lovinger. "Longitudinal Measures of the Intelligence of Disadvantaged Negro Adolescents," *School Review*, 76 (March 1968), 60-66.

Havighurst, R. J., and J. E. Moorefield. "Nature and Needs of the Disadvantaged: Disadvantaged in Industrial Cities," *National Society for the Study of Education Yearbook*, Part 1 (1967) pp. 8-20.

Howard, D. R. "Needs and Problems of Socially Disadvantaged Children as Perceived by Students and Teachers," *Exceptional Children*, 34 (January 1968), 327-335.

Inman, T. H. "Educating Teachers for the Disadvantaged," *Journal of Business Education*, 43 (April 1968), 268-269.

Johntz, W. F. "Innovation and the New Concern for the Disadvantaged," *CTA Journal*, 63 (January 1967), 5-6.

Jones, W. E. "View from the Counselor's Corner," *Contemporary Education*, 39 (March 1968), 224-225.

Jordan, D. "Upward Bound," *Teachers College Journal*, 39 (October 1967), 21-23.

Jordan, D. C. "Academic Year Phase of the Program: Upward Bound," *Teachers College Journal*, 38 (January 1967), 174-175.

Joseph, E. A. "Selected Aspects of the Internality of the Negro in Education," *Education*, 88 (November 1967), 149-152.

Justman, J. "Assessing the Intelligence of Disadvantaged Children," *Education*, 87 (February 1967), 354-362.

Katz, P. A. "Acquisition and Retention of Discrimination Learning Sets in Lower-Class Preschool Children," *Journal of Educational Psychology*, 58 (August 1967), 253-258.

Kirman, J. M. "Teaching Culturally Deprived Negro Children: Higher Horizons Program," *Journal of Negro Education*, 36 (Winter 1967), 81-82.

Klopf, G. J. "Follow-Through Program," *Childhood Education*, 44 (September 1967), 72.

Kozal, J. "Halls of Darkness: In the Ghetto Schools," *Harvard Educational Review*, 37 (Summer 1967), 379-407; *Discussion*, 37 (Fall 1967), 644-646.

Lammers, C. C. "Save the Slow Learner: Improvement of Instruction at Inner-City Secondary Schools," *Clearing House*, 41 (January 1967), 296-300.

Levine, D. U. "Cultural Diffraction in the Social System of the Low-Income Schools," *School and Society*, 96 (March 30, 1968), 206-207.

Lewis, H. E. "Disadvantaged College Youth," *Art Education*, 20 16, (May 1967), 13-16.

Lin, S. C. "Disadvantaged Student? or Disadvantaged Teacher?" *English Journal*, 56 (May 1967), 751-756.

Long, C. M. "Working with the Disadvantaged: Questions and Answers," *Instructor*, 76 (August 1966), 34; (October 1966), 30; (November 1966), 28;

(January 1967), 24; (February 1967), 24 Jan.; 34 Feb.; 34; (March 1967), 26; (April 1967), 28.

McReynolds, G. "Upward Bound," *School and Community*, 53 (February 1967), 21.

Meltzer, J. "Impact of Social Class," *Educational Leadership*, 25 (October 1967), 37.

Moore, W., Jr. "Cultural Barrier in the Classroom," *School and Community*, 53 (November 1966), 26.

"New Dimension for the Silent Ones," *Minnesota Journal of Education*, 47 (January 1967), 22-23.

North, G. E., and O. L. Buchanan. "Teacher Views of Poverty Area Children," *Journal of Educational Research*, 61 (October 1967); 53-55.

Norton, M. S. "After Project Head Start, What Next?" *Elementary School Journal*, 67 (January 1967), 179-183.

Nuhlicek, A. L. "Orientation Centers for In-Migrants and Transients," *National Elementary Principal*, 46 (January 1967), 34-38.

Olson, A. U. "Teaching Culturally Disadvantaged Children," *Education*, 87 (March 1967), 423-425.

Ornstein, A. C. "Cynicism or Witticism: Professors of Education and Ghetto School Teachers," *Journal of Secondary Education*, 43 (April 1968), 162-164.

Ornstein, A. C., and S. S. Rosenfeld. "Environmental and Other Factors Which Mitigate Against Disadvantaged Youngsters in School," *Contemporary Education*, 39 (January 1968), 156-160.

Ornstein, A. C. "Reaching the Disadvantaged," *School and Society*, 96 (March 30, 1968), 214-216.

Ornstein, A. C. "Teaching the Disadvantaged," *Educational Forum*, 31 (January 1967), 215-223.

Ornstein, A. C. "Techniques and Fundamentals for Teaching the Disadvantaged," *Journal of Negro Education*, 36 (Spring 1967), 136-145.

Ornstein, A. C. "Theory as a Basic Guide for Teaching the Disadvantaged," *Clearing House*, 42 (March 1968), 434-442.

Paschal, B. J. "Anti-Push Theory: Best for Deprived Children," *Instructor*, 77 (December 1967), 38.

Price, K. "Problem of the Culturally Deprived," *Record*, 69 (November 1967), 122-131.

Puder, W. H., and S. E. Hand. "Personality Factors Which May Interfere with the Learning of Adult Basic Education Students," *Adult Education*, 18 (Winter 1968), 81-93.

Rader, H. "Ghetto Child's Self-Image," *Illinois Education*, 56 (March 1968), 298-300.

Rauch, S. J. "Ten Guidelines for Teaching the Disadvantaged," *Journal of Reading*, 10 (May 1967), 536-541.

Reed, Horace B. "Skidmore and PEP—Where the Action Is," *Skidmore Alumnae Quarterly*, 46 (Fall 1967), 12-15.

Rieber, M., and M. Womack. "Intelligence of Preschool Children as Related to Ethnic and Demographic Variables," *Exceptional Children*, 34 (April 1968), 609-614.

Rogers, D. W. "Visual Expression: A Creative Advantage of the Disadvantaged," *Elementary School Journal*, 68 (May 1968), 394-399.

Rooney, M. T. "Undereducated Adult: How Can We Reach and Teach Him to See Beyond Today?" *Loretto NCEA Bulletin*, 64 (May 1968), 25-29.

Rowland, M. K. and P. Del Campo. "Values of the Educationally Disadvantaged: How Different Are They?" *Journal of Negro Education*; 37 (Winter 1968) 86-89.

Rudnitsky, C. W. "Concern Is Yours," *Pennsylvania School Journal*, 116 (February 1968), 318-319.

Savitzky, Charles. "S.T.E.P. Program for Potential Dropouts," *Bulletin of The National Association of Secondary School Principals*, 47 (December 1963), 51-58.

Schwartz, S. "Failure Strategies and Teachers of the Disadvantaged," *Teachers College Record*, 68 (February 1967), 380-393.

Scott, P., and G. Petrie. "Screening Children for Compensatory Education," *Education*, 87 (March 1967), 395-401.

"Self-concepts of Some Disadvantaged Students at Inner City High School," *Contemporary Education*, 39 (March 1968), 229-232.

Singleton, C. M., and S. M. Brown. "To the Hills and Hollows: Story of the Appalachia Educational Laboratory," *American Education*, 3 (July 1967), 22-25.

Smith, C. R. "Breakthrough from Poverty: Post High School Technical Education for the Disadvantaged," *American Vocational Journal*, 42 (February 1967), 18-19.

Smith, D. H. "Speaker Models Project To Enhance Pupils Self-Esteem," *Journal of Negro Education*, 36 (Spring 1967), 177-180.

Smith, M. "Education of the Disadvantaged," *Wilson Library Bulletin*, 42 (February 1968), 587-592.

Smith, P. M. "Drop-out Prone Feelings with Urban and Small Town Culturally Disadvantaged Pupils," *Journal of Negro Education*, 37 (Winter 1968), 79-81.

Sonquist, H. D., and C. K. Kamii. "Applying Some Piagetian Concepts in the Classroom for the Disadvantaged," *Young Children*, 22 (March 1967), 231-238.

Squires, S. I., and E. B. Reingold. "Portrait of the Artist as a Disadvantaged Child," *New York State Education*, 55 (February 1968), 38-43.

Stodolsky, S. S., and G. Resser. "Learning Patterns in the Disadvantaged," *Harvard Education Review*, 37 (Fall 1967), 546-593.

"Training Programs for Teachers of Culturally Disadvantaged Children," *NEA Research Bulletin*, 44 (December 1968), 125-126.

Trout, L. "We Ain't Unteachable . . . Just Unteached," *NEA Journal*, 56 (April 1967), 24-26.

U.S. Office of Education. "Ten Research Lessons That Are Shaking Educational Programs," *Nations Schools*, 81 (February 1968), 55-64.

Van Til, W. "Comments During Meeting of National Teacher Corps Team Leaders," *Contemporary Education*, 39 (March 1968), 233-234.

Venditti, F. P., and M. Y. Nunnery. "Civil Rights Institutes Can Change Attitudes," *Nations Schools*, 78 (September 1966), 23.

Venn, G. "Remedy for Ghetto Unrest," *American Education*, 4 (May 1968).

Waddles, B., and D. Robinson. "Teaching in Inner City Schools," *NEA Journal*, 57 (March 1968), 38-40.

Wagner, G. "What Schools Are Doing: Helping Disadvantaged Children and Youth," *Education*, 37 (January 1967), 313-318.

Welter, P. R. "Case Study: Summer Counseling with Disadvantaged Junior High School Students," *Personnel and Guidance Journal*, 46 (May 1968), 884-888.

Wilcox, P. R. "Teacher Attitudes and Student Achievement: In Ghetto Schools," *Teachers College Record*, 68 (February 1967), 371-379.

Wilkins, G. "Improving Self-Images," *Pennsylvania School Journal*, 116 (September 1967), 9-11.

Williams, A. "Teacher Visits the Homes of Disadvantaged Children," *Teachers College Journal*, 37 (October 1965), 12-13.

Windoes, F. "What Deprived Kids Are Teaching Their Teachers," *Contemporary Education*, 39 (March 1968), 217-218.

"Working with the Disadvantaged," *Instructor*, 77 (August 1967), 44-45; (October 1967), 46-47; (November 1967) 37; (December 1967), 38-39; (January 1968), 37; (February 1968), 60; (March 1968), 38-39; (April 1968), 34-35.

Zwier, M. D. "Disadvantaged Child or Teacher," *Education*, 88 (November 1967), 156-159.

Index